Talitha Cu....

Theologies of
African Women

Talitha Cum!

Theologies of African Women

Edited by

Nyambura J. Njoroge
and Musa W. Dube

Cluster Publications
2001

ISBN 1-875053-25-5

First published in 2001

Published by Cluster Publications
P.O. Box 2400
Pietermaritzburg 3200
South Africa
  Tel. & fax: (033) 345 9897
  E-mail: cluster@futurenet.co.za
  Internet: http://www.hs.unp.ac.za/theology/cluspub.htm

*Cluster Publications is a non-profit publishing enterprise
of the Pietermaritzburg Cluster of Theological Institutions,
aiming to produce good scholarship and accessible and
inexpensive resources for contemporary theology.*

Cover design by Kaburo Kobia

Typesetting by Lou Levine of *Stylish Impressions* - (033) 3869584

Printed by Natal Witness Commercial Printers (Pty) Ltd, Pietermaritzburg, South Africa

Contents

Contributors

Rose Teteki Abbey, a Ghanaian and Ordained Presbyterian Minister is in charge of a church in Osu, Accra, Ghana.

Esther E. Acolatse, a Ghanaian, is a Pastoral Theology Doctoral Candidate at Princeton Theological Seminary, New Jersey, USA.

Bernadette Mbuy Beya, a Congolese, is a Religious Sister in the Roman Catholic Church.

Musa W. Dube, a Motswana, is a senior lecturer in New Testament Studies in the Department of Theology and Religious Studies, University of Botswana.

Grace Rose Imathiu, a Kenyan and Ordained Methodist Minister, is a New Testament Doctoral Candidate at Vanderbilt Divinity School, Nashville, Tenessee, USA.

Musimbi R. A. Kanyoro, a Kenyan, is the General Secretary of the World Young Women's Christian Association (World-YWCA) in Geneva, Switzerland.

Kabamba Kiboko, a Congolese and Ordained Methodist Minister is a Doctoral Candidate at the University of Denver, Iliff School of Theology, USA.

Christina Landman, a South African, is Professor of Church History, University of South Africa (UNISA).

Nyambura J. Njoroge, a Kenyan and Ordained Presbyterian Minister, is the Executive Secretary of Ecumenical Theological Education Programme of the World Council of Churches, Geneva, Switzerland.

Gomang Seratwa Ntloedibe-Kuswani, a Motswana, is a lecturer in the University of Botswana, Gaborone, Botswana.

Mercy Amba Oduyoye, a Ghanaian, is the Director of the Institute of African Women in Religion and Culture at Trinity Theological Seminary, Legon, Ghana.

Preface

Nyambura J. Njoroge

During the last decade of the twentieth century, African women theologians were busy searching for and discovering their written voices by articulating their theological and ethical concerns. An outcome of this daunting task was the publication of a number of anthologies that have introduced readers to the Circle of Concerned African Women Theologians. These women are concerned to ensure that their many unrecorded experiences, perspectives and reflections in different fields of theology and ethics become visible in bookstores, in libraries and on the shelves of students, scholars, women and men of faith who congregate to hear the Word of God. Whilst African women cannot stop others from researching and writing about them, they yearn to develop their distinctive written voices and to have their rightful place in the academic world. Moreover, they want to invite all those who care about African affairs to engage with them in critical listening and conversation as they creatively articulate the many oppressed voices of children, youth, women and men.

Through their written testimonies these women attempt to carry out the functions of the theologians as described by Professor John Pobee: "Theologians are located in their community of faith as its articulate individuals in its womb" (Pobee 1996:163). These women do not write for the sake of writing. These concerned women theologians have decided to enter and operate in the context of oral-Spirit. According to Musa W. Dube Shomanah:

> The oral-Spirit framework can be a creative space, then, where women articulate their own sacred, life-affirming and liberating words of wisdom....The oral-Spirit framework needs to be employed to invite women from diverse cultures to completely rewrite, create, hear, speak, sense and feel new sacred words of life, wisdom, liberation and justice. (Dude Shomanah 1998:53)

Concerned African women theologians are not giving voice

to the so called "voiceless". Instead they are affirming that women have already spoken about their inner feelings and experiences of sorrow in songs, dances, novels, stories, tears, deep silences and through the stripes on their bodies. Unfortunately these voices have fallen on the deaf ears of Christians and their churches. With Jesus the women sigh and shout "*Eph'phatha*", meaning, "Be opened!" (Mark 7:31-35). By doing so these concerned women theologians are challenging the deafness and muteness and also the blindness of Christians and churches to the plight of African women and their children. They are calling churches to listen and engage in conversation with African women in order to look for solutions to the endless and senseless woes facing African women. By translating these voices into articles and books, concerned African women theologians hope to reach many people and to move beyond solidarity to accountability and action.

In the chapters of this volume eleven women have opened yet another space for listening, conversing and action, in the hope that many more African women will get up, arise and echo the cries of the people who exist in their context of pain and suffering, exclusion and marginalization, violence and hopelessness. The eleven women are determined to make a contribution by transforming the practices and attitudes that condemn many Africans to life-threatening activities and premature death. By engaging in this process, the contributors join their forebears in faith in embracing the gifts of healing, wellness and wholeness in the midst of despair, violence, disease and death.

Together these doctors of theology, ministers, messengers of the good news and church leaders invite us to combat self-hatred, ignorance, greed and exploitation. Together, we will soil our hands in our efforts to achieve the goals of dignity, liberation and fullness of life in Africa.

Africa - Talitha Cum! Amka! Arise!

References

Pobee, J. S. (1996). "Bible Study in Africa: A Passover of Language". *Semeia, 73*, 161-179.

Dube Shomanah, M. W. (1998). "Scripture, Feminism and Post-colonial Contexts". *Concilium, 3*, 37-59.

Introduction:
"Little Girl, Get Up!"

Introduction:
"Little Girl, Get Up!"

Musa Wenkosi Dube

He took her by hand and said to her, "Talitha Cum", which means, "Little girl, get up!" And immediately the girl got up and began to walk about. (She was twelve years of age) (Mark 5:42).

I believe that we must all work together to transform the patriarchal model into one of shared power, power that lifts up and strengthens others, not power that depends on keeping others down.[1]

She heard her own beloved child singing, calling out, "Who is there? Who is there? Who is cutting here? Please, go and inform our parents that we have been buried here in our own land and left to die." Seized by anger, Africa called out, "Talitha Cum.... And behold, the bellies of the earth opened. Utentelezandleni jumped out." (Dube Shomanah 1999:13)

Who Touched my Clothes?

In Mark 5, Jesus is on an "emergency call" to Jairus' house, to heal a little girl "who is at the point of death" (Mark 5:23). In this emergency setting, another woman delays Jesus, thereby asserting that her own situation was equally critical. The story tells us that the woman had been bleeding for twelve years and she had lost all her money visiting one professional healer after another without being healed. She hears that Jesus is passing by, and she sees the crowds that throng about him, but she is determined to be healed. She pushes through the thick crowd, seeking to touch the garment of Jesus, for she believes that "If I but touch his clothes, I will be made well" (Mark 5:28). She touches his clothes and power leaves Jesus, forcing him to stop and ask, "Who touched my clothes?" (Mark 5:30). While the investigation is taking place, the daughter of Jairus dies and the messengers come to report this, saying to Jairus: "Your daughter is dead. Why bother the teacher any further?" (Mark 5:35). Jesus, however, bids Jairus to have faith. They continue towards his house, where Jesus takes the hand of the dead daughter and says, "Talitha Cum", which means "Little girl, get up!" She then rose.

Apart from these two women, a number of other characters appear in the story. They are accorded various classifications and degrees of social power. Jairus is identified by name and social position: he is a leader of the synagogue, a father and a husband. Jesus is a teacher of great power as attested by Jairus' approach, the appreciative crowds, the attitude of the bleeding woman and the way he brings a dead girl back to life. Jairus, who is a leader of the synagogue, "fell at his feet and begged him repeatedly" (Mark 5:23) to come and heal his daughter. The very large crowd that followed and pressed around Jesus also highlights his fame. The bleeding woman who, for twelve years, had visited numerous healers and lost all her money, suddenly believes that being healed, through touching the hem of Jesus' garment, is only a hand's stretch away. Indeed, she is then healed! When Jesus returns life to a dead little girl by calling her back to life, we see that even death flees at the voice of Jesus. There are other male characters in this story, including disciples of Jesus, some of whom are identified by name as Peter, James, and John.

There are other characters as well, some whose gender cannot be established, and who were both men and women. These are the many professional healers visited by the bleeding woman and the messengers from Jairus' house. While their gender cannot be easily identified from the narrative, they belong to distinct classes. Some were servants while others were physicians who made money, and were professionals of some sort. Others present are the mourners in Jairus' house. Lastly, there is the mother of the dead girl, who is neither named nor accorded any public profession or identity apart from being identified through her role of mother.

Reaching Out to Touch and Being Touched

The story, however, revolves around two females: one, a young girl, another an adult woman. They are both nameless, associated with sickness, and are not identified through having any professional roles. Both of them have the number twelve in common: one suffered for twelve years, while the other one had lived for twelve years, when she experienced sickness, death and resurrection. Thus the bleeding woman's illness could be dated from about the time when the little girl was born. Both women were cured by a man, Jesus, of ill health and were restored back to life and society. But they are not named, nor are they accorded any professional roles. On reading this story, African women would elect to believe that they (the woman and the young girl) have been freed to explore and engage in the professions of their choice. It is this unfinished business in the story "Talitha Cum" that fascinates African women theologians, as they strive to take her story further and to give each a name, a voice, a life beyond the protective power of Jairus and Jesus. African women theologians have become the bleeding woman who reaches for power, they are the ones calling out "Talitha Cum!" to the unfinished business of a young girl's life.[2]

The story of the little girl who is called back to life has thus come to symbolize the theological struggles, and the quest for empowerment of African women theologians in God's household. Quite a number of African women theologians' works have revolved around this story, including Oduyoye (1997) and Oduyoye and Kanyoro (1992). Most African women find themselves nameless, without professions, associated with illness in their respective societies and institutions, and are living in poverty. More often than not they are daughters to their fathers; they are mothers to their children; and they have male leaders in their churches and homes. Furthermore, they are left without any money in their pockets after the daily struggle for survival, that is, after paying many healers to be healed. The African women writers of this volume are seeking for power sharing in the household of God, but they have come to realize that power is in the hands of men, in both the biblical world and contemporary societies. Like the bleeding woman, they know that Jesus has the power to heal, they see that Jesus is surrounded by a massive crowd and they are pushing their way to Jesus - the source of power. Yet Jesus, whom they seek to touch and be healed, is a man too. The fear and suspicion is still there that, as with other healers, one might pay and still not benefit from any positive results. But as they, like the bleeding woman, try to touch Jesus, African women may have run out of purchasing power. Dube Shomanah (1999) suggests that African women are without financial power. They are in a desperate economic situation, one in which they realize that they must now get economic power for themselves, with or without the consent of those in power. Thus their decision to touch the garments of power is meant to change the direction of power, and thereby enable power to flow from the powerful to the disempowered. This touch is a transformative act: it seeks to shake the halls of power and lead the powerful to ask: "Who touched me?"

Jesus' response is significant in this story. While the woman comes openly, though in fear and trembling, and confesses that she "touched" the clothes of Jesus, he does not rebuke her for this daring, self-empowering act. Instead, he commends her act: "Daughter, your faith has made you well; go in peace, and be healed of your disease" (Mark 5:34). In addition, Jesus' readiness to travel with a synagogue leader, Jairus, to his house to bid a little girl arise, is an assurance to many African women theologians that Jesus supports both their moves towards self-empowerment and their call to those in power to distribute power to the disempowered. Jesus' and Jairus' journey challenges all those who are empowered, particularly the males, to scrutinize how they use their power: and to ask whether they are empowering others or not.

The story in Mark 5: 21-43 offers a model of transforming power, which calls for the active involvement of the powerless and the powerful. It is a model that involves reaching out to touch and being touched. It suggests that the powerful and powerless must work together to redistribute power, to share it and to use it positively. Jesus and Jairus represent those who hold power and who were willing to seek the empowerment of the disempowered. The bleeding woman, however, represents the powerless and the exploited. They are equally responsible for transforming power, by ensuring that it flows to their deprived circles too. The healers who took her money and failed to heal her, reminds us painfully that there are many who are in power who will use their positions to further exploit the least privileged. The story challenges the reader to take a certain position in relation to power. It challenges the reader to identify the group to which they belong: to those who run around and beg repeatedly for their dying daughters; to those who are willing to reach out to the places of power and redistribute it to those who need it; to those who are prepared to feel power leave them and flow elsewhere, and accept it; to those who are ready to exploit the weak and powerless; and to those little girls who are lying dead, and who must, nonetheless, hear the voice of life calling "Little girl, get up!" The little girl must start walking around and speaking. She must. To this task, African women theologians are committed.

The Girl Child, Power and Transformation

The plight of the girl child has recently been highlighted in the international forums where the gender struggles aimed at bringing about the empowerment of women take place. Beijing Platform for Action named the girl child as one of the twelve critical areas in the global struggles to empower women. It is recognized that in many societies "the girl child often faces discrimination from the earliest stages of life, through childhood and into adulthood." *("The girl child", 2000, p.)*. It is, therefore, acknowledged by many involved in the struggle today that the empowerment of women in society will be achieved if we also focus on the girl child, and seek to remove all the social constructions that disadvantage her. The many women, who find themselves poor, nameless and without professions in their societies endure this oppression because of gender socialization that begins from their birth and continues to mark their whole lives. African women have been "socially sick" since their birth due to the ascribed discriminative gender roles they carry out. They are just as sick as the little girls in many houses, who are at "the point of death". Because of this they have to struggle to touch the garments of power, and to redirect and redistribute power.

The powerlessness of many African women, their lack of material and financial resources, their non-involvement in the money making professions and public positions of influence, all render them sick and in search of healing. It forces them to search for the transformation of power in God's households - in the churches, synagogues, academic halls, in the private space of the home and in the open public spaces. They seek for the transformation of our current understanding, distribution and use of power so that it will allow women in public places to reach for power and those in the homes to arise from sickness and death. As used here, the term power can be defined as "the ability to bring change. Power is the ability to speak and be heard as well as the ability to implement your ideas in social institutions for public availability."[3] In Mercy A. Oduyoye's words, power is "the ability, skill and know-how and the strength to do something or make something happen."[4]

Power in itself is not negative; how it is used and allocated is important. If power is denied to certain groups of people, they are susceptible to manipulation by the powerful. They are exposed to the oppression of the powerful. It is only when power is distributed to all members of the society that there can be dialogue and respect for one another. Certain groups such as black people, women, children, many indigenous populations, people in the lower classes, homosexuals and the "Two-Thirds World"[5] populations have been systematically and historically kept from power. The writers of this volume are mostly at a distance from power through their social locations as women, black people and citizens of the Two-Thirds World. Being a black African, in particular, means being associated with economic poverty, illness and backwardness. Such is the image depicted in movies such as "Out of Africa", "Far Away Places", and "The

Gods Must be Crazy". In these days, one is seen to wear the "badge" of HIV/AIDS by virtue of geographical and racial identity. It is therefore fitting that African women theologians' quest for liberation should wrestle with, "transforming power" in God's household.

Transformation is a term that incorporates the will to change something. Transformation is not reformation, which maintains the basic structure. To transform is an attempt to inaugurate *metanoia*, a complete changing of the current situation. Transforming power thus can only describe the intention to change all the known aspects of power to a new understanding, use and allocation of power that affirms the involvement of all members of a society.[6] In the quest for this change, "the overriding question is how we, the women of Africa, can be attentive and receptive to God's power so that the concerns of women and their needs would be addressed by the larger community" (Kanyoro 1997:17).

The writers of the chapters in this volume have made the attempt to transform power by focusing on and in various social spaces. They scrutinize the imbalances of power, showing how black and white African women have been forced to occupy places of powerlessness in God's household. But since the whole creation is God's *oikos* - both the public and private spaces - African women seek to touch Jesus and shake all other places of power, thus asserting their right to human dignity. They seek to be part of the movement towards healing the world and themselves by transforming power to empower all people, regardless of their gender, age, race, class, religion, nationality and culture. They have heard the voice of Jesus calling "Get up" and they have risen.

Method and Theoretical Frameworks

The African women theologians who have contributed to this volume are from various parts of the continent. Collectively they bring different training, concerns, persuasions, nationalities, ethnic groups, classes and religious affiliations. It follows that their methods and theoretical frameworks will differ in their quest for transforming power in God's household. For example, some employ the term "feminist theology", while others prefer "African women's theology". The phrase, "women's theology", is mostly used by the Two-Thirds World women to distinguish their work from that of "First-World" or "Western" women. Feminism is sometimes associated with Western women. This has led some men in Two-Thirds World contexts to associate it with discourse concerning women's call for liberation and their quest for empowerment. These men have dismissed this discourse on the pretext that it is another Western imposition. Some women use the term, women's theology, and prefer to undertake "gender analysis" as opposed to "feminist" analysis. The choice is therefore, determined by a number of factors, such as one's context, the rhetorical ends sought, as well as theoretical understanding and dispositions. Similarly, some authors speak of "Africa" or "African women" while others prefer to be specific to their countries, regions and ethnic groups. The use of such categories as Africa or African women is open to question, for it suggests uniformity where there is enormous diversity (Appiah 1992). It is also a colonial and colonizing category, and one that is more often than not racist. It is racist because it does not give proper regard for the great differences in and among African people. Nonetheless, it is used in this volume as a category since it enables our discussion to address issues of concern that cut across the continent, and commands solidarity in the quest for liberation.

In terms of methods, the authors have also employed different tools. Some authors have used ideological readings of texts (Imathiu), narrative analysis (Njoroge), story-telling methods of analysis (Dube, Landman), autobiographical (Kiboko), documentation of historical and literary cases (Oduyoye). Others have critically (and discriminately utilized) and assessed the available standard theological frameworks (Ntloedibe-Kuswani, Acolatse and Abbey), and others have used fieldwork research methods (Beya). Most writers, however, employed a range of methods and categories of analysis. Gender analysis is central to each paper, and this is complemented by highlighting colonial encounters, and the socio-economic concerns of the continent. For the purposes of guiding the reader, through providing a working structure to the volume, these articles can be divided into the following three categories:

1. Circle transformative biblical hermeneutics
2. Circle transformation of theological frameworks
3. Circle transformation of the church and society.

Circle Transformative Acts

The term "circle" refers to the name "Circle for Concerned African Women Theologians" but it also serves as a theoretical framework. As used in this context, it describes African women theologians in various contexts, methods and concerns, who work together for the empowerment of women and the recognition of human dignity. A "circle of women" describes those who are seated together, who are connected and who seek to keep the interconnectedness of life. It signifies life as a continuous flowing force, which must continue to be nurtured by all and at all times. A circle of women pursuing theology together in different African contexts is an approach that insists that African women are also part of the life force in creation: they are in the circle of creation. It is an approach that pays attention to all that denies the fulfillment of women's lives and the assertion that African women are part of the circle of life. It is a circle for it seeks to ensure that power flows from all and to all among those who are in the circle of life.

The chapters in this volume, therefore, highlight some of the circle strategies of reading and practicing theology. Circle transformative acts seek to confront all the factors that deny African women and others on the continent their human rights and dignity. Circle transformative acts also seek to clear a space for transformation, and space for liberation and power sharing. In the following I shall briefly highlight the various methods employed by the authors, give a brief synopsis of each chapter, and relate them to the three categories identified above.

Circle Transformative Biblical Hermeneutics

This section features four writers: Grace Rose Imathiu, Musa W. Dube, Nyambura J. Njoroge and Christina Landman. They have undertaken various forms of biblical interpretation that focus on ways of reading whereby women can be empowered to become agents of self-actualization in their worlds.

In her chapter, "Reading Between the Lines: Power, Representation and Luke's Acts", Imathiu, who sees herself as a complex subject with many faces, recounts how, "the early images of the world constructed in [her] grandmother's house are significant to [her] self-understanding and her way of doing theology"(1). In her grandmother's house she learnt to value people for who they are: she learnt that as a woman one was expected to be "silent" and to express good behavior towards male persons. Imathiu also recalls how colonial pictures, from various parts of Africa, have shaped her way of reading. In these pictures, she notes that if Africans appeared with one or two Europeans they might be identified but their names were not mentioned. If identified it was through labels such as "natives," "chiefs" and "witch doctors". Further, the white males were often depicted as masters - being carried or served by Africans. These pictures often left her wondering, "who these people were and what their unwritten stories were". But she only heard the "deafening silence in the gaps of the recorded story"(2). Although well instructed in the mainstream methods of biblical analysis, Imathiu has come to realize that her training was infused with "elitism, patriarchy and Eurocentrism" and "western values of aesthetics and ethics"(2). It is the former experience of being a silenced woman and unnamed African that informs her reading practices. In her quest to transform power in this world of many silenced women and unidentified Africans, she has learnt to read between the lines. Imathiu maintains that: "A reading strategy of those who live on the peripherals of power is very different to the readings of those in power." For those who live in the margins, the focus in the narrative would be the unnamed persons and silent narrative. There is identification with the Other and the struggle to find God's word in such a situation. Imathiu demonstrates her method by interrogating the depictions of Samaritans in Luke's Acts. For Imathiu, African women readers can transform the discriminatory acts of silencing certain groups of people by reading in solidarity with the unnamed and articulating their suppressed voices.

Musa W. Dube's chapter is entitled "John 4:1-42: The Five Husbands at the Well of Living Waters: The Samaritan Woman and African Woman." She embarks on reading the story of the Samaritan woman through a storytelling method. Dube adopts this method because as she explains, for Southern African women, "storytelling has always been our language. We have always told stories by the fireside to pass wisdom and express ethics of living" (John 4:5). The re-telling of the Samaritan woman's story becomes the re-telling of the stories of Southern African women covering "the pre-colonial times, colonial times, the struggles for independence, post-independence, neocolonialism and globalization"(4). Each of these periods is characterized by a husband spending time with the Samaritan/Southern African woman and then passing on. Dube thus activates the five husbands of the Samaritan/Southern African woman and the current one, who is not hers (Globalization) to expose the exploitative relationships that they have had with the woman. Yet the re-telling does not end with the exploitative husbands. A liberating relationship is envisaged in the seventh scene of the story, when the woman encounters Justine. Here Dube makes the effort to dream of a new world that empowers both women and men.

Nyambura Njoroge's chapter, "A Spirituality of Resistance and Transformation", discusses the story of Rizpah within the African context, a context that is characterized by the violence and destruction that affects women and children more than anyone else. Njoroge points to the fact that Christianity is growing faster in Africa than elsewhere in the world, yet this is a glaring contradiction as increasing violence, exploitation and destruction mar the continent. With the plight of African women and children in mind, Njoroge travels with the Rizpah in search for a spirituality of resistance, which can "lead us to engage in restoring our human dignity and respect for life". She is struck by the strategy that Rizpah - a powerless woman and Saul's concubine - adopts in the face of male violence, the death of her children and the rampant disrespect for life. Rizpah, whose sons and those of Merab are killed and left unburied to satisfy the wronged Gibeonites, decides to sit by these dead bodies and guard them against being eaten by birds of the plains. This is, indeed, not only a form of mourning for a mother, but also a public statement of protest against violence and the injustice committed to the dead. Rizpah's act finally led King David to agree to the burial of the dead. To Njoroge, Rizpah is "a woman, a mother, who demanded action from the highest authority in the land in spite of her lowly status as a concubine". Njoroge's reading thus calls upon African women theologians to foster a "theology, which attempts to capture the spirit of Rizpah", one that turns "these tears, wailing and vigils into prophetic voices".

In the "Implementation of Biblical Hermeneutics", Christina Landman argues that biblical women characters were often invisible and without human dignity. Landman holds that they are often depicted as complying with their own victimization. This, she argues, hardly makes them viable as liberation role models for today's women, who are openly calling for their own empowerment. Landman thus maintains that there is a world of difference between ancient and contemporary women. She seeks for alternative women and finds them in extra-canonical books, such as "The Gospel of Mary Magdalene, The Acts of Thecla and The Book of Norea," which depicts women characters as public players, who often resisted patriarchal subordination. For Landman, these alternative women empower us to read the women in canonized gospels differently. They enable us to see that women in the early church were not always silent, submissive and confined to the domestic sphere: hence we must tell their untold stories.

Circle Transformation of Theological Frameworks

In this section four writers focus on transforming power by interrogating widely accepted or standard theological frameworks and concepts. In so doing the writers expose the patriarchal and colonial features of these constructions. They also move away from subscribing to oppressive and exploitative paradigms by proposing liberating frameworks that do not embrace gender discrimination or eurocentricism. Articles in this section include those of Gomang Ntloedibe-Kuswani, Esther Acolatse, Rose Teteki Abbey and Musimbi Kanyoro.

In her chapter, "The Religious Life of An African: A God given *Praeparatio Evangelica?*", Ntloedibe-Kuswani interrogates the presuppositions of a widely celebrated and established African theologian, John Mbiti. Her principal focus is on Mbiti's argument that African Religions are/ were a "preparation for the Christian gospel", not a self-contained and complete system of religious thought in their own right, which is also salvific. Ntloedibe-Kuswani investigates the historical background of this derogatory working assumption in Mbiti's theological thinking, and traces it back to the arrival of Christianity in Sub-Saharan Africa with its colonialist connotations. She holds that racism characterized the colonization of the continent to the degree that scientific, anthropological and missionary discourse concurred in painting a "very negative picture of anything African". Mbiti argued that African Religions are a preparation for the Christian gospel rather than the absolute opposite of Christianity. In reality, Mbiti's defense of African Religions operated within the colonial paradigm. It does not assert the individual existence, completeness and salvific character of African Religions, whereas the Christian religion is accorded the status of such privileges.

Ntloedibe-Kuswani further asks how such a construction affects African women. This construction of African religions, she argues, affected women negatively by distancing them from leadership in the church and society. While most African religions did not exclude women from the spiritual realm of leadership, Christianity and its male God, His son and male church leadership disempowered African women in church and society. Ntloedibe-Kuswani sees hope in the transformative paradigm articulated by the African Independent Churches that have given equal power to African religions and Christianity and to women. Further, she calls for a theological discourse that does not subscribe to patriarchy, colonialism or globalization. African Religions, she asserts, must be acknowledged in their own right.

In "Rethinking Sin and Grace: An African Evangelical Feminist Response" Esther E. Acolatse joins other western feminists to explore and analyze Niebuhr's construction of sin and grace. Acolatse holds that it is legitimate and necessary for an African woman to interrogate a western theologian's approach to these areas, for much of the theological thinking in mainline churches in Africa has been shaped by western theologians through missionaries. According to Acolatse, Niebuhr's doctrine of sin held that the "basic sin of humanity is pride"(5), which consists of three forms: power, knowledge and virtue. He regarded sensuality as the gratification of sensual appetites, which is an act of pride and self-centeredness. Niebuhr also understood grace to be the "shattering of the self, self-sacrifice and love of the other".

Acolatse addresses the problems raised by this theological construction, arguing that "Neibuhr's understanding of sin speaks primarily to men who are in the position of power and authority proffered by patriarchal societal structures". Acolatse thus argues that "Niebuhr describes male sin rather than sin generally"(6). She holds that sensuality as sin has been projected to women by men, leading to such atrocious practices as genital mutilation, also regarded as a sin by many who are religious. Accordingly, Acolatse questions Niebuhr's understanding of grace, holding that it cannot save women because it is inappropriate in the various patriarchal contexts that often places an onus on them to occupy positions of self-sacrifice, love of others and self-denial. This understanding of grace is misplaced because it can only endorse the patriarchal status quo for women. Further, Acolatse argues that Neibuhr's understanding of sin is not only patriarchal but is also class-ridden and white.

In her attempt to transform power so that it recognizes the humanity of both genders, all classes and all races, Acolatse strives to show that the understanding of grace and sin should be formulated in dialogue with a variety of other identities, and in their social locations and associated settings of power. For women in patriarchal societies, Acolatse maintains that "giving heedlessly" and "self-immolation for the sake of others" should be seen as sin, whereas self-assertion befriends grace. For women, grace should be "a journey towards self-hood, a coming into themselves, even self-love". In short, the way we articulate sin and grace should provide us with:

> practical steps of living together within the household of God in a way that edifies all who belong to the community. This means that men, women and children together live in such a way that accords full humanity to all participants in the *oikos* of God. (12)

Rose Teteki Abbey's "Rediscovering Ataa Naa Nyonmo - The Father Mother God" explores the naming of God in our biblical translations in the light of the fact that many African languages have gender-neutral names of the Divine. Abbey thus challenges the concept of the dominant male face/image of God. She looks at the biblical and Ghanaian metaphors of God and identifies the factors that determined why translators leaned towards male images of God rather than using inclusive ones. Abbey acknowledges that the dominant biblical metaphors of God are male, yet female ones also exist. The biblical feminine face of God is, however, suppressed "because it challenges the patriarchal nature of our societies"(3). Exploring the names of God amongst Ghanaian ethnic groups, Abbey highlights that the Supreme God is often accorded both gender neutral and specific names but is not presented exclusively in male images. Abbey prefers the image of Ataa Naa Nyonmo, Father Mother God, for "it speaks of God neither exclusively as Father nor as Mother, but takes the whole humanity into account"(4).

Abbey asks why African Christianity, despite the prevalence of gender-neutral names, has not adopted such images for itself. She points to patriarchy in the Bible, in

African cultures and to the arrival of Christianity in colonial contexts as the factors at work in this. The latter factors led to a dismissal of African cultures and did not lead missionaries to appreciate that African cultures have something to offer. Yet they used African names in their translations, but notably selected the male and "macho-oriented" ones. This male view of God, Abbey maintains, distances women from church leadership and it has also distanced from God those who have been abused by their earthly fathers. It creates a male oriented theology. In addition, in the African context whiteness is added to the picture of the divine, as attested by the widely promoted image of Jesus, who is projected as a white blond male.

In her attempt to transform power, Abbey joins Mercy Oduyoye's call for a theology that "flies on two wings". Abbey asserts that:

> Our theology, conversation about God, can only be said to have two wings when the Motherhood as well as the Fatherhood of God can be expressed freely by men and women doing theology. (10)

But to transform power in God's *oikos* such that it is spread across our diverse identities and affirms all of us, Abbey writes:

> the task of Christian theology...is to allow God to be black as well as white, gentile as well as Jew, poor as well as rich, crucified as well as risen, male as well as female. This will not only enhance our relation to God, it will also change the way we relate to each other. It is when we "see" God in these contradictions, these opposites that our theology will fly in two wings. (11)

Indeed, the task involves seeing God beyond the "constructed opposites", but across the wide spectrum of colors of our identities and cultures. Further, Abbey's paper challenges those African theologians, such as Lamin Sanneh and Kwame Bediako, who have acclaimed the translation of the Bible and the gospel into native tongues and cultures as something that brought Christianity home to the various African people. Abbey's study of translations of the Christian gospel, however, highlights that these translations did, in fact, distance African women from their accepted positions in social and spiritual realms.

"Engendered Communal Theology: African Women's Contribution to Theology in the 21st Century" places African women theologians' quest to transform power at the crossroads of African and feminist theologies. The writer, Kanyoro, suggests that African theologians have sought to articulate inculturation hermeneutics, which is the meeting point of biblical and African religious/cultural point of view. On the other hand, African women do not and cannot concentrate on similarities between African cultures and biblical stories, for they, more often than not, concur in endorsing patriarchal oppression. Kanyoro thus argues for an "engendered communal theology" that rises from the culture of the community, which nonetheless considers both the culture and the Bible from a gender perspective.

Kanyoro stresses that inculturation is insufficient for African women. Rather, women should apply a method that "puts culture to a thorough exegesis"(3). African women, Kanyoro argues, cannot work from premises that celebrate "all cultural practices regardless of their negative impact on women". Rather, in their quest for transforming power in God's household, African women need to carry out gender analysis of both the Bible and their cultures. They also need to "build solidarity with others in community for ... change of oppressive systems has to be done within the community"(3).

Circle Transformation of the Church and Society

This section features three writers, Bernadette Mbuy Beya, Kabamba Kiboko and Mercy Amba Oduyoye. Their papers are different from the others because they focus on practical examples of transforming and using power.

In "Women in the Church in Africa: Possibilities for Presence and Promises" Bernadette Mbuy Beya describes a strategy that involves fieldwork research to document the activities of women and men in the church, and the role of academic forums, such as Circle of Concerned Women

Theologians and EATWOT (Ecumenical Association of Third World Theologians) in transforming power. Mbuy Beya focuses on Roman Catholic women in the Democratic Republic of Congo, who are actively providing leadership in the church. She documents their stories of involvement, achievement and the difficulties that confront them. This presentation is a persuasive testimony and indicates the contribution of those involved in acts whereby power is transformed. Her approach is also a form of action-oriented research, an approach that confronts us with facts and recommendations from the field. It calls on those in power to respond by putting in place space for women in the church to serve God freely and with all their gifts.

Mbuy Beya's approach also focuses on the structures of power and how they can create the space for transformation. She discusses official statements from the Vatican that promise power sharing, and that contain the potential to transform power. She also identifies both the activities of the Circle and EATWOT as structural spaces that can inaugurate transformation in the use, allocation and sharing of power in God's *oikos*.

In her chapter, "Sharing Power: An Autobiographical View", Kiboko, another DRC theologian, highlights a strategy for church women to create space for transforming power. Kiboko focuses on United Methodist Women, their solidarity and their struggle to empower the girl child by undertaking an interventionist strategy of providing room and board for poor female students, and those from homes far away. The strategy protects female students against sexual exploitation and enables them to finish their educational training. Kiboko then relates this national story to her own life and her village of Dilambwe, and introducing us to Sanga women. She shows us how they read the Bible together, how they examined power amongst themselves, and how they have been a constant form of support to her, even up to her doctoral studies. In telling this story of "sharing power" Kiboko provides us with a model of transforming power. Instead of women sitting and bemoaning that they are women, excluded and marginalized by patriarchal institutions, they can be seen to act together to examine how they are involved in the same oppressive uses of power. They can thus begin to actively empower each other and the girl child by undertaking projects that empower them against gender oppressive social systems. In this way they too are calling "Little girl, get up!" Kiboko's approach thus provides us with a model of women as agents of change in the transformation of power.

Mercy Amba Oduyoye's chapter, "Transforming Power: Paradigms from the Novels of Buchi Emecheta," searches for models of women in power in the novels of Buchi Emecheta. She uses the cases of the women in the novels to explore and document their use of power, and the possible models of transformation they may offer. These models of power from Emecheta's novels highlight how African women are depicted in relation to traditional expectations. Oduyoye explores how they are creating new spaces and new uses of power, by developing the capacity to confront and examine their designated places in society.

This coverage of Buchi Emecheta's work is significant, for it highlights women's contributions to the construction, deconstruction and reconstruction of social reality. Similarly, history has indeed been "his story", a story that has excluded women's story and their perspectives. Oduyoye's account of women and power serves to deconstruct the patriarchal gaps that continue to marginalize and silence women.

New Horizons: Calling Talitha Cum!

The writers of the chapters in this volume make a contribution to African theology in a number of ways. First, they provide new insights and methods of reading, and they widen the categories of inquiry. Of particular note is the authors' use of storytelling and its associated ideological inquiry in biblical reading strategies. They tell biblical stories, and in their socio-economic stories of the African continent, gender oppression is highlighted, and new visions of the world are advanced. Second, the close scrutiny of the choices for the names of God in the Bible highlights how renowned translations of theologies have, for Africa, subscribed to patriarchal and colonizing frameworks. Instead of bringing the gospel home to women, translation of the Bible in Africa has, in fact, marginalized African women and excluded them from social and spiritual spaces. Third, inculturation is also questioned. It is shown to involve the oppression of women and there is a call to extend repertoires and to widen its boundaries through adding the tools of gender analysis. Fourth, African women's use of action oriented research also underlines their social engagement in and commitment to social transformation. As Kanyoro maintains: "For us in Africa, it does not matter how much we write of our theology in books, the big test before us is whether we can bring change in our societies."(2)

In their writings the contributors also embrace global theological levels. First, while white feminist theologians have championed gender analysis aimed at dismantling patriarchy, they have, more often than not, failed to demonstrate an equal commitment to the global oppression inherent in colonialism, neocolonialism and globalization. These essays take these forms of oppression into account, together with other categories such as race, class, age and religion (See Imathiu, Ntloedibe-Kuswani, Kiboko, Abbey and Kanyoro). The authors offer penetrating critiques of widely accepted theological frameworks, to which even women subscribe, thus showing how embedded they are in a colonial and patriarchal mind-set. In so doing the contributors collectively call for the decolonization and depatriarchalization of African theological discourse as a whole. Second, while Western feminists have argued for inclusive language in biblical translations, more often than not they did not have the necessary prerequisite gender inclusive names for the Divine. In this volume African women theologians propose gender-neutral names of God from their languages, names that provide much needed and credible alternatives. These alternatives challenge Bible translators to confront their own patriarchally informed translations and the impact they may have on the lives of women.

Third, the storytelling method makes a major contribution to feminist discourse. The call to re-tell biblical stories so that they tell the untold stories of women was sounded long ago. Yet, little work has been done to further this. This has, perhaps, been due to the pressure on feminists to write in an academically acceptable idiom. Dube's elaborate story on the Samaritan woman, and her interaction with the many husbands of her life, is an attempt to rewrite and to articulate the Samaritan/Southern African woman's untold experiences. It also proposes a vision of a just world.

Fourth, the authors undertake to analyze biblical and African religions. They call for a feminist gender analysis that pays attention to both traditions. In so doing, they underline the multicultural character of our existence, and call for feminist biblical narrations that take cognizance of the diverseness for our global village.

These chapters, and the pledges contained to transforming power, come through the voices of Talitha Cum, the little girl who was called to life. This Talitha Cum, who energizes African women theologians, therefore, is not the one who awaits the saving touch of Jesus and Jairus. Rather, she is the one who is already alive: she is one who is up and walking about. African women theologians seek to travel with Talitha Cum, to name her, to give her a voice to speak out in public and private spaces. They seek to empower her in the process of seeking out their own empowerment. The chapters in this volume, and the work of African women theologians as a whole, continue to articulate the unfinished business of the little girl who rose from death and who is up and about. They continue to stretch their hands to touch the garments of power. They continue to call, *a luta continua* - the struggle continues!

Endnotes

1.   Kiboko, K. Sharing Power: An Autobiographical View. p.

2.   See Dube Shomanah (1999) where we find "Mama Africa's surprising assumption of power, when she calls Thalitha Cum! to those who have been buried by the various forms of oppression" (p. 11).

3.   Imathiu, R. T. p. 3

4. Oduyoye, M. A.

5. The term Two-Thirds World is preferred here rather than Third World.

6. Transforming Power: Women in God's Household was the theme of the 1996 general meeting of the Pan African Circle of Concerned African Women Theologians held in Nairobi. Two-thirds of the articles in this book were written for, and presented at, this conference.

References

Appiah, K. A. (1992). *In My Father's House: Africa in the Philosophy of Culture.* New York: Oxford University Press.

Dube Shomanah, M. W. (1999). "Fifty years of Bleeding: A Storytelling Feminist Reading of Mark 5:24-43." *The Ecumenical Review,* 51(1), 11-17.

"The Girl Child: Fact Sheet No 12." (2000) in *Women 2000.* New York: United Nations.

Kanyoro, M. R. A. (1997). "Celebrating God's Transforming Power", in M. Oduyoye (Ed.), *Transforming Power: Women in the Household of God.* Accra: Sam Woode, 7-27.

Oduyoye, M. A. (Ed.). (1997). *Thalita Qumi.* Ibadan: Daystar Press.

Oduyoye, M. A., & Kanyoro, M. R. A. (Eds.). (1992). *The Will to Arise: Women, Tradition and the Church in Africa.* New York: Orbis Books.

Circle Transformative Biblical Hermeneutics

Reading Between the Lines: Power, Representation and Luke's Acts

Grace Rose Imathiu

Introduction: A Woman's Experience

I am an African woman from the Meru community on the slopes of Mt. Kenya. I am educated in the ways of the west having lived in the USA and England for eleven years. I am third-generation Christian and second-generation clergy. I am the second daughter of my mother, and I am therefore named according to Meru tradition after my maternal grandmother, my *ntagu*. When my parents were in England for further studies, my maternal grandmother was responsible for me. My grandfather was a successful businessman who lived in town and visited us occasionally. It was understood that the home I was growing up in belonged to *ntagu*.

The early images of the world constructed in my grandmother's house are significant to my self-understanding and the way I do theology. In my grandmother's house each person was valued for whom they were, not in proportion to the size of their contribution: when we walked to fetch water at the river, my grandmother carried a big tin drum and I carried a bottle; when we cooked she peeled the bananas and I shelled the peas; the days we had meat for a meal, I held one end of the piece while she cut the meat into stew pieces. Even at five years of age, I was allowed to participate in the life of the community and understood myself to be a valued member of the community.

Although all my formal studies of scripture have been carried out in Western institutions of learning, it is this socio-cultural location that has informed the foundation of my theology. My formal studies in biblical studies have failed to take seriously my socio-cultural location. I have been in a program of instruction that proposes to make me into a "critical scholar" who is apparently able to transcend my own prejudices and able to adapt a reading strategy that is objective, value-free, and rational. I have been instructed in linguistics, since my research involves foreign languages, instructed in procedures of literary criticism, since I deal with written texts, and I have a working knowledge of the social scientific method, such as is used in archaeology, history, and computer science. The induction of critical scholars like myself not only shortens the radius of the circle of those who can sit in discussion on biblical studies: it also places a greater value on written texts over and above other legitimate traditions.

With time I have become suspicious of this approach to biblical studies. It is an approach to biblical studies that has an agenda, one that must be exposed, denounced and brought to justice in the way it propagates elitism, patriarchy, and Eurocentrism. The end product of these methods is "written and coherent narrative", a narrative that is, for the sake of coherence, selective, interpretative, editorial, and manipulative of events. The coherency of the narrative in turn is based on a matrix of meaning. When this matrix of meaning is interrogated, it is found to be deeply located in western consciousness, and imbued with western values of aesthetics and ethics.

I do not know if you have ever looked at those historical photographs taken during colonial times in various parts of Africa where there are one or two Europeans and African people. These photographs may range from a white hunter displaying a leopard skin, a white couple enjoying a bush tea party to a white man being carried on a rig on the shoulders of African people. Have you noticed that these photographs identify Europeans by name and often refer to Africans as "natives" or ignore their presence altogether? Have you ever noticed that the only African people named in these photographs are the chiefs and so-called "witch doctors"? When I look at these photographs I am disturbed.

I have come to the conclusion that the photographer, a European, composed pictures based on what he thought was of importance. Thus the man "behind the camera", in neglecting to identify the African people by name as individuals, has succeeded in making Africans a group of people who lack identity as individuals. Just as the group was seen to represent the individual, an individual African was understood to represent the group. The chiefs and witch doctors on the other hand were perceived as individuals because they were identified as members of a powerbase, individuals with whom Europeans had to contend.

If you are like me, you might have spent hours peering into the African faces wondering who these people were and what their unwritten stories were. You, too, might have felt the deafening silence in the gaps in the recorded story, in the "heroic" model of grand history, a model that ignores their story.

All these observations and reflections are pertinent to biblical studies, especially to the theme of power, and specifically as it is reflected in relationships. At the outset, there is the challenge of defining power clearly, and in succinct terms that help illustrate how power dictates whose voice is to be included and whose voice is to be excluded. Power is the license to construct the picture presented and the capacity to edit, manipulate, exclude and include in order to represent what is seen as the other. Power is the capacity to choose to name and choose not to name. Power is the capacity to bring change. Power is the capacity to present or dismiss the other. Power is the authority to speak and be heard as well as the capacity to implement your ideas in social institutions for public usefulness.

The systematic dismissing of the others present by refusing to name them is consistent with the experience of Meru women. The Meru women are the "Other" in my society. Women are known as their father's daughters when unmarried, their husband's wives when married, and are also referred to as the mother of their firstborn child after motherhood. Women are denied presence as individuals in their own right by the patriarchal model's refusal to name them.

At that early age, I noticed that the household was unusually quiet when my grandfather visited us from his residence in town. I also learned that my grandmother respected my grandfather greatly, and respect was shown through the code of silence. Because she was silent over her trials and tribulations, my grandmother was praised as a good wife. My grandmother never spoke about any of my grandfather's weaknesses although I often glimpsed tears in her eyes and a biting of the lip. I, too, was expected to respect my grandfather at all times. I was expected to be silent in the presence of my grandfather: a child seen but never heard. My grandfather regarded my silence with praise, often commenting what a polite child I was, and promising to take me visiting since he was sure I would not embarrass him.

The code of silence was established in our relationship with my grandfather as the greatest tool of patriarchal thoughts, colonialism and Western civilization in general. Oppressive reigns depend on a silencing of the Other and the passive acceptance of the pain and oppression in their lives as their lot. The Other is silenced in various ways, all of which are geared into devaluing and invalidating any of his/her experiences. A helpful example is in the attitude towards women's work.

Traditionally sociologists have assumed that women's work behavior is gender-based but that men's is not. Family and parenting have traditionally been viewed as female issues alone. Since women perform the domestic tasks with no special and formal training, women's work is understood as something anyone could handle. Women's work is therefore overloaded, undervalued, and often invisible. These erroneous presumptions carry over to the public employment sector where women's work is often supportive, caring and care taking. The leading jobs for women have traditionally been primary school teachers, secretaries, registered nurses, typists and bookkeepers. Such work often includes service to others, and often parallels the kinds of tasks women are expected to do because of their gender.

My suspicions about such issues began when I constantly found that there were biblical passages that were particularly meaningful to my community, which were superficially dealt with or totally ignored by commentary after commentary. For a long time I respected the commentaries and assumed that my community had made a mistake and that these passages and characters were really not as important as we had assumed. But I had to deal with the reality as a pastor, that my community found itself addressed in many of the gaps and silences in the text as well as in the peripheral characters of the narrative. Thus began the journey towards undertaking a reading of the text whereby my community's experience was taken seriously and valued. This would be a reading that took the flesh and blood of the various backgrounds of readers seriously. It would be a reading approach that would lengthen the radius of the circle of those who could interpret scripture to include even the rural African woman.

African biblical hermeneutics interested in the experiences and hopes of African women must take seriously a reading strategy that takes into account the text's silent characters - a reading strategy that "reads between the lines" using women's experience as a resource. The reading strategy of those who live on the periphery of power is very different from that of those in power. For those who live on the margins, the focus in the narrative would be the unnamed persons and the silent characters of the narrative. There is identification with the Other and a struggle to find God's word in such a situation. I will now give an example of my reading strategy.

Reading Between the Lines of Luke's Acts

In the Christian Scriptures the treatment of the Samaritans as the Other in Luke's Acts is of particular interest. There are four stories mentioning the Samaritans in Luke's Acts: the parable of the compassionate Samaritan traveler (Luke 10:25-37); the grateful Samaritan leper who returned to give Jesus his thanks (Luke 17:11-19); the refusal to offer

Jesus hospitality by a Samaritan village (Luke 9:51-56); and the story of Simon the Magician's conversion (Acts 8:5-25). My focus is on the last text.

Acts 8:5-25 presents an exceptionally interesting encounter with the representation of the Other when the Other is seen as a object of resistance to Christian missionary activity. Paying particular attention to the rhetoric and characterization of the Samaritans in their position as the Other yields the bigotry lurking in the heart of missionary outreach. For those of us who are not included in the larger recital of our own histories, there is consistency in a reading strategy that pays careful attention to the text's omissions and gaps, and the exclusion and editing out of certain voices. These gaps are to be understood as programmatic, leading to an examination as to whom the text has excluded and why. My particular social location and historical context has especially sensitized me to the various ways of excluding the Other. My own location has made me aware of the omission of names of persons and places in discourse, the negative labeling of the Other's cultural practices, and the voices of characters in a narrative - who speaks, when and to whom they speak, what is said and whose words are recorded.

The narrative in Acts 8:5-25 is a seemingly straightforward story of a successful Christian mission to the Samaritans and the subsequent establishment of a Christian community in Samaria. The story begins with Philip preaching to the Samaritans in general but moves to the particular and specific evangelizing, conversion, baptism, laying on of hands and rebuking of Simon. Simon is the only named Samaritan actor in the narrative in contrast to the naming of Phillip, Peter, John and Jerusalem. At the beginning of the narrative, Simon has powerful magic and is held in awe by many in Samaria. Simon also has economic resources, and he offers to buy the gift of imparting the Holy Spirit from the apostles. Peter discounts Simon's magic and money. At the close of the narrative Simon is impotent, shamed and groveling at Peter's feet: his magic has been taken.

This is a particularly disturbing narrative for me. In the first instance, the historical tensions and hostility between the Samaritan and Jewish communities raise concern that the "missionaries" to Samaria – Phillip, Peter and John – are Jews. The history of political tension, religious schism, and ethnic and cultural hostility between Jerusalem and Samaria cannot be suspended. Centuries of rivalry between these two communities form the backdrop to the narrative. There was theological and political rivalry between Samaria and Jerusalem, which led to schism between the two groups. Discrepancies exist in the traditions of the two groups, one of which is of the origins of the Samaritans. The Samaritan tradition maintains that they are the direct descendants of the faithful nucleus of ancient Israel.[1] According to this tradition, the breach with the Judeans started in the time of Eli who founded at Shiloh an apostolic sanctuary dedicated to Yahweh. However, the Law of Moses assigned Mount Gerizim as the true "chosen place". This Samaritan infamy was later reinforced by the "accursed Ezra" who falsified the sacred text thereby seducing the people, on their return from the Babylonian exile, to erect the second temple beside the Judean capital. The Jewish traditions on the other hand link the Samaritans to the colonists from various Mesopotamia towns who settled in the Northern Kingdom following the conquests of the Assyrians. Jewish tradition maintains that these colonists adopted the Israelite faith alongside their own religions. These were the basic reasons why the Samaritans obstructed the efforts of Ezra and Nehemiah to rebuild Jerusalem and re-establish the sanctuary of Yahweh (Ezra 4:2; Nehemiah 2:19; 4:2).

In light of the conflicting traditions on the origins of the Samaritans, any missionary enterprise originating from Jerusalem to Samaria must be considered suspect and thoroughly interrogated. Jerusalem was not and cannot be seen as a neutral entity *vis-à-vis* Samaria.

Luke records the lack of welcome and reception Jesus received in a Samaritan village "*oti to prosopon autou hen poreuomenon eis Ierousalem*" (Luke 9:53). Peter and John "went back, returned, made their way back" to Jerusalem. The text identifies and affirms Jerusalem as the seat of power from whence apostles would come and to where they would return. Consequently, while the narrative is Christian, its allegiance to Jerusalem inherently influences its characterization of the Samaritans.

According to Acts 8:4-5, Phillip was one of those forced to leave Jerusalem after the martyrdom of Stephen. He fled to Samaria where he became successful as a missionary. Simon Magus is said to be one of his converts. Philip instructed and baptized an Ethiopian eunuch, a non-Jew, and preached in every city from Asdod to Caesarea on the sea. Phillip was a deacon and not a disciple. He appears first as one of the Greek-speaking Christians, set apart to perform certain administration tasks in the Jerusalem community (Acts 6:5). According to Acts 21:8-9 he had four daughters whom were known as "virgin prophetesses".

In Acts 8, Phillip is presented as a successful missionary, preaching the good news and performing miraculous signs in a Samaritan city. The Samaritan city is not named. The omission of the Samaritan city's name is pronounced and in blatant contrast to the recognition given to Greek and Roman cities that are named in Acts; including Seleucia (Acts 13:4), Paphos (Acts 13:6), Perga (Acts 13:13), Phrygia and Galatia (Acts 15:6). This omission of the name of the first site where a Christian missionary breakthrough took place is both curious and suspicious. There are two things of note. First, there is suspicion as to the credibility of this text as a factual and accurate report. One might argue that the city was unnamed because there was no such city; no such evangelization; and no such conversions. The credibility of the report is therefore put in question by the omission of the name of the Samaritan city.

It is not inconceivable that this missionary report was fictional but functional. The report served a purpose in that the Samaritan city was a generalization for all Samaritan cities. A Christian mission breakthrough in only one unnamed Samaritan city was intended to imply that the entire Samaria region had been successfully evangelized. The individual thus becomes the representative of the group.

This successful and triumphalistic mission to Samaria counters the earlier Lukan text of the Samaritan rejection of the Christian message by an unnamed Samaritan village in Luke 9:51-57. The narrator's intention of portraying a complete and total evangelization of Samaria is further demonstrated by the lack of any further mention of Samaria or Samaritans in Acts.

A second matter to note is that Luke, in refusing to name the Samaritan city, demonstrated bigotry and consciously plotted a strategy whereby Samaria would be disenfranchised. The Samaritan city is not named. To name a place is to give it power. To ignore a name is to disenfranchise and dismiss the place as insignificant. This strategy is similar to the recent colonial ones discussed above.

Phillip's preaching leads to the conversion and baptism of many in the Samaritan city. In whichever way one may choose to understand Phillip's activity, it was something that brought a complete change of heart to the Samaritans in this unnamed city. The narrator defines Phillip's work as "miracles" *vis-à-vis* Simon's magic. This is consistent with the determined distinguishing of the Christian mission from the magic practiced in the Greco-Roman world. C. E. Arnold defines magic as:

> a method of manipulating supernatural powers to accomplish certain tasks with guaranteed results. Magicians would not seek the will of the deity in a matter, but would invoke the deity to do precisely as stated. (Arnold 1993:580)

B. L. Blackburn, who holds that supernatural events transcend ordinary happenings, associates them with divine power: they are manifestations of God's power. According to him, they manifest God's saving or judging purpose (1992).

This term "magic" functions as a disclaimer of the miracles performed by non-Christian groups. The term should be regarded as a convenient propagandist label constructed to discredit the Other. In this text, Simon becomes the supreme example of the magus, a construction that carries over in the narrative's polemic and in non-canonical texts.

Magi are mentioned only three times in the New Testament, but the word appears frequently in the Greek translations of the Old Testament for such terms as "enchanter", "diviner" and "necromancer". Originally Magi were a shaman caste of the Medes. They then became the Zoroastrian priests of Persian. Some scholars argue that in the Mediterranean world the term had lost its national connotation and it was used to refer to the profession of persons engaged in such activities as astrology, necromancy, exorcism and incantations.

Simon has come to be known as "Simon Magus" in Christian literature and interpretation. The word "magus" does not actually occur in the story. The participle *mageuwn* - practicing as a magus- and the noun *tais mayais* - works of a magus - indicate clearly enough that Simon was a magus by profession. He ought to be compared with Elymas-bar-Jesus (Acts 13:6-12), a magus and false prophet and associated with the Proconsul. Joseph mentions another magus, Atomos, who is associated with Governor Felix.[2]

The later generations of Christians regarded Simon Magus as an impostor whose becoming a Christian only from base motives is obvious. But Acts states simply that Simon believed and was baptized and continued his association with Phillip, who was deeply impressed by the signs he showed. His only major mistake was that he thought he could buy the ability to impart the Holy Spirit, of which the apostles held a monopoly. For this error, Peter pronounced a merciless denunciation, yet it appears that even Phillip did not possess this power. One motif of the story seems to be that only the apostles could impart the Holy Spirit.

Speculation on Simon gripped the imagination of the early Christians. They wove about him a romantic saga, one that expressed various Gnostic ideas. Eusebius says that Simon was the author of sacrifices and lamentations.[3]

Justine first says Simon moved around with a woman named Helena who had been a prostitute in Tyre. Justine also says the Romans worshipped Simon and had set up a statue for him on the island of Tiber. Irenaeus adds that Helena was held in captivity by the Lower angels and archangels and Simon had assumed the form of the lower powers in order to redeem her. Irenaeus further ascribes three identities to Simon and that he had three followings: Simon appears to the Jews as the Son, to the Samaritans as the Father, and to others as the Holy Spirit.[4]

There have been questions raised as to whether Simon actually existed or whether he was mythical figure. The text has incomprehensible features. For instance, no commentary has given an acceptable meaning to his *legwn einai tina eautou megan* (Acts 8:9) or the people saying, *Outos estin n dunamis tou Qeou h kalumenh Megalh* (Acts 8:10). These words, because of their mysterious nature, have fallen on fertile ground and germinated a luxuriant crop of legends.

The text surprisingly presents Phillip's successful mission of preaching the good news, persuading and baptizing many, both men and women, as incomplete. Conversion and baptism do not set adequate boundaries for Christian self-definition in the church represented by the narrator. Hence it becomes necessary for Peter and John to come down from Jerusalem to visit the Samaritan mission.

Peter and John find that although the Samaritans are baptized, they have not received the Holy Spirit. The narrative suggests that the converted and baptized Samaritans are not complete. It takes the authority of Jerusalem to complete the process. John and Peter become the agents for this second phase of setting a boundary for the Samaritan Christian community. These two leaders pray for the converted Christian Samaritans, lay hands on them, and they receive the Holy Spirit.

Simon, the newly converted ex-magician is thoroughly impressed by Peter and John's ability to impart the Holy Spirit with the laying-on of hands. He offers Peter and John money in exchange for this "magic," so that he too might be able to have the ability to impart the Holy Spirit with the laying on of his hands. Peter is appalled and offended by Simon's offer and he rebukes him in stern and scathing terms. Simon is frightened, cowers before Peter, and submits to Peter's authority.

The narrative creates a hierarchy by playing characters off against each other. For instance, on the one hand, Simon

Magus is described as powerful and awesome, and on the other hand, he is presented as astounded by Phillip's acts of power. What is of critical concern here is that this is much more just individuals battling for power. It is a cultural battle.

The naming of characters in narratives is a powerful tool for exercising control. The image of the Other can be manipulated by the narrator into silence or total absence. Names are devices that the narrative uses in exerting domination over the Other. The lack of names for Samaritan characters and villages in Luke's Acts offers us an opportunity to see the operative nature of this paradigm. Any powerful characters are downgraded with negative labeling. Simon the Samaritan is therefore labeled as a magus whereas Phillip is said to perform miracles.

African women are a welcome recourse in biblical hermeneutics because of our experience of alienation as the Other in our cultural contexts. This experience has involved living in societies where we are not named as individuals but as men's daughters, men's wives or mothers. Our claim to individuality is a claim to our God-given right. Our reading strategy must therefore be one of seeking out the gaps and silences in the text and re-imagining the unspoken stories. The text will thus become our departure point for our speaking about our own unspoken stories.

Endnotes

1. See the discussion that Jesus held with the Samaritan woman in John 4 1-42.

2. See the observations of Josephus in Antiquities of the Jews IV, 1.

3. This claim is made by Eusebius in the History of the Christian Church, from the earliest times to AD 461, F.J. Foakes Jackson, 1957, III, 31, 3-4, V. 24.

4. For this observation see Eusebius in Antiquities of the Jews XX, VII, 2.

References

Arnold, C. E. (1993). "Magic" in G. F. Hawthorne, R. Martin, & D. Reid (Eds.), *Dictionary of Paul and His Letters*. Leicester: Intervarsity Press.

Blackburn, B. L. (1992). "Miracles and Miracle Stories" in J. Green, S. McKnight, & H. Marshall (Eds.), *Dictionary of Jesus and the Gospels*. Leicester: Intervarsity Press.

John 4: 1-42 - The Five Husbands at the Well of Living Waters: The Samaritan Woman and African Women

Musa Wenkosi Dube

Samaritan Woman

The sun is in the midsky
Its rays pour down harsh, hot air
Yet you walk to the well, there is no siesta for you
You walk to the well in the hot day
For you are thirsty

Hush, woman, hush
For no more shall you braze the rays
Not again shall you thirst; this day you quit
Carrying a pail of water to the well
You shall leave your pail

Hush, Samaritan woman
For no more shall you drag your feet
Under the hot sands and weights of pails of water
Today you shall spring into the village
To proclaim the good news

Spring, Samaritan woman
For there is no more this race and that mountain
No more Jew or Samaritan, no male nor female here
Only Truth and Spirit are in the ripe fields
Awaiting your harvest

Introduction: The Samaritan Woman and Samaria

Biblical scholars have noted that the five husbands of the Samaritan woman and the woman herself are featured as symbols.[1] The five husbands stand for the foreign powers that ruled Samaria. The last husband, who is not hers, refers to the Roman Empire, which was the contemporary political power. The woman character represents the land, Samaria. The story, therefore, embodies a comment about various political powers that ruled Samaria. Indeed, the identification of a woman with the land is quite common. For example, we often speak of Mama Africa, Mother Africa or the Motherland. The land, like a woman, gives birth to and nurtures life. The land, like a woman, is something that we enter, take and possess: something we try to control and own. Nonetheless, many studies have shown that the identification of land and female gender reinforces the subjugation of women, wherever such narratives are read or such thinking is found. Just as much as male political powers will strive to enter, own, control and possess the land, the same will apply to women. Both the land and the woman are victims of social exploitation and subjugation. What about Africans and African women!

Africa and African Women

In the following dramatic re-telling, the Samaritan woman shall stand for both the woman and the land. The woman shall stand for both Africa and women of Africa. The story is now retold as a comment on the various political regimes that have come through Southern Africa, converging in the present day Zimbabwe. Despite this specificity, it is expected that many African women can read the story to tell their own regional and national stories of exploitation and the struggle to survive. In this re-telling, the story of the Samaritan woman is our story. Her experience of many husbands is our experience. In short, the economic and political crisis of African countries, under foreign and local political powers alike, is a story that we share with the Samaritan woman. This situation exposes most African women to multiple forms of oppression. Most African women are oppressed because of gender, racial/ethnic and religious tensions as well as the economic and political crisis suffered by the whole continent. This politically unstable context manifests itself in colonialism, neo-colonialism, coups, ethnic and civil wars, crime, diseases and globalization. In the past and present times African women have been the hardest hit. In colonial times, African women were systematically marginalized from education, church roles and clerical jobs, and, like the whole continent, they were dispossessed and denied their basic human rights. In contemporary times, African women are the hardest hit: they are in refugee camps; they live with poverty and starvation; they are caught in the violent civil and ethnic wars and oppressive international financial policies; and they live with and die of AIDS. As Southern African women we find that, together with the rest of Africa, we have had many husbands, but we have not yet had one to call our own. As the dramatic re-telling will show, even the husband we have now is not our own. Our struggle against exploitative forces and our search for liberating interdependence, both at national and international levels, is an on going story.

"How Can You a Jew Ask a Drink of me, a Woman of Samaria?" (John 4:9)

Another point raised by the Samaritan woman is that of racial and ethnic tension. The Samaritan woman poses a crucial question to Jesus: "How can you, a Jew, ask a drink of me, a woman of Samaria? (Jews do not share things in common with Samaritans)" (John 4:9). The relationship between Samaritans and Jews was characterized by racial tension. The question of ethnic tension and racial discrimination based on fear and suppression of differences is a painful experience of all African countries at local and international level. In Somalia, Rwanda, Burundi and many other countries we are plagued by the sin of having "no dealings" with our neighbors.

We practice various ways of discriminating against our neighbors. In Botswana we have Basarwa, or the so-called Bushmen, whom we exploit because of their different lifestyle. In Zimbabwe, we had segregation of land policies that dispossessed the black masses for the benefit of a minority of white settlers. As we speak, the land question is yet to be solved in Zimbabwe. In South Africa, apartheid was a plague for many decades. Indeed, the apartheid government was toppled in the 1990s, but the decades of structural marginalization and deprivation are a wound that will remain with us for a long time. We are struggling with the many years of systematic deprivation of black South Africans. Generations of young people who were denied education and access to professional training can only resort to crime, which is currently affecting the whole region. As in Zimbabwe, the dispossession of black people of their land is yet to be addressed. Apartheid, both in South Africa and Zimbabwe, was certainly an economic system of exploitation designed to appropriate the resources and labor of black people for the benefit of minority whites.

Internationally, as Africans, we are discriminated against on the basis of our color. Since imperial times when Africa was "constructed" as "the dark continent" and its people were portrayed as "savage" and "childish" in colonial literature, we live with this international discrimination. Such constructions served to justify colonial oppression, for then colonizers could claim to bring light to us and to rule us since we were children who needed guidance. We still live with this overt discrimination. People of African descent, living in the Diaspora, struggle with racial marginalization and oppression. Many African travelers can tell their stories of crossing the borders in the airports and of living overseas. Yet this racial discrimination continues to validate our economic marginalization in a world that is largely becoming globalized. For instance: the glaring absence of black faces among the G7; our unrepresented face in small things such as international weather prediction presented on first world television; and in "Grammy" Awards. These reflect that we are not represented or we are simply ignored by structures that affect our lives. While it seems that the First World has "no dealings" with Africa, they are constantly designing economic policies and projects that makes us the market of their goods and provider of a cheap workforce to feed the labor demands of their multi-national corporations. Their multi-national companies, which supposedly create jobs for us, specialize in suppressing our small businesses, and maximizing profit for themselves. Racial discrimination, therefore, always carries an economic face, and it is one evil suffered by black Africans, regardless of their gender, class, religion and geographical location.

The story of the Jewish and Samaritan relationship of "no dealings" is, therefore, close to us. It touches our hearts, for we have had our own Jewish and Samaritan relationships, both internationally and locally. Our experience makes us identify with the Samaritans, who were also despised and marginalized. We read this story with a keen eye to understanding how racial and ethnic discrimination works. We read the story of "no dealings" as a story that authorizes economic exploitation. But above all, we read this story with a keen search for healing, for a revolutionized world, a just world of loving our neighbors, as we love ourselves.

"Our ancestors worshipped on this mountain... but you say that ... people must worship in Jerusalem." (John 4:20)

Let us now turn to the question of religious tension, which is also pertinent to our context. The Samaritan woman also posed a question of religious differences and tension to Jesus: "Our ancestors worshipped on this mountain, but you say that the place where people must worship is in Jerusalem," (John 4:20). The Samaritan woman's statement indicates that the relationship between Jews and Samaritans was also characterized by religious tension.

Questions of religion and ways of worship are familiar to us. Indeed, the coming of Christian missions in the past two centuries was characterized by an absolute denial of the validity or even existence of African religions. Consequently, we ask the following questions: Is there only one religion? Can we be Christians without downgrading our African religions? What about Islam? How should different religions relate? Is it acceptable for one religion to derogate another? Moreover, as Southern Africans and Africans in general, who witnessed the coming of Christian mission twinned with colonialism, we realize that "this mountain and Jerusalem" are not only religious centers - they are also economic centers. That is, religious contest is also a competition for economic power. Religious centers are intertwined with certain economic centers, for our very spirituality is inseparably tied together with our economic interests. The struggle to convert or win people to one's religion often entails (consciously or unconsciously) the attempt to expand one's economic market. Who gets converted to new religion is also related to economic power in the world. The inseparability of religion with economics is attested evident in the Genesis creation story. It states that when God created humankind, God placed them in a garden with rich fruits and gave them dominion over the earth (Genesis 1:27-28). Similarly, at the very inception of the early church, the economic factor immediately became an issue: the early church decided on sharing its wealth equally and those who diverted from this were sent to death (Acts: 4-5). Our dramatic re-telling, therefore, highlights economic investment that accompanies religious competition, tensions and conversion. Our dramatic re-telling of the story, therefore, seeks to detect religious intolerance and to encourage an approach that celebrates God's cultural diversity.

"I sent you to reap that for which you did not labour." (John 4:38)

The story also speaks explicitly about economic interests, a point that we shall now consider. In a story that began with a discussion of ethnic tensions, then moved to religious tension, we are not surprised that it closes with reference to explicit material interest. Here, the Johannine Jesus invites his disciples to look at the ripe fields, which could be Samaria or the whole world. These fields are ready for harvest. These fields were not planted by the disciples, but the disciples are invited to enter them. This invitation arrests our attention as Southern African readers, for here we are touching on international (Jewish and Samaritan) ethics of trade. How does our historical experience, as Southern Africans and Africans of various countries, who underwent various forms of colonialism, neo-colonialism, and now, globalization, inform our reading of this passage? Of course, we realize that this is a religious conversation in a sacred text, yet our social location as people who experienced the arrival of Christianity with colonialism, and the current fundamentalist religious movements from major trade centers of the world, leads us to investigate the ethics of trade advocated in the passage. We seek to understand whether it encodes exploitative ethics, or not. If so, we ask how we can re-read the story so that it revolutionizes the terms of international trade. How can our international trade be designed in such a way that it becomes a relationship of liberating interdependence to all the involved parties?

These are the questions behind our dramatic re-telling of the Samaritan woman's story. And as many other women take the story back to their regions, districts, and nations, it is hoped that they shall struggle with these questions in their attempt to be participants in building a just world.

"His disciples ... were astonished that he was speaking with a woman." (John 4:27)

Let us now return to the issue of gender that we mentioned earlier. The Samaritan woman is indeed a woman and Samaria all at once. She is situated within all these issues of racial and religious tension; she is part and parcel of the economic history of many husbands. But how is her role gendered? Is she a symbol of victimization or an agent of empowerment to Southern African women? Or is she both? Our text tells us that when the disciples arrived, they were astonished that Jesus was talking to a woman (John 4:27). This indicates that gender is also a factor here. Male disciples do not think it proper that Jesus should speak directly to or with a woman. In this re-telling, therefore, her gendered role will be subject to preservation in so far as it tells our stories of the marginalization and oppression of women. It shall also be subject to transformation, in so far as we want to tell her story as an articulation of our dreams and struggles for liberation and self-empowerment.

As Southern African women, we travel in her story and with her. We take the Samaritan woman's journey to the well. We seek to understand our various oppressions, our strength and our possibilities in this journey. We read her story to ask her questions as our questions. We ask questions about racial/ethnic and religious tension and of the ethics of international economic trade. We seek to discover how she encountered God. As we journey with the Samaritan woman to the well, we realize she encountered God through following an inquisitive path. She is not a silent or docile believer. She questions, asking about issues of her day and her society. She is also well informed about the issues of her society. She invites people to come and see the Messiah, without surrendering her questioning approach (He cannot be the Messiah, can he? (John 4:29)). Moreover, when Jesus promises waters that could quench her thirst permanently, she is quick to ask for this. When Jesus announces himself as the Messiah, she is very quick to respond by rushing to the city. It is this model of a socially informed and engaged faith that we have to adopt to understand God's will for our world.

Method of Re-telling

The above factors inform the following re-telling of the Samaritan woman's story. Her story is our mirror of the past, present and future. The re-telling covers the pre-colonial times, the colonial times, the struggles for independence, post-independence neo-colonialism and globalization.

Our telling and re-telling of the Samaritan woman's story considers all the factors above, for they define our lives as Southern African women and African people at large. Gender, class, religious, racial and ethnic issues are inseparably tied with political and economic interests. We are, therefore, traveling with the Samaritan woman to the well, in search of the water that could quench our thirst permanently. Together with her we say, "Give us this water, so that we may never thirst or have to keep coming here to draw water" (John 4:15).

This re-telling is, of course, not a factual account of history, but it works within concrete historical frameworks, by employing historical characters. Some of the characters are still alive. It is also based in the physical setting of Southern Africa. And, lastly, it employs historical phrases or ideology that characterized each particular character or period under discussion. In short, it is a comment on history and the present world systems from a story-telling point of view. Why, one may ask? The re-telling is a critical assessment of yesterday's world system and an expression of our dreams and prayers for the present and the future.

As Southern African women, we also re-tell the Samaritan woman's story because we are storytellers. Storytelling has always been our language. We have always told stories by the fireside to pass wisdom and express ethics of living.[2]

With this introduction, we turn to the dramatic re-telling of the Samaritan woman. Here the five husbands come alive under the titles of Mzilikazi, David Livingstone, Cecil

John Rhodes, Ian Smith and Canaan Banana, all of them are historical or contemporary figures. Lastly we have Globalization and Justine, who are personified concepts. The dramatic re-telling concludes by the arrival of Justine who receives and gives water that promises to quench our thirst permanently. The latter scene carries our vision of a just world.

Scene I: The First Husband

Now when Mzilikazi heard that Shaka's army was close to him and was defeated by the Dutch white farmers (Boers) at Mosega, he left Ekuphumuleni and went further north. Passing through the Batswana kingdoms he crossed Limpopo and came to the Inyati well in the Rozwi area in Mashonaland. Mzilikazi, tired out by his journey, sat by the well. It was 1837. A Rozwi woman came to draw water, and they began to talk.

Mzilkazi: "Give me a drink." (His disciples had gone to the city to spy on it).

Rozwi woman: "How is it that you, a Nguni, ask a drink from me a woman of Rozwi?" (Rozwi had no dealings with Nguni people since the days of Zwangendaba.)

Mzilikazi: "If you knew my gift and who is it that is saying to you, 'Give me a drink' you would have asked him, and he would have given you living water."

Rozwi woman: "*Baba*, you have no bucket, and the well is deep. Where do you get that living water? Are you greater than Mambo, who gave us this well, and with his sons, daughters, and flocks drank from it?"

Mzilikazi: "Everyone who drinks of this water will soon die, for Sebetwane, Shaka and the Boers are coming to seize all these wells. But all those accept the living waters of my power will never thirst."

Rozwi woman: "*Baba*, give me this water, so I may never be thirsty, or have to keep coming here to draw water."

Mzilikazi: "For this reason, I have come. I have also brought
my disciplined armies, who can protect you. I have
brought my *Izangoma* and *Inyanga*³, who are seasoned
rainmakers and diviners. Every morning they divine for
any impending enemies."

Rozwi woman: "I see that you are a priest. You say your
nganga can make rain and foretell things. But we worship
Mwari at the mountain of *Thaba zi ka Mambo*. Our spirit
mediums are very skilled."

Mzilikazi: "Woman, believe me, the hour is coming, and is
now here, when all who worship Mwari will worship in
my kraal and on the mountain of my choice. All spirit
mediums, *inyangas* and *sangomas* will not dance in their
usual places, but in the kraal of great Mzilikazi ka
Khumalo."

Rozwi woman: "We know that a great warrior called
Mzilikazi is coming. When he comes he will seize all
things from us."

Mzilikazi: "I am he, the one who is speaking to you."

Just then his disciples came. They were armed warriors,
carrying ripe mangos and bananas, on their assegais (short
spears) and shields. Seeing them, the woman left her water
jar and ran back to the city. She said to the people, "Come,
see Mzilikazi who says he can protect us from all our enemies
and droughts. He cannot be the Messiah, can he?" They
left the city to meet him. Meanwhile, Mzilikazi and his
disciples spoke.

The disciples: "*Nkosi*, eat something."

Mzilikazi: "My food is to do the will of Khumalo, who left
me behind to protect my people and make sure they have
a place of rest. But I tell you, look around you and see
how the fields are ripe for harvesting. One sows, another
reaps. I sent you to reap that for which you did not
labor. Others have labored and you have entered into
their labor."

Many Rozwis, Kalangas and Mazezuru came from the
city. And when they saw Mzilikazi surrounded by his armed
warriors, they said, "We know that you will be our protector.

You are the Saviour of the Rozwi." So the Rozwis invited Mzilikazi to stay with them.

Scene II: The Second Husband

Now when David Livingstone heard that Dutch white farmers were taking more land in the Transvaal areas than the British white farmers of the Cape, he left the Bakwena Kingdom to open up Africa for commerce, Christianity, and civilization. He came by the falls of *Mosi u Thunya*. He sat there by the falls, tired by his journey and captivated by the beauty. It was 1856. And a Shona woman came to draw water. They began to talk.

Livingstone: "Give me water to drink." (His disciples had gone around to survey the land for navigable rivers).

Shona woman: "How can you a white man ask a drink from me a black Shona woman?" (For white and black people have no dealings.)

Livingstone: "If you knew that I discovered these Victoria Falls, and who is saying to you 'Give me a drink,' you would have asked him and he would have shared with you the living waters of commerce, Christianity, and civilization."

Shona woman: "You are a foreigner here. You have no land and no wells here. Where do you get that living water? Are you greater than our ancestor Mwene Mutapa who gave us the well, and with his sons, daughters, and flocks drank from it?"

Livingstone: "All who drank from these falls have never discovered them or named the land. They have never known how to drink from these springs. But all those who drink the waters that I shall give to them shall never be thirsty again."

Shona woman: "Give me this water that I may never thirst again, or have to keep coming here to draw water."

Livingstone: "I bring you, and Africa as a whole, the living waters of Christianity, commerce and civilization."

Shona woman: "I hear that you are talking about Christianity and commerce and civilization. But our ancestors have always worshipped Mwari in the mountain of *Taba zi ka Mambo.* Mwari has always provided us with living water that keeps our crops and cattle alive. Mwari keeps our land self-sufficient and well protected. This belief is our culture and our civilization."

Livingstone: "Woman, believe me, you worship what you do not know, for salvation comes from the white people. But the hour is coming, and is now here, that all you people must accept Christianity, commerce and civilization from Europe."

At that point the disciples of Livingstone, who were his guides, arrived with beads, mirrors, guns and gunpowder. Livingstone showed them his portrait of the *Mosi u Thunya Falls.* He had drawn the land on paper. Seeing this taking of land, the woman departed to inform the village, saying, "Come and see a man who told me he knows everything Africans ever needed. He cannot be the Messiah, can he?"

Meanwhile the guides of Livingstone spoke to him.

The guides: "Morena, eat something."

Livingstone: "My food is to do the will of England who sent me and to complete the work of the God."

And David Livingstone captivated by the falls, scribbled a letter to Britain saying:

> Look at this picture, and you will see how the fields are ripe for harvesting. Today, I have discovered something for our Queen and named it Victoria Falls. I am going ahead to open Africa for Christianity, commerce, and civilization. Come over, for I am opening the land. One sows and another reaps. I am calling you to reap that for which you did not labour. Others have laboured, and you have entered their labor. And even now, I declare that Christianity, commerce and civilization are the salvation of Africa.
>
> *Yours in the Service of the Queen and God,*
>
> *David Livingstone.*

Many from the village came to see Livingstone. But he had already gone into the interior of Africa.

Scene III: The Third Husband

Now when Cecil John Rhodes realized that there were many rich minerals in Africa (although they were primarily in the area now called South Africa), and when he realized that the Dutch white farmers were taking more land from the blacks in the Transvaal area and that the Germans were also advancing from South West Africa taking more land, he feared. Rhodes feared that his dream of building a railroad from Cape to Cairo would be hindered, for it had to pass through Bechuanaland, Matebeleland, Mashonaland and towards Cairo. Rhodes had to urge Britain to declare a Protectorate over Bechuanaland. Taking his British South Africa Company and going towards Cairo, he had to pass through Matebeleland.

So he came to a Matebeleland city called KoBulawayo, near the well that Mzilikazi had given to his son Lobengula. And Rhodes, tired out by his long journey and his poor health, sat by the well. It was on the 30th of October, 1888. A Ndebele woman came to draw water and here is their dialogue.

Rhodes: "Give me a drink." (His disciples had gone to the city to barter or negotiate for land concessions for mining.)

Ndebele woman: "How is it that you a white man ask a drink of me, a black woman of Matebeleland?" (Ndebele restricted their dealings with Southern African whites since the days of the Mosega War.)

Rhodes: "If you knew the power invested in me and who it is that is saying 'give me a drink,' you would have asked him and he would have given you the right to draw living waters from this well or to live in this land."

Ndebele woman: "Sir you are a foreigner and you have no well and land rights in this place. Are you greater than Mzilikazi, our ancestor, who gave us this well, and who with his sons, daughters and flocks drank from it?"

Rhodes: "Every king who lived in this land has never known how to use the riches of their land or to run the country. But the British people have a Christian duty to bring the springs of civilization, justice and liberty to the world."

Ndebele Woman: "I see that you are a British Christian. Our ancestors worship Mwari on the mountains of Matopo, who gives us rain for our crops and cattle. But you and the British missionaries say that people must follow Christianity as the only religion."

Rhodes: "Woman, believe me, the hour is coming and now is here when all Africans will neither worship Mwari or from the Matopo mountain. You worship what you do not know. We worship what we know for salvation comes from Britain."

Ndebele woman: "We know that there is a scramble for Africa and that Cecil J. Rhodes is colonizing Africa from the Cape to Cairo. When he comes, he will take all things from us."

Rhodes: "I am he, the one who is speaking to you."

Just then his disciples returned from the kraal of Lobengula rejoicing and waving a piece paper: "Sir, he gave us the approval. We gave him some few beers, mirrors and promises of rifles and he granted us all mineral rights in the Matebeleland and Mashonaland!"

Hearing about the contents of the contract, the woman left her bucket, and ran to the village to sound the alarm. "Come, see the man who told me that Britain has the best rule for the whole world, and he is coming here to rule us! He cannot be the Messiah, can he?"

Meanwhile his disciples spoke to Rhodes.

The contractors: "Sir, rejoice and eat something."

Rhodes: "My food is to carry out my duty to God and to England. I want to ensure that her rule and civilization abounds in Africa from Cape and Cairo. Indeed, British governance is the best in the whole world and the best for all humankind. I tell you, look around you, and see how the fields are ripe for harvesting. One sows and another reaps. I sent you to reap that for which you did not labor. Others have labored, and you have entered into their labor."

Just then many AmaNdebele from the city of Bulawayo came to hear for themselves what the woman had said. As they arrived, they saw the British South Africa Company busy prospecting the land for minerals. Then Charles Rudd, James Maguire, Frank Thompson and other disciples of Rhodes stood up to address the AmaNdebele saying, "This land shall be named Southern Rhodesia after Cecil John Rhodes from now onwards. The Barotseland shall also be called Northern Rhodesia after him, for he is indeed the Savior of Africa."

Scene IV: The Fourth Husband

Now when Ian Smith heard that the British Empire was accepting "the winds of change" and giving power back to black nationals in Malawi and Zambia - although they were not giving it back to them in Zimbabwe - Smith left the British government and came to Rhodesia. Smith, tired from his strategies against black nationals, came to the city of Salisbury, near the well that white minority settlers had taken from black populations. It was on 11th November, 1965. A Ndebele-Shona woman came to draw water and here is their dialogue.

Smith: "Give me a drink." (His disciples had gone to declare the independence of white minority rule at the city.)

Ndebele-Shona woman: "How is it that you a white man ask a drink from me a black native woman?" (White and black people stayed in separate lands.)

Smith: "If you knew my gift, and whom it is that is saying to you 'give me a drink', you would have asked him and he would have given you living waters."

Ndebele-Shona woman: "*Baba*, you have no bucket, and the well is deep and dry. Where do you get that living water? Are you greater than our ancestors Mambo and Mzilikazi who gave us the well of living waters that you white minority settlers have taken from us? This is the well that our ancestors, with their daughters, sons and flocks, drank from."

Smith: "Every black person who drinks of this water will soon move to the Reserves or stay in white farms as servants. Yet all those who accept the living waters of my power will never thirst again."

Ndebele-Shona woman: "*Baba*, give me this water, so that I may never be thirsty, or have to keep coming here to draw water."

Smith: "For this reason I believe in the policy of 'white supremacy ... for the foreseeable future.' In this country of Cecil John Rhodes' dreams, white Christian rule of the minority is the living waters."

Ndebele-Shona woman: "I see that you believe in the white Christian minority rule. But our black national movements are seized by the Spirit of *Chimurenga* and they are pressing for independence from the British Government."

Smith: "Woman believe me, the hour is coming, and now is here, when we shall become an independent white-run state, and all blacks must worship in the religion of their masters. You worship what you do not know, but we worship what we know, for salvation comes from white settler Christians."

Ndebele-Shona woman: "We know that Ian Smith is coming into power. And when he comes, he will push us further into the crowded and infertile reserves and turn us into servants of white farmers."

Smith: "I am he, the one who is speaking to you."

Just then his disciples came. They were white Rhodesian farmers.

Smith: "Have you announced my Unilateral Declaration of Independence over the radio? Have you rounded up all ZANU and ZAPU leaders and imprisoned them?"

The woman, hearing this, left her water jar and ran back to the city. She said to the people, "Come see Ian Smith who says he declares our country to be an independent country ruled by the white settler minorities. He cannot be the Messiah, can he?" They left the city and sought refugee status in Zambia, Botswana and Mozambique, while pressing for their liberation.

Scene V: The Fifth Husband

Now when Ndabanigi Sithole, Joshua Nkomo, Josiah Tongogara, Robert Mugabe and other black nationals realized that the British Government was not going to repeal Ian Smith's Unilateral Declaration of Independence - after all the Rhodesian white settlers were its kith and kin - they decided to undertake an armed struggle for their liberation.

Now when Canaan Banana led military strikes against white minority rule from Mozambique, he came into a white farm. He was tired and sat down by one of the springs of a fertile farm that Cecil John Rhodes had taken from black people and given to white settlers. It was in the late 1970s. A white woman came to the well and they began to talk.

Banana: "Give me a drink." (His disciples had gone to the farms to launch attack against white minority rule.)

White Rhodesian woman: "How is it that you a black boy can ask me a white mistress to give you water?" (Black people were supposed to serve all whites.)

Banana: "If you knew my gift, and whom it is that is saying to you, 'give me a drink', you would have asked him and he would have given you living waters - the right to some of this spring."

White Rhodesian woman: "Black boy, you belong to the Reserves and you have no land rights in this area. Where do you get that living water? Are you greater than our ancestor, Cecil John Rhodes, who gave us this well, and with his British South Africa Company and their daughters and sons drank from it?"

Banana: "Every white person who drinks from these stolen wells will soon be thirsty again. But those who accept the living waters that I bring will never thirst again."

White Rhodesian woman: "Black boy, give me this water, so I may never thirst again, or have to keep sending my boys and girls to draw water for me."

Banana: "For this reason I have come. I bring liberation for the whole country by the mighty spirit of Mbuya Nehanda, the daughter of Mwari."

White Rhodesian woman: "I see you are a priest of your pagan god, Mwali. But we worship the universal Christian God, who gave us this land, since we are God's chosen people."

Banana: "Woman, believe me, the hour is coming, and now is here, when all who worship the Christian God, must realize that all creation is holy and all religious shrines of the world are manifestations of God and must be respected. The hour is coming, and now is here, when all those things in the Bible that oppress women, suppress other religions and support colonialism must be edited out. The Bible must be re-written and extended to reflect the diversity of God's world. This is liberation and respect for God's diversity."

White Rhodesian woman: "We know that a great socialist leader is coming. When he comes, he will seize our farms and homes from us."

Banana: "I am he, the one who is speaking to you."

Just then his disciples came out of the trees. They were armed black guerillas, wearing their camouflage attire. They began to sing *chimurenga* songs of liberation. The woman, seeing and hearing them, ran back to the farm and to the city of Salisbury. She said to the white people, "Come, see a socialist who says he will redistribute our land to black people. He cannot be the Messiah, can he?" They left Salisbury and flew to Britain to meet with freedom fighters in Lancaster House. Meanwhile the disciples of Banana spoke to him.

The disciples: "Comrade, eat something."

Banana: "My food is to do the will of him who sent me and to make sure that all creation is treated as holy. But I tell you, look around you and see how the fields are ripe for harvesting. You have sown and others have reaped your crops. I am sending you to reap that which you labored for. You have labored for too long and others have entered into your fields."

Just then Robert Mugabe and Joshua Nkomo arrived from Lancaster house declaring, "We have won independence of our country. Its new name is Zimbabwe!"

Scene VI: The Sixth Husband "The One you Have Now is not Your Husband!" (John 4:18)

Now when the West heard that the East was making and baptizing many disciples with communist thinking in Southern Africa - although it was not the East who baptized them, rather the oppressed were attracted by its ethics - Mr. Neo-colonialism came quickly down. Mr. Cold War also came down and instigated civil wars in Mozambique, Angola and other Marxist oriented African countries.

But just then the Berlin Wall collapsed, followed by other eastern icons. Mr. Cold War had to leave Africa. Then Globalization realized that capitalism had no rival in the world markets, except for the expensive labor of his own countries. He left the Western centers and went to Two-Third World countries. He had to pass through to Southern Africa. Then Globalization arrived at Victoria Falls, tired by his long journey from the United States. As we speak, Globalization is sitting by the Falls, just where David Livingstone sat. We are in the 1990s. A Zimbabwean woman has gone to draw water, and they are talking.

Globalization: "Give me a drink." (His disciples are talking with the SADC ministers of foreign affairs to acquire trade permission for his multi-national companies in the region.)

Zimbabwean woman: "How is it that you, a North American, ask a drink of me a black woman of Zimbabwe? (North America has no defined trade relations with Africa.)

Globalization: "If you knew my gift, and whom it is that is saying to you 'give me a drink', you would have asked him, and he would have given you living water of coca cola."

Zimbabwean woman: "Sir, you have no bucket, and the well is deep. Where do you get that living water? Are you greater than our liberators Nkomo-Mugabe, who with all the sons and daughters of Zimbabwe fought for the independence of our nation, and gave us this well back again?"

Globalization: "Everyone who drinks water within the confines of their national boundaries will be thirsty again. But those who drink the water of coke regardless of borders that I shall give them will never be thirsty. The water that I give is a spring of water gushing up across the globe, unlimited by any national boundaries."

Zimbabwean woman: "Sir, give me this water, so that I may never be thirsty or have to keep coming here to draw water."

Globalization: "I will create for you, and Africa as a whole, jobs. My living waters of free trade - my borderless trade - will flow freely around the globe leading you to realize heaven on earth. The global TV Christian ministries, the soap operas, the internet and the like that I bring, shall teach you that God has called you to abundant riches."

Zimbabwean woman: "I hear you are talking about free trade, which disregards all borders, and North American TV Christian ministries. But our liberators together with the many daughters and sons of Zimbabwe fought for our own national independence helped by the Mwari priests. We fought against the federation and minority rule, in order to have our national borders secure. Moreover, our African Independent Churches fought to be free from Christian cultural imperialism."

Globalization: "Woman, believe me, you worship what you do not know and you defend economic policies that are useless, for the world economic structures are determined in and by North America. You have to follow suit, or you will marginalize yourself. But the hour is coming, and now is here, that all nations must regionalize. There should be international production networks, that is, competitive free trade and mobility unlimited by national boundaries."

Zimbabwean woman: "We know that Globalization is coming. When he comes, he will take our national independence away from us - the very independence that we fought and died to attain."

Globalization: "I am he, the one who is speaking to you."

Just then his disciples returned from the cities of SADC, one waving a business file. "Sir, we have the approval to set up our multi-national companies in the whole region of Southern Africa. There is plenty of cheap labor and hardly any competition from their small businesses. The latter will disappear before our mega companies."

Hearing about this, the woman left her bucket and ran to sound the alarm to Southern African nations. "Come, see the man who told me that free trade - borderless trade - is the best economic strategy for the whole world. He cannot be the Messiah, can he?"

Meanwhile the disciples spoke to Globalization.

The disciples: "Savior of the whole world, eat something."

Globalization: "My duty is to remove all the barriers to free the flow of capital. I want a borderless economy for my multi-national corporations. I want enlarged markets that will amass giant profits for us. I want cheap labor. I tell you, look around you. See how the fields are ripe for harvesting. One sows and another reaps. I am sending you to reap that for which you did not labor. Others have labored, and you are entering into their labor."

Currently, many Southern Africans from the SADC countries are trying to understand what the woman is saying and to hear about Globalization for themselves. As we speak, Coca Cola, Pepsi, Hyundai, Macdonalds, KFC and many other disciples of globalization are already painting the global landscape with their colors. Even now you can hear the voice of multi-national corporations saying, "Globalization is the Savior of the World, invite him to enter and stay in your regions."

Conclusion: "Give me this water that I may not thirst again!" (John 4:15)

As Southern African and African women as a whole, we are still journeying to the well. We are still thirsty. Together with the Samaritan woman we are saying, "Give me this water that I may not thirst again" (John 4:15). Yet, as the above scenes with the six husbands show, our journey is not in any way close to its end. We have been to the well several times. We have met and co-habited with several husbands. We have been given promises, but we have yet to drink the water that will quench our thirst permanently.

Indeed, there is something shocking in finding a stranger, with whom you have "no dealings", sitting by your well and asking for a drink! It is even more shocking when this very stranger promises to give you better water! But as the above scenes indicate, we Southern African women will do better to keep the inquisitive faith of the Samaritan woman who says, "He cannot be the Messiah, can he?" Such faith does not withhold its inquisitive edge. Rather, it is a call for careful assessment of promises that are advanced to us. Indeed, many husbands have visited our wells, promised us living water and then took the very wells we owned away.

It is also instructive for the church and Christians, both locally and internationally, that most of the exploitative husbands were also practicing Christians (David Livingstone, Cecil John Rhodes, Ian Smith and Globalization). In short, the church is implicated in international structures that are oppressive and exploitative to God's creation. This portrait is, therefore, a call for self-examination and to repentance. It is a call to responsible Christian practice. The dramatic re-telling forces us to ask the following questions: How can we learn to avoid the sins of yesterday? How can we be part of dreaming, birthing and building a just world? How can we bring God's kingdom on earth as it is heaven? How, indeed, can we find the way to a well that will quench our thirst permanently? We conclude, then, with a dialogue between a Southern African woman and Justine, which is our effort to hear God's will for the world.

Scene VII: Justine at the Well of Living Waters

Now when Justine learned that Selfish Exploitation was making and baptizing more disciples than Justice - the world had chosen unjust ethics for itself - she left her abode and traveled towards love. But she had to pass through Southern Africa. So she came to the Great Zimbabwe ruins near the mountain that Banyachaba had given to her son Lunji. And Justine, tired out by her journey, is sitting by the well. It is in the present future. A Southern African woman comes to draw water, and they begin to talk.

Justine: "Give me a drink." (Her disciples had gone to the city to give and receive love.)

Southern African woman: "How wonderful that you, a woman of the tribe of Justice, ask water from me, a black woman of Southern Africa." (Black Southern African women had suffered many injustices for almost two centuries.)

Justine: "I know that you know the gift of God, and that it is Justine who is saying to you, 'Give me a drink.' I have come that we can talk and plan on how we can give our world - each other - the living waters of Justice."

Southern African woman: "*Iyo Sisi Wethu*, you have no selfish intentions, and the well of your wisdom is deep. *Qiniso sibili!* Where else can we get living waters of Justice, unless we both talk and plan to give it to ourselves and to our world? Justice is greater than the wells of Selfish Exploitation, which we are drinking from right now."

Justine: "Everyone who drinks from the wells of Selfish Exploitation, collecting massive profits at the expense of the whole world, will lead the whole earth to great thirst. But those who drink of the waters of Justice that they must give to each other, and to everyone, will never be thirsty. The waters of Justice that they give to each other will become in them a spring of Love gushing up to eternal life."

Southern African woman: "*Qiniso, Sisi Wethu.*" This world needs to drink this water. But how can we bring our world to drink from this well so that it may never be thirsty, or keep drawing from the wells of Selfish Exploitation?"

Justine: "Go, call your husband, and come back."

Southern African woman: "I have no husband."

Justine: "You are right in saying, 'I have no husband': for you have had five husbands, and the one you have now is not your husband. What you have said is true!"

Southern African woman: "*Sisi Wethu*, I see that you are a prophet from God. Most of our exploiters are from Christian countries and they call themselves God's children, who bring light to the whole world. They have lit the world with darkness."

Justine: "Woman, believe me, they have neglected the weightier matters: the fact that God demands justice, mercy and faith. The hour is coming, and now is here, when all true worshippers, who call themselves children of God, must turn and repent from drinking from the wells of Selfish Exploitation."

Southern African woman: "We are praying and working for God's Reign to come on earth as it is in heaven. When God's Reign comes, Justice will conquer selfish Exploitation."

Justine: "I am she, the one speaking to you."

African Woman

The sun is in the midsky
Its rays pour down harsh, hot air
Yet you walk to the well, there is no siesta for you
You walk to the well in the hot day
For you are thirsty

Hush, woman, hush
For no more shall you braze the rays
Not again shall you thirst; this day you quit
Carrying a pail of water to the well, this day
You shall leave your pail behind

Hush, African woman, hush
For no more shall you drag your feet
Under the hot sands and weights of pails of water
Today you shall spring into the city
To proclaim the good news

Spring!
African woman, spring!
For there is no more this man or that woman
There is no more black or white, Ndebele or Shona
No more reaper of foreign fields,
no more Mwali or God,
No more African Religions, or Christianity or Islam
Today we will all drink from God's deep wells, all
We will be God's Springs of Truth, all
Springing to the Spirit of Diversity
Look the fields of Justice are ripe
Awaiting your harvest,
Spring! Woman
Spring!
Africa

Endnotes

1. This essay was initially published in Kanyoro, M., & Njoroge, N. (Eds.). (1998). *A Decade in Solidarity with the Bible.* Geneva: World Council of Churches. It is reproduced here with permission.

2. For my other articles on the storytelling perspective see (1999) "Fifty Years of Bleeding: A Storytelling Feminist Reading of Mark 5:24-43" (pp11-17) in *The Ecumenical Review*, Geneva: World Council of Churches, 51(1) and (1999) "The Unpublished Letters of Orpah to Ruth" (pp.145-150) in A. Brenner (Ed.), *Ruth and Esther: A Feminist Companion to the Bible.* Sheffield: Sheffield Academic Press.

3. Please note that words of indigenous language are deliberately not translated. This is a postcolonial "english", meant to remind the reader that the writer and audience are not English. It is a strategy that allows the postcolonial readers to have "secret" talk amongst themselves within the dominance of such factors as colonial languages, trade and media.

A Spirituality of Resistance and Transformation

Nyambura J. Njoroge

Any spirituality that does not lead to engagement in the making of peace, the crafting of non-violent responses to contemporary events and relationships is not worthy of being called a spirituality. (McKenna, 1994:204)

Introduction: In search of a Metaphor

In 1997, Ghana celebrated 40 years of political independence. It was the first African country to become independent from the cruel hand of colonial rule, after the infamous 1884 Berlin Conference that brought about the partitioning of Africa between the colonial powers. Since then each and every single country in Africa has flown an African flag, the last being South Africa in 1994, with the exception of Western Sahara the status of which remains unresolved. These have been years of struggles for nationhood from the ashes of exploitation, domination and oppression. Several of these countries have fought guerrilla (liberation) wars including Kenya, Algeria, Zambia, Zimbabwe, Angola, Mozambique, Namibia and South Africa. Other countries have witnessed ethnic strife, civil wars, military dictatorship and, the worst of all, genocide in Rwanda and Burundi. Genocide has also been a feature of the most recent wars in Liberia, Sierra Leone, the Ethiopia/Eritirea border dispute, and the strife in the Democratic Republic of Congo.

Despite the apparent economic growth in the 1960s and 1970s, the continent has continued to experience disquieting economic crises that have caused untold poverty and dehumanization. Drought, famine, floods and ecological disasters have accompanied the political and economic crises thus making the situation more unbearable. The continent is known to have the highest number of refugees and internally displaced persons in the world. Confrontation, war, violence, great suffering and loss of human dignity have marked the last half of twentieth century. As a result, many Africans live in perpetual insecurity and fear for their lives and those of their children. This is not to say that Africa has a monopoly of violence. But certainly its enormous propensity for destruction demands special attention, particularly by Africans.

Yet, these have also been years of religious growth for both Islam and Christianity. This growth has witnessed the birth of written African theologies and codes of ethics by Africans. Missionary-founded churches have become autonomous under African leadership, many new African Churches have been instituted, and there has been much reorganizing, and restructuring of existing churches. African Christians have become more conscious of their African traditional religiosity and the need to be firmly grounded in their cultural values and heritage. Community life, as opposed to western individualism, has been upheld as a central element in African culture and religion as well as respect for life, all life. On the other hand, Christians struggle to understand the contradiction that is reflected in the on-going violence and destruction as opposed to the growth of Christianity in the continent. Perhaps the contradiction most challenging is to the growth of the religious movement is the genocide in Rwanda and Burundi. In these African dilemmas, women and children are affected most.

This chapter is based on a personal struggle to articulate, within a biblical and theological framework, the dilemmas presented in the African context in the last fifty years, especially in the last decade of the 1990s. My reflections are undertaken as an African Christian woman in search of a metaphor or metaphors that will lead us to engage in restoring our human dignity and respect for life. This chapter was written during Easter-tide of 1996, but most of my ideas were gathered during the 40 days of Lent and the Holy Week. Meditations on the baptism, temptations and ministry of our Lord Jesus Christ, and his journey to the cross, sustained my sense of disillusion as I reflected on the many woes afflicting Africans, particularly the HIV/AIDS pandemic. For the first time in my life I attended an Ash Wednesday worship service to mark the beginning of Lent. As the words "Remember O Mortal that you are dust and to dust you shall return" were whispered to me by the pastor, and as the ashes were smeared upon my brow in the shape of the cross, I experienced God's presence and empowerment to go forth in search of God's will.

During this Lenten journey, I encountered several biblical images. But, with the plight of the African woman and her children in mind, the one that captured my attention most was the image of Rizpah, daughter of Aiah and concubine of King Saul. Rizpah became a companion who has opened my eyes and helped me to articulate the plight of the African continent. Instead of a metaphor, I found a spirituality. I first discovered Rizpah in 1994 in the article, "Re-imagining the Church as Worshipping Community," by Ofelia Ortega (1994), a Cuban Reformed pastor and theologian.

Why Rizpah?

Let us listen to the only biblical texts that speak for Rizpah!

> While there was war between the house of Saul and the house of David, Abner was making himself strong in the house of Saul. Now Saul had a concubine whose name was Rizpah daughter of Aiah. And Ishbaal said to Abner, Why have you gone in to my father's concubine? The words of Ishbaal made Abner very angry; he said, "Am I a dog's head for Judah? Today I keep showing loyalty to the house of your father Saul, to his brothers, and to his friends, and have not given you into the hand of David; and yet you charge me now with a crime concerning this woman. (2 Samuel 3:6-8)[1]

Rizpah lived in a time of hatred, bitterness, revenge and violence. Israel was in its early stages as a kingdom, and Saul was king. But we only meet Rizpah after Saul's death.

When the Israelites came into the promised land, it was already occupied. The First and Second Books Samuel are part of a larger work known as Deuteronomistic History that traces the history of Israel from the conquest to the exile. This is found in the books of Joshua, Judges 1 and 2, Samuel 1 and 2, and Kings 1 and 2. Israel, it appears, was always at war, either keeping its hold on its territory or engaged in other battles to extend them.

In this text, Rizpah is invisible and muted. We get to know her from an ugly dispute over her, between Saul's son, Ishbaal, and the commander of Saul's army, Abner. Because Saul had died Abner, wanted to inherit Rizpah as his concubine, as a way of demonstrating his ambition to become King Saul's successor. David too was involved in this power struggle although he could claim that he had been anointed by God to take over when Saul was rejected by God (1 Samuel 15 & 16). It is within the context of this power struggle that we encounter Rizpah. We have no idea how Rizpah felt about this incident, her relationship with Saul or even how she faced Saul's death. Although King David and the people of Israel mourned the death of Saul and his three sons (2 Samuel 1), David did not make the effort to give them a decent burial. Rizpah remained invisible until she lost all she had to live for: her two sons.

The genesis of her plight is found in 2 Samuel 21:1-14. A famine had prevailed for three years in Israel and, in seeking help from God, King David had been told that there was bloodguilt on the house of Saul. This was attributed to Saul's treatment of the Gibeonites and David sought their advice as to how this guilt could be expiated. They refused to countenance being paid silver and gold, and did not seek to put anyone to death in Israel. However, they did express strong desire to be revenged on Saul who had planned to destroy them and drive them out of Israel. They wanted seven sons of Saul to be handed over so that they could "impale them before the Lord at Gibeon on the mountain of the lord". King David agreed to this but spared Mephibosheth, the son of Jonathen, because of the bond between Jonathen and David. The two sons of Rizpah and the five sons of Merab were given to the Gibeonites who

impaled them on the mountain before the Lord. The
seven of them perished together. They were put to death
in the first days of harvest, at the beginning of barley
harvest.

    Then Rizpah the daughter of Aiah took sackcloth, and
spread it on a rock for herself, from the beginning of
harvest until rain fell on them from the heavens; she did
not allow the birds of the air to come on the bodies by
day, or the wild animals by night. When David was told
what Rizpah daughter of Aiah, the concubine of Saul,
had done, David went and took the bones of Saul and
the bones of his son Jonathan from the people of Jabesh-
Gilead, who had stolen them from the public square of
Bethshan where the Philistines had hung them up, on
the day the Philistines killed Saul on Gilboa. He brought
up from there the bones of Saul and the bones of his son
Jonathan; and they gathered the bones of those who
had been impaled. They buried the bones of Saul and of
his son Jonathan in the land of Benjamin in Zela, in the
tomb of his father Kish; they did all that the king
commanded. After that, God heeded supplications for
the land. (2 Samuel 21:9-14)

    Biblical scholars place this passage as preceding chapter
9, which tells the story of Jonathan's son Mephibosheth,
the only survivor in king Saul's household after this violent
death by the Gibeonites. That means the killing of the seven
took place in the early stages of David's reign, when a three-
year famine sent led to King David to seek the help of the
Lord God. The payment was to expiate the bloodguilt on
Saul and his household. When David approached the
Gibeonites and let them decide the terms of restitution the
outcome was inevitable. What else could have been
expected? Out of many years of bitterness came the
opportunity for revenge! Without any negotiation, David
agreed, and two sons and five grandsons of Saul were placed
in the hands of Gibeonites. It is hard to tell from the text
whether David made the concessions out of malicious self-
interest, thereby ridding himself of Saul's household. One
is left to wonder why he did not consider negotiating with
Gibeonites, since they were not at war. God did not prescribe
the form of restitution; it was David's task to seek it out.

Finally we get to see Rizpah although she remained mute throughout. Rizpah's presence and action spoke louder than words. Ofelia Ortega writes:

> In 2 Samuel 3 Rizpah is presented as a passive victim and considered an object of barter. But here her very presence is eloquent. We can imagine her: there she was invisible, but here her act is an act of covering, protecting the bodies, and it was so impressive and notorious that even David, who represented power and authority, could not ignore her. She really changed the course of history. (Ortega 1994:43)

Rizpah had seen enough death in Saul's household. She must have been grieved beyond words or tears when David gave away her sons. She had nothing to fear even the danger of her own death from the wild animals. The reader is left to imagine how long the vigil lasted, and what was running through her mind. Keeping vigil must have been Rizpah's way of protesting against the senseless killings on the mountain before the Lord. Revenge and bloodshed were not the way of absolving Saul's sins. It was a way of telling King David that he should have negotiated with the Gibeonites and repented the wrongs done by his predecessor. Rizpah might also have been reminding David that the remains of the seven would be left in the hands of the enemy just like their fathers before them. They had no burial place since Saul and his other dead sons had not received a decent burial. It could as well be that as Rizpah kept vigil over the dead bodies, she prayed for Saul's forgiveness and repented for Israel's sins. Edith Dean writes:

> Some commentators interpret the spreading of the sackcloth as a sign that the land had repented because of drought and famine. When Rizpah spread it out to protect the bodies of her sons, she probably made a pledge with God that she would watch over them until God relented and the rains came. (Dean 1955:111)

Whatever it was that Rizpah was saying, her action moved David to action. David recognized that Rizpah might have understood the situation more clearly than he did, and he accepted that God had sent her to change his mind towards

Saul. David acknowledged Rizpah's resistance to revenge and bloodshed as the way of solving conflicts with the neighbors. David changed his mind and reconciled himself to Saul by collecting his remains and those of his son Jonathan. The bones of Saul and all his slain sons were gathered and buried in their rightful place, in the tomb of Saul's father Kish. Despite death, dignity was restored to the house of Saul and in Israel. We are told that only after Rizpah's vigil and David's response did God heed supplications for the land. It rained and the famine ended. Consequently, David recalled the oath of the Lord that was between him and Jonathan and sought after any remaining offspring of Saul so that he could show kindness, which is reflected in the narrative (2 Samuel 9).

In my imagination I joined Rizpah at the vigil, in the presence of death, great loss and deep emptiness. As I did so I encountered a woman of courage, determination and great inner strength: a woman who, despite death or because of it, was not afraid to confront the ugly face of revenge, violence and death; a mother who demanded action from the highest authority in the land in spite of her lowly status of concubine. In my struggle to understand what Rizpah's action meant or demonstrated, I could only imagine her strong awareness of the presence of God, who alone could deliver her from her deep grief and experience of loss. I encountered a "human spirit", that inner dimension that can only be God-given. I felt a spirituality that guided a helpless mother to gather all her courage to do her best for her dead sons. In the presence of death, there was still hope and something to live for. In my view, Rizpah demonstrated a spirituality of resistance and transformation: a spirituality that demanded the restoration of human dignity and respect for life in the midst of death. For Rizpah, revenge and death were not the last words. There was an alternative. In God, transformation of our attitudes, beliefs and values is possible.

Despite the historical distance between Rizpah's context and mine, she helped me understand Africa in a new way. I was able to see Africa for what it is, a continent that seems always at war, either fighting against foreign occupation and exploitation or engaged in territorial disputes. In such circumstances, power struggles, hatred, revenge and violence are inevitable. It seems that African countries have been going through the days experienced by Israel as described in Deuteronomistic History, particularly during the reigns of Saul and David. Although there are major differences between the stories of Israel and Africa, it is clear that in both cases, peace, justice and forgiveness have been given little chance to flourish.

In the Christian church, Rizpah remains unknown and one of the least studied female characters in the Bible. It did not surprise me, therefore, to discover that Jo Ann Hackett, the commentator on the two books of Samuel in *The Women's Bible Commentary*[2] is silent on Rizpah's story even in a book that gives prominence to the women in the Bible (*Newsom & Ringe*, 1992). Yet Rizpah's action has a powerful message for those who find themselves in the midst of violent death. Rizpah knows, even in the midst of injustice, that revenge and the shedding of innocent blood do not appease God. She knows, in the gift of wisdom given to her, and demonstrated in her vigil, that David had the chance to negotiate for a peaceful course with the Gibeonites. Wearing her sackcloth, Rizpah challenges the powers that be about the injustice done to Saul's household.

This image of Rizpah mirrors the African woman who has refused to succumb to the violence and death experienced by her children. This African woman has defiantly refused to accept revenge as the way to solve the African crises. This image of Africa has been little analyzed and most misunderstood, and has been ignored by those who come to Africa to help solve its problems. Even Africans themselves have not paid attention to the African woman and her experience of God in the presence of death and injustice inflicted on her children.

Rizpah: A Sister in the Struggle

Both the image of Rizpah as an invisible and muted concubine and the defiant Rizpah in sackcloth in the presence of death capture vividly the plight of the African woman who has refused to accept violence and death as a way of life. Like Rizpah, for many decades the African ' woman was spoken for and commented on while she remained faceless and voiceless. She has continued to produce and nurture African off springs for her male counterpart but her humanity has never been taken into account. When Africa's new social institutions, such as schools, hospitals and churches, were introduced by missionaries and the colonial powers, the social, religious and cultural milieu of the African woman was taken for granted, and little notice or heed was taken of her.

Similarly, when Africa regained its political independence, the African woman remained faceless and voiceless. Development programs of the1960s and 1970s paid little attention to, or undertook little critical analysis of, African woman's contributions in the shaping of the economy. When Africa's biographies began to emerge, they were androcentric (male centered) with occasional mention of a few women. When African theology emerged in the 1960s, it was completely silent on women's experiences of God and their contributions to the shaping of the African church. Theological institutions and seminaries left the African woman to thè pew and in the churchwomen's organizations. The only time she appeared on the seminary campus was in the kitchen and bedroom of the male student or lecturer as a spouse. In the church governing bodies, female organizations and females themselves were totally absent. In some churches this practice, whereby the woman remains invisible and muted, continues as this is being written.

In textbooks on Africa, the African woman, to a large extent, was depicted as a passive and helpless victim - if she was included at all. At worst, her efforts to resist and take action to change things were ignored or dismissed as ineffective. Rather than watch closely, listen attentively and affirm her efforts, many scholars turned a blind eye to the African woman. Any acts of resistance and yearning for transformation were labeled anti-cultural. She has been rejected as a moral and historical agent. She is the one who has no right to decide her own destiny and that of her children. Thanks to the worldwide women's movement, the way has been paved for women to have a voice and tell their stories. Within this women's movement are women theologians who have given us the language and courage to read the scriptures with feminine eyes, and this is what has helped me to discover Rizpah.

As I explored Rizpah's vigil, she helped me to see beyond the marginalized and neglected African woman. I found the defiant African woman who, in a variety of ways, has refused to be ignored when her children succumb to violent death. Instead of wearing sackcloth, the African woman traditionally sits on a *kanga*[3] and covers and protects her dying children from wild animals, hunger and violent governments. Like her sister Rizpah, an African woman's inner strength and spirit that, despite of death or because of it, continues to fight for life, remains unknown to and ignored by the world. When her husband, sons and brothers die in battle or are imprisoned for life, the African woman does not take the path of revenge and death, but continues to struggle for life and human dignity. African woman's spirituality of resistance and transformation has yet to be researched or documented.

While I was keeping vigil with Rizpah during Lent, our conversation remained non-verbal. But when I followed her to the tomb of Kish to lay to rest the remains of Saul and his household, Rizpah finally spoke to me with a big sigh of relief. She embraced me, took my *kanga* and bound the two of us together. She whispered in my ears: "At last they can rest in peace!" Then Rizpah said: "As you enter Holy Week, keep close to the women who followed Jesus all the way from birth, his ministry on earth, on the way to Jerusalem, at the cross, burial and at the empty tomb. There you will encounter the living Christ who will travel with you as you search for human dignity and life for your children in Africa."

Rizpah introduced me to Jesus, his mother Mary, Mary Magdalene, and Salome in a new way. This way was one that I had never experienced before in my journey of faith. Like Rizpah and the African woman, these sisters demonstrated a spirituality of resistance and transformation. I was therefore moved to pay attention to these women in the gospels and Jesus in the light of a spirituality of resistance and transformation. How did Jesus understand his encounter with violent death and the trauma of the resurrection? My encounter with Rizpah is incomplete without reflecting on Jesus' passion story and the women around him. Let us briefly, take heed of Rizpah's advice.

"Daughters of Jerusalem, do not Weep for me"

> A great number of people followed him, and among them were women who were beating their breasts and wailing for him. But Jesus turned to them and said, "Daughters of Jerusalem, do not weep for me, but weep for yourselves and for your children. For the days are surely coming when they will say, blessed are the barren, and the wombs that never bore, and the breasts that never nursed. Then they will begin to say to the mountains, 'Fall on us' and to the hills, 'Cover us'. For if they do this when the wood is green, what will happen when it is dry?" (Luke 23:27-31)

Rizpah is no longer alone. Many other women today are heard and seen: beating their breasts and wailing. Like Rizpah, their great sorrow and grief demonstrate resistance to injustice and violent death. Their actions are full of compassion and humanness. Communally, these women share with Jesus in his suffering. But Jesus responded by telling them that even they have their own cross to bear. He wanted his followers, especially the women who openly displayed their remorse, to understand that it was not just him who was affected by the social, political and religious injustices that he confronted. Jesus wanted them to reflect on the context which shaped their own lives, and to follow his example by working for peace, justice and restoration of the Kingdom of God. What exactly did Jesus mean when he spoke to the women?

Let us pause and ask why did Jesus have to die on the cross: what does his death mean to us as Christians and as women, bearing in mind Rizpah's experience? Megan McKenna, an American theologian, has reminded us that when we make the theological statement: "Jesus died on the cross for our sins", it is based upon the light of past reality, the experience of a believing community, and after the occurrence of Jesus' death and resurrection. But she goes further and cautions that merely repeating this statement can rob the story and person of Jesus' life and death of any power to transform us. McKenna's argument is perceptive:

> When Jesus spoke of the cross, the images he evoked had nothing whatsoever to do with the theological notion of dying for sin. They were images of execution: long, tortuous, painful, public, and humiliating. Crucifixion was a form of capital punishment, legal - though unjust - that the Roman, the oppressor, the powerful used on the helpless, the poor and the oppressed, slaves, revolutionaries, anyone who spoke out against injustice. To say Jesus died on the cross for our sins is often to ignore or forget that he died because he was dangerous to a society that wanted to hold unto its power. Jesus died on the cross for his beliefs, his idea of God, his preaching, his siding with the poor and the outcast. He died on the cross because he told the truth to power, putting himself in jeopardy for others, so that they might know life and the hope of freedom. His command to be ready to experience crucifixion as part of discipleship says that this is not just an historical account of one innocent man dying or a theological statement about why he died; it is a present-day reality that his disciples - all of us - must accept and deal with consistently. (McKenna 1994:223-224)

African Christians have lived with the theological statement of Jesus dying on the cross for our sins, which we inherited from missionary theology without much scrutiny. Consequently, we have failed to articulate the theological meaning of Jesus' life and death on the cross through the eyes of the suffering masses in Africa. We have ignored being informed, and convinced by the words of Jesus to the weeping women:

> Daughters of Jerusalem, do not weep for me, but weep for yourselves and for your children. For the days are surely coming when they say, blessed are the barren,

and the wombs that never bore, and the breasts that never nursed. (Luke 23:28-29)

Even though for many centuries in Africa we have experienced many painful violent deaths and many crosses (including the slave trade, colonialism, neocolonialism, civil wars and genocide) we have yet to come to grips with the meaning of the cross and what is meant by carrying our own cross. We have to learn to resist the evil forces in our midst and to struggle for transformation of our lives. But through Rizpah and in Africa we encounter women who are not afraid to say no to these evil forces.

As mentioned in the introduction, many Africans have been condemned to lives of poverty, oppression, violence, disease and premature violent death at the hands of the powers that be. Daily, many Africans are forced to carry the cross of hunger, torture, humiliation, and rape, while others watch or blame them for their suffering. Despair and hopelessness have sucked away our humanness and compassion and in the last years of the twentieth century, this has been clearly expressed in the wars in Liberia, Sierra Leone, Somalia, Angola, Sudan, Burundi, Rwanda, the Democratic Republic of Congo and the Ethiopia/Eritirea border conflicts. However, in the midst of all these crises we have seen people who have accompanied those who are suffering and dying, especially the women who provide for, and also keep vigil at the side of, malnourished children in refugee camps, hospital corridors, at home and with the sick and elderly. It is essentially the woman who keep the African spirit going in the darkest of the days, when the demons are released and destruction wipes away so many of their children.

Our theology and Christianity must pay attention to these women in the scriptures and in Africa who demonstrate compassion and remorse at what we do to each other through violence, through rejection and in sin. We need to articulate in theological terms these women's actions and lay them bare in the life and mission of the church, where their cries have also been neglected and rejected. Needless to say, actions speak louder than words but the language of silence should not always be seen to mean powerlessness. For instance, we see the power of Ripzah's silent vigil over her sons' bodies, and the courage of the women who followed Jesus beating their breasts and wailing. There was no fear in these women, they did not worry what the authorities would say, and their way was to identify with the suffering and the dying and to demand for justice, human dignity and life in their land. Such powerful actions by women in the Bible and in contemporary life situations could be re-enacted in liturgical language to enable Christians to capture and nurture a spirituality of resistance and transformation. Such a spirituality will engender the struggle for justice, peace and reconciliation even if it means death in the hands of the authorities. In the light of this powerful symbolic language of resistance, we also need to relearn the meaning of baptism as a symbol of resistance to injustice and our faith in the transforming power of grace. In baptism, we accept to follow the path of Jesus, his beliefs, his idea about God and his siding with the poor and outcast. We should also commit our lives to the struggle for life in the midst of torture and death.

If this theology, which attempts to capture the spirit of Rizpah and the wailing women, does not reach the women, children and men in the pews, Africa will continue to destroy itself. We need to turn these tears, wailing and vigils into the prophetic voices that will name those who inflict death and destruction and profit from it. We also need to acknowledge our complicity when we watch helplessly and fail to take action against the evil forces in our midst. We must learn what it means to take the cross and follow Jesus in the African context. Rizpah's vigil and the tears of the women following Jesus reveal humanness, compassion, and God's desire for us to resist evil and to transform the misery of the human condition to one of life and dignity. The tears of women have for long been rejected: yet they were the ones who accompanied Jesus to the cross and all the way to the tomb.

These daughters of Jerusalem rose early in the morning on the third day to anoint the body of Jesus, an act of mercy and solidarity with the departed. But what they found astonished them. They encountered the risen Christ who greeted them, and once again sent them, this time not to weep for their children, but to give a message to the male disciples of Jesus, some of whom had denied and abandoned him. "Do not be Afraid; go and tell my brothers to go to Galilee; there they will see me" (Matthew 28:10).

Do not be Afraid: Go and Tell

A spirituality of resistance and transformation demands that we share the good news of the possibility of new life in the presence of death here and now. It is a spirituality that invokes a passion that believes positive change is possible. In Africa, as we watch the escalating anarchy in many countries and in our streets, it is difficult to comprehend how we can end violent death and proclaim new life in Christ. We even wonder where God is when such chaos and destruction take place. We therefore need a zeal that believes - unless we are determined to use the rule of the gun as a means of remaining independent - that we can sit down together and engage in dialogue over our differences. Passionate commitment is needed whereby we are not afraid to try new ways of relating to our neighbors and our enemies. Such zeal would be willing to listen to the word of God in the scriptures that require that we trust in God and act justly.

Like the daughters of Jerusalem, we must not be afraid, to proclaim what we have seen and heard in the scriptures and in our walk with God we must proclaim that in Christ there is new life. Christ has not abandoned us in Africa, but has given us the gift of the Holy Spirit to help us transform our lives to restore dignity and wholeness in our countries. We need to retell the resurrection story to recapture its redeeming grace, mercy, faith, hope and love which alone can help us to witness to the world of the power of God in history. Following the example of Rizpah and the women at the tomb, we should go to our brothers in the church and tell them that we must re-read and re-interpret the scriptures to hear afresh the message of Jesus: "The thief comes only to steal and kill and destroy. I came that they may have life, and have it abundantly" (John 10:10). Through the resurrection event, Jesus has assured us of his presence and power to overcome death. We should therefore not accept that death has the last word in Africa.

Conclusion: In the Company of Courageous Women

I began in search of a metaphor; instead I found a spirituality: a spirituality that calls us to engage in peace-making and the transformation of Africa. This chapter has introduced us to one of the most forgotten and neglected woman in the Bible, Rizpah, whose courageous act demonstrated her great love and suffering for her children. Rizpah's experience pointed us to a similar act at the cross of Jesus as his mother and her friends watched from a distance as he breathed his last (Mark 15:40-41; John 19:25-27). As Christian women, this link between Rizpah and the women in the gospels is crucial for our ongoing search for fullness of life. In company with these courageous women and the many others we encounter in our search for fullness of life, African Christian women must rise to the occasion and say no to all life-destroying activities in our homes, churches and societies. Today we must spread our *kangas* to protect all those whose lives are threatened by the HIV/AIDS pandemic, and the ever-growing violence and criminality in our societies. As acts of defiance and resistance we must provide protection to the defenceless who suffer, such as orphans, widows and widowers. We must comfort all those who have been maimed by mines, whose limbs have been chopped off in the Sierra Leone war and through the carnage on our roads and railway tracks. We must not succumb to those who accuse and silence us African women by claiming that we are merely the agents of western feminism. We know the pain of nurturing life, through bearing it in our wombs and by hard labor, merely to see it destroyed.[4]

Like Rizpah and the women at the cross, we must resist evil and give birth to new life-affirming theologies and ethics. We must also journey with Jesus to rediscover anew the joy of resurrection and the meaning of Christianity in Africa. This way we will nurture a spirituality of resistance and transformation that will lead us to engage in peace-making activities in our homes, churches and societies.

Endnotes

1. All Bible references are from the New Revised Standard Version.

2. This is a surprising omission as this work was one of the first works to focus the attention of theologians on the role of women in the Bible.

3. *Kanga* is a rectangular piece of pure cotton cloth with a border all around it, printed in bold designs and bright colors. It is also known as *leso*, which is widely used in Africa in numerous ways. For more information see Handy, J., & Bygott, D. (1984). *Kangas: 101 Uses*. Nairobi: Lino Typesetters.

4. We should note that in Africa, one does not have to be a biological mother to shoulder the responsibility of motherhood and nurturing life.

References

McKenna, M. (1994*). Not Counting Women and Children: Neglected Stories from the Bible*. New York: Orbis Books.

Ortega, O. (May/June, 1994). "Re-imagining the Church as a Worshipping Community." *Church and Society* (Presbyterian Church, USA), 40-51.

Dean, E. (1955). *All the Women of the Bible*. London: Independent Press.

Newsom, C., & Ringe, S. (Eds.). (1992). *The Women's Bible commentary*. Louisville: Westminster/John Knox Press.

The Implementation of Biblical Hermeneutics

Christina Landman

What do we have to do with the Women in the Bible?

For the past twenty years women theologians have imaginatively endeavored to place the women of the Bible on the agenda of scientific inquiry. The aim of this inquiry was never simply academic. Most of these women theologians were, and still are, church feminists, aiming with their research to change the position of women in churches with a vision towards influencing women's image in society.

The Biblical Women were Invisible and Without Human Dignity

The time has come, however, to ask the question whether the study and proclamation of women in the Bible can and has been effectively implemented in church and society to make women more human and visible. Indeed, the uncomfortable truth is that women in the Bible had not been treated as humans during their own times and their current visibility can be fully attributed not to the Bible authors, but to the efforts of their twentieth century sisters.

In terms of humanity and visibility the women in the Bible are an embarrassment to their modern sisters. In fact they can only be used today as negative sources to demonstrate the lack of human dignity and visibility with which these women were treated in their societies. They are typical of what women today want to free themselves from.   Even women who are visible in Biblical texts, like Esther and Herodias, affect us because of the lack of overt power available to them.   Even they had to employ traditional female wiles to fulfill their aims and to affect decision-making in the royal courts.

The women mentioned in the Bible are excellent examples of the negative influence religion can exercise on women's lives and the miseries patriarchal religion can cause.   Their examples cannot empower the uplifting of women today because they themselves did not offer alternatives to female oppression.   It seems that the only thing we share with women in the Bible is oppression.   But then again we do not even share a consciousness of oppression with them.   The women in the Bible are not depicted as people who were aware of, let alone reacting against being oppressed.

The Women in the Bible are From Foreign Contexts

Furthermore, our contexts differ vastly from these women. Very few of us today share the experience of nomad women in an ancient desert; or peasant women in an impoverished country under Roman rule; or women in the harem of a Middle-Eastern king; or women in slavery or semi-slavery with no chance of leading a life of human dignity, let alone a vision of taking on leadership roles.   Some of us may, on a superficial level, share with some of these women some forms of social discrimination.   Some of us are, for instance, subjected to tribal customs prohibiting women inheriting from their fathers' estate, just as many of them were.   But on the whole these women's experiences, of which we only have second-hand reports, are far removed from ours.

What is more, modern or rather post-modern feminists no longer believe in "women's experience" as a definable entity, which is universally valid for all women.   Women's experiences are diverse.   This was precisely the problem with patriarchy: it did not allow women's experiences and expertise any diversity and molded them into uniform styles based on an undiversified notion of "woman's nature" or "womanness". Feminists do not want to repeat this insult of stylizing women uniformly, even from a liberative perspective.

We cannot, then, claim that we share "being a woman" with women in the Bible, not only because of the diversity of human experiences but also because women in the Bible do not have their own voices. Their experiences are described by male authors who obviously wrote from the perspective of a negative ideology, one that alleged the existence of a common female nature.

In summary, we do, indeed, have very little to do with women as they are portrayed in the Bible. In their Biblical characterization they show no vision of being liberated from inhuman treatment and invisibility. Using these women to empower women today contradicts the textual analyses of feminist theologians themselves. Furthermore, our social contexts differ vastly from that of theirs and so do our experiences. As the experiences of women in the Bible differed from one another, so our experiences differ not only from that of our contemporaries, but even more so from women from ancient cultures.

Who are the Alternative Women of Biblical Times?

Selectivity and the Early Bible

There is, surely, a reason why women's experiences are fenced in and framed into specific styles in the Bible. Furthermore, there must be a reason why women's willingness to conform to traditional lifestyles is taken for granted in the Bible and, even worse, why their unwillingness to conform to cultural discriminatory practices is not even treated as a theme.

The reason can be found in the men who eventually determined the contents of the Bible. The fourth century church fathers took the job of compiling a book containing the original teaching of Jesus, Paul and their disciples on themselves in order to combat what they regarded to be heretical teaching in the church at the time. Women teaching, preaching and officiating in the church were *per se* heretical to these men who themselves were ascetic and monkish (Schüssler Fiorenza, 1994). Books referring to such women or written by them were left out of the Bible.

Examples of Alternative Women

What were the women like who should have been included in the Bible, on grounds of their close affinity to Jesus or Paul, but who threatened the old fathers? Would their inclusion in the Bible have changed the fate of the millions of women who came after them over the next two thousand years and suffered inferiority in church and society because of the sexist orientation and sections in the Bible? And were they women with whom at least some of us can identify today?

The Gospel of Mary (Magdalene), (King 1994b) was written more or less at the same time as the gospels that were included in the Bible. In this gospel Mary Magdalene is depicted as a leader amongst Jesus' disciples. Jesus dialogued extensively with her before his ascension and appeared in visions to her thereafter. In *The Gospel of Mary (Magdalene)* we find her teaching the other disciples on the subject of Jesus' thoughts, with Peter, in particular, hanging to the words from her lips. However, the depiction of Mary Magdalene as a disciple is not found in the Bible.

In *The Acts of Thecla* (McGinn 1994) that originates from the second century AD, we find the story of the life and work of another woman of substance who was not featured in the Bible. Thecla became greatly attached to Paul and his teaching when he visited Iconium in Asia Minor on one of his missionary tours. She decided to devote her life in full to this teaching, thereby enraging her fiancé. He then convinced the governor that she should be burnt at the stake for transgressing the cultural boundaries set for women in that society and at that time. But with Thecla on the pyre, God sent a massive hailstorm, which quenched the flames, setting Thecla free to follow Paul to a deserted grave on the road to Corinth.

On moving to Corinth, another man fell in love with her and he, too, was offended by her lack of interest in him. He also persuaded the local governor to execute her, this time by throwing her to wild beasts in the arena. The backlash against an independent woman in this city was as intense as in the previous one and Thecla was pushed naked into the arena in front of a massive crowd. It turned into a battle of the sexes with the female animals in the arena fighting for Thecla against the male beasts. The day belonged to the females, and Thecla baptized herself in front of the crowd in a bath full of killer seals that did not touch her. Not only was the story of Thecla left out of the Bible, in the fourth century monks created a cult of a soft-spoken, over-motherly Mary, to counteract the cult of Thecla that had been spreading like wildfire. This cult had inspired women from all over the world to travel to churches named after her where *The Acts of Thecla* was read daily.

The Book of Norea (King 1994a) is an example of a book from the first century AD of Jewish origin which was left out of the Old Testament to make space for the much more favored version of the story of the fall. In this version Eve, the first woman, introduced sin into the world, thereby discrediting all religious women who came after her. In *The Book of Norea*, however, Eve's daughter Norea, who is not mentioned with her brothers Cain and Abel in the Old Testament, tells a story contradictory to the account of the fall in Genesis. In this story the snake in paradise was the vehicle of the Spirit of God and it was this Divine Spirit who advised Eve to eat from the fruits of wisdom, so that women could become wise and convince men to share with them in this wisdom. However, this story of the wise woman was abandoned in favor of an image of the first woman as ignorant and an easy prey to the devil and his agents.

The Contribution of Alternative Women

Is Mary Magdalene the disciple, Thecla the teacher and preacher, and Eve who introduced wisdom into the world, more useful to us than the women who eventually came to be mentioned in the Bible? They are, because they testify to a religious culture in the early days of Christianity in which women participated on different levels and in accord with their talents and expertise. These selections are examples of the religious behavior of women that have been kept from us through their exclusion from the Bible and the church's tradition of suppression them.

Furthermore, the main contribution of these stories and the women they feature is that they empower us to retell the stories of some of the women in the Bible from a liberative perspective. Knowledge of the existence of these strong and strongly spiritual women, and the reasons for the suppression of their voices, inspire us not only to call for them to be read alongside the Biblical canon, but also to retell the stories of women in the Bible as stories of liberation, even when this means neglecting their patriarchal setting.

A Commentary on the Extended Bible by African Women

Commentaries from America and Europe

Women have endeavored before to write a commentary on the whole of the Bible from a liberative perspective. A little more than one hundred years ago, in 1895, Elizabeth Cady Stanton published *The Woman's Bible* in which she commented on extracts from the Bible in which reference is made to women. She had a vision that recovering and recycling the accounts of women in the Bible would liberate women from social and ecclesiastical invisibility and inferiority.

To commemorate *The Woman's Bible,* one hundred years after it was published, Carol Newsom and Sharon Ringe (1992) published *The Women's Bible Commentary.* This is an anthology of commentaries by women on every book in the Bible as well as on some so-called apocryphal material. This publication testifies to the development in women theologians' historical-critical, social and gender-sensitive readings of the Bible. Although Elizabeth Cady Stanton's *The Woman's Bible* was not well received one hundred years ago, Newsom & Ringe brought to reality many of the goals Stanton envisaged for women's theology. Indeed, Stanton might even have inspired some of the insights of this commentary. Newsom and Ringe's commentary has also been translated into Dutch under the title *Met Eigen Ogen: Commentaar op de Bijbel Vanuit het Perspectief van Vrouwen.*[1] Thus Dutch women theologians have added their own contribution to biblical interpretation through this translation.

Also in commemoration of *The Woman's Bible*, Elisabeth Schüssler Fiorenza (1994) published *Searching the Scriptures: A Feminist Commentary.* However, she wanted to liberate the Bible from the boundaries set for it by the women-unfriendly fathers of the fourth century. Her anthology therefore includes commentaries on the work of the strong women of early Christianity that are found in such texts as *The Book of Sophia, The Book of Norea, The Daughters of Job, The Gospel of Mary (Magdalene), The Acts of Thecla,* and *The Passion of Perpetua and Felicity.*

The Tenets of African Women's Theology

What, then, is left for African women theologians to do? What sort of commentary can African women write on the (extended) Bible that can make contributions in addition to those European and American women have already made?

African women's theology, as is the case with Third World women's theologies in general (Ortega, 1995)[2], displays the following characteristics:

(a) African women's theology is a theology of relations. The female theologian in Africa wants to replace the hierarchical relations of patriarchal theologies and customary practice with relations based on mutuality. She is society-sensitive.

(b) African women's theology is a theology of inter-relatedness. It acknowledges the inter-relatedness of men and women, and of people and nature. African women theologians are ecology-sensitive.

(c) African women's theology is also culture-sensitive. It encourages dialogue between cultures and within cultures in order to criticize what is oppressive and to develop what is liberative in African customs.

(d) African women's theology implements its research findings through a ministry of storytelling. An African woman theologian wishes to break down the barriers between theological meta-language and literary language and to convey her ideas through a narrative theology.

A Narrative Commentary by African Women Theologians

A Ministry of Story Telling

This is the contribution African female theologians can make. They can write a narrative commentary on the (extended) Bible, consisting of stories of its women, stories told, and retold, in such a way that women (and men) today can make some contextual identifications with them in terms of relations, inter-relatedness and social practice.

The following are examples of stories that can be told that keep in mind the concerns of African women theologians concerning relationships, the inter-relatedness of all beings, and the customs whereby people subdue one another.

Hannah's story (in I Samuel 1) is a story of a woman who first conformed to custom and then abandoned it in order to be at odds with society. Hannah was childless. She called on God's help to bear a child and thus to conform to what was expected of her as a woman. Then she gave the child Samuel back to God, not because she regarded children as property to dispose of at the parent's will, but because she saw no future for him in a context where the relations between people - in this case between her and her husband's other wife Peninnah - were based on jealousy. In Hannah's story we find woman using culture against woman, and a woman using another woman's infertility to disempower and ridicule her. But Hannah refused to be subjected to this cruel play with custom that forced her to conform and she therefore gave her only child to God. The child Samuel eventually became a great man of God and leader of the people, but this was only because his mother dared not to acquiesce to custom.[3]

Jezebel's story (in I Kings 19) is a story of a very religious woman who wanted to consolidate the land of the peasants into big state-controlled farms that would have been very advantageous for the people in the cities. However, apart from the fact that the gods she worshipped were foreign gods, Jezebel ignored the inter-relatedness of city people to the people of the rural areas and the inter-relatedness of God, people and nature in these rural areas. She therefore lost the support of the peasants and eventually her life.[4]

Mrs. Job's story (in Job 1) is a story of a woman who lost everything in life. She was, furthermore, deemed of so little value that when Satan took everything from her husband, he did not even bother to take Job's wife. She herself lost faith in life and was therefore not present when her husband's tribulations came to an end, and life became bearable again.[5]

Lydia's story (in Acts 16) is the story of a woman who was empowered by Paul to start a congregation in Philippi. She was a woman who made a difference in a city hostile to Christianity. Tabitha's story (in Acts 9) is the story of a woman who made a difference to the lives of poor widows by doing something very traditional, like making clothes for the deprived.

The story of Mary and Elizabeth (in Luke 1) is the story of women who supported one another when the eyes of society were looking with malignant curiosity at one of them. However, the story of Mrs. Wisdom (in Proverbs 7) is the story of a woman who peeps at other women with an eye towards the gossip market.

The story of Samson's mother (in Judges 14-16) is the story of the only woman who survived her relationship with Samson. All the other women, his bride, the prostitute and even Delilah suffered in their relationships with Samson.

Only his mother survived emotionally, because she placed her role as mother alongside his role as son and did not allow herself to perish as a human being when her son was struck down.[6] The Story of Mary (Luke and Acts) is the story of a woman who was not only mother to the Son of God, but who primarily is the mother of all believers because of the role she played amongst the very first Christians after Jesus' death and resurrection.[7]

The story of the man and woman of the Song of Songs is the story of a black woman and a white man who restored paradise for themselves through their relationship and their inter-relatedness with nature and her animals. This was achieved in spite of customary prejudices.[8]

Conclusion

In this paper I have argued for the implementation of Biblical hermeneutics as a narrative commentary on the (extended) Bible by African women. The implementation of this research by African women on Biblical hermeneutics should, however, not end at publication but should be part of a broader ministry of story telling, thereby invading the liturgy, the preaching and the counseling of the church.

Endnotes

1. Translated and introduced under the editorship of Mieke Heijerman & Caroline Vander Stichele. (1995). Zoetermeer: Meinema.

2. This paragraph is dependent on a summary of the whole of this book.

3. Inspired by Klein, L. (1994). "Hanna: Marginalized Victim and Social Redeemer" in A. Brenner (Ed.), *A Feminist Companion to Samuel and Kings.* Sheffield: Sheffield Academic Press, 77-92.

4. Inspired by Jobsen, A. (1990*). Izebel en Achab: Verklaring van een Bijbelgedeelte.* Kampen: Kok.

5. Inspired by van Wolde, E. (1991). *Meneer en Mevrouw Job: Job in Gesprek met Zijn Vrouw, Zijn Vrienden en God.* Baarn: Ten Have.

6. Inspired by Reinhartz, A. (1993). "Samson's Mother: An Unnamed Protagonist." in A. Brenner (Ed.), *A Feminist Companion to Judges.* Sheffield: Sheffield Academic Press, 150-170.

7. Inspired by Graef, H. (1985). *Mary: A History of Doctrine and Devotion.* Maryland: Christian Classics.

8. Inspired by Goitein, S. D. (1993). "The Song of Songs: A Female Composition"; Trible, P. (1993). "Love's Lyrics Redeemed"; and Meyers, C. (1993). "Gender Imagery in the Song of Songs" in A. Brenner (Ed.), *A Feminist Companion to Judges).* Sheffield: Sheffield Academic Press, 58-66, 100-120, 197-212.

References

Schüssler Fiorenza, E. (Ed.) 1994. *Searching the Scriptures: A Feminist Commentary.* New York: Crossroad.

King, K. 1994a. "The Book of Norea, Daughter of Eve" in E. Schüssler Fiorenza (Ed.), *Searching the Scriptures: A Feminist Commentary.* New York: Crossroad, 66-85.

King, K. 1994b. "The Gospel of Mary (Magdalene)" in E. Schüssler Fiorenza (Ed.), *Searching the Scriptures: A Feminist Commentary.* New York: Crossroad, 601-635.

McGinn, S. (1994). *The Acts of Thecla* in E. Schüssler Fiorenza (Ed.), *Searching the Scriptures: A Feminist Commentary.* New York: Crossroad, 800-828.

Newsom, C., & Ringe, S. 1992. *The Women's Bible Commentary.* Louisville: Westminster/John Knox Press.

Ortega, O. (Ed.) 1995. *Women's Vision: Theological Reflection, Celebration, Action.* Geneva: World Council of Churches.

Stanton, E. C. 1895. *The Woman's Bible.* Boston: Northeastern University Press

Circle Transforming Theological Frameworks

The Religious Life of an African: A God-given Praeparatio Evangelica?

Gomang Seratwa Ntloedibe-Kuswani

Introduction

> "*Anima(e) naturaliter Christiana(e)*". If the intention of
> this dictum by Tertullian is to express, not that
> Christianity corresponds to man's natural religion, but
> that every religion has evolved features - and may create
> in its adherents an inner attitude - which paves the way
> for an understanding of the Christian message, and
> which find their full realisation in the Gospel of Christ,
> then it may justly be applied to African religions.
> (Westermann 1937:64)

This is the same kind of argument put forward by John
Mbiti (1970a), that the adherents of African religions have
an "inner attitude", which paves the way for an
understanding of the Christian message. Mbiti does not
term it *"O testimonium animae naturaliter Christianae"* as
Tertullian does, but he appears to mean the same thing:
that the religious life of an African is a "God-given"
praeparatio evangelica (preparation for the Christian gospel).

We need to ask ourselves why Mbiti had to argue that
African religions are a preparation for the Christian gospel.
What really necessitated this argument? Probably Mbiti is
trying to correct the colonial impressions that held that
indigenous religions are not God-given or divine, but are
evil and must be eliminated. During the colonial missionary
era, most of the missionaries who took the Christian gospel
to Africa were very negative about anything African.
Missionaries like Robert Moffat held that Africans had no
consciousness of their own until it was formed by them -

the missionaries - and had no knowledge of God and of future life (Seaver 1957; Moffat 1842).

Background to the Missionary Era

The missionary era became part of the wider phenomenon of Africa-Europe contact. The missionary shared a similar understanding of Africa with any European of the time. By the early nineteenth century, Europe had a fixed image of Africa, as explained by Philip D. Curtin in *The Image of Africa*. Curtin noted that different races inhabit the world and race difference plays a role in history:

> Some people, perhaps most people, have been conscious of their own racial type. Some have assumed that they were a "chosen people", especially favoured by God. Some have assumed that they and they alone were human. Most have preferred their own type as the aesthetic standard of human beauty. Most have assumed that people of their own type were physically or mentally or culturally superior to other races. (Curtin 1964:29).

Nineteenth century European science was also misused to support some of the unfounded racial views. It was assumed that race determined the course of human history. Skin color was an outstanding feature used against the Africans. Their skin color was associated in some way with the lower and inferior way of life and the status of slavery (Curtin, 1964). Color prejudice was used as a basis for assessing African peoples, their culture, and traditions. Curtin comments that the scientists of the time, such as the early nineteenth century French biologist Lamarck, continued to hold the colonialistic European belief that the Christian God had arranged creation in a "Great Chain of Being"; that is, a hierarchy of beings. Curtin also states that, previously, the Swedish biologist Linnaeus and the natural scientists of the eighteenth century had developed a color classification based on race in keeping with the Great Chain of Being. The black race was dumped at the bottom of humanity and the white Europeans placed on the very top. The blacks were not only at the bottom, they were also placed side-by-side with orangutans and only separated from them by the fact that orangutans could not speak. In 1774, Edward Long claimed that Europeans and Negroes did not belong to the same species (Curtin 1964). In other words his claim suggested that God created Europeans as humans, but Africans, if created by the same God at all, were created as "animal-like creatures". This kind of claim was used as justification of the enslavement of Africans and the destruction of their identity. This is the historical background that has made it necessary for African theology to be dominated by themes of liberation and identity.

Theories from some European anthropologists also contributed to the shaping of the missionary image of Africa. Sir E. B. Tylor (1930), for example, classified the religions of the so-called primal societies as (lower) animism. At that time the two other religions acceptable to Christian Europe were Judaism and Islam. Asian and African religions were dismissed as pagan and animistic because of the status of their societies as compared with those of Europe. What European missionaries inherited from Tylor's classification of religion is reflected in the Commission IV Report of the 1910 Edinburgh Missionary Conference in Scotland:

> Negroes all over the continent of Africa; Indians in the Americas; and Islanders from all the tropical and Southern oceans hold various forms of animistic beliefs. Indeed the religions of China and Japan are, to some extent, but civilised and moralised forms of animism. (Gairdner 1910:139)

As with the 1884 Berlin colonial conference on the partitioning of Africa, no African was present at the 1910 Edinburgh Missionary Conference, when African religions were excluded, marginalized, and condemned for destruction by an imperial power. Some missionaries were filled with this imperial spirit and came to Africa thinking of destroying what they regarded as animism. However, other European missionaries in Africa started to see things differently. The truth and facts about African religions were such that they forced the Africa-based white missionaries to call another conference in Belgium to share with their counterparts in Europe what they had discovered about African "animism" (Smith 1926).

This historical background gives us a clear picture of the kind of missionaries and Christianity that Africa received. Though at times the missionaries have been and are praised as the humanitarians of Europe, who accepted Africans as humans and fought for the abolition of slavery, their background helps us to understand why it was still difficult for some of them to accept anything African as God-given. This is reflected in the initial aggressive encounters between Christianity and African religions. In the colonial period Christianity was presented as the only true religion. It was the one given by God to be the tool that was to be used conquer and get rid of African religions. In other words, the process of making Africans a "new creation" (2 Corinthians 5:17) could also be understood as the destruction of what was African and replacing it with what was thought to be "superior". Various Christian writers have considered the non-Christian traditions: some have thought them to be perfect specimens of absolute error, masterpieces of hell's invention, and Christianity was simply called upon to oppose, uproot, and destroy them (Gairdner 1910).

For some missionaries, the Christian gospel was no longer the message of Christ but the message of the chosen or superior groups. But using the Christian gospel to destroy what was African was tantamount to destroying the African people themselves. Africans are, in general, religious beings and one cannot destroy their religion without destroying them. In the event it was difficult to destroy African religions: instead both the African people and their religions became forces to be reckoned with. The encounter between the missionary enterprise and African tradition fed the root of African theology from which theologians like John Mbiti emerged.

John Mbiti was born in Kenya, East Africa. He was ordained as an Anglican priest. In the early 1960s, he studied for a doctoral degree in New Testament studies at Cambridge University. Mbiti later became a professor of

Theology and Comparative Religion at Makerere University in Uganda. In 1972, he was appointed the Director of the World Council of Churches, Ecumenical Institute Bossey, Céligny, Switzerland. He was a pastor in a Swiss Reformed Church and lectured at the University of Berne in Switzerland. He has published many books and articles. Though a New Testament scholar, John Mbiti's publications show a wide range of interests, particularly in African traditions and religions. In common with his contemporaries, Mbiti tries "to affirm the integrity of an African point of view in religious apprehension where it has been underestimated or despised in Africa's missionary history" (Bediako 1992:304).

In spite of the fact that Mbiti sees some aspects of African religions as incompatible with Christianity, he was one of the early African theologians who saw little antagonism between African religions and the Christian gospel (Mbiti 1970a). Instead, Mbiti celebrated the African religious past as a preparation for the Christian gospel. He saw the Christian gospel as a fulfillment of African religions. This is what influenced Mbiti's shift of interest towards African religions and away from the New Testament (Bediako 1992).

Unlike other African theologians, Mbiti does not continually protest about the ills and mistakes caused by the missionaries (Bediako 1992). To him, missionaries brought to Africa a religion that is historically African. He argues that when missionary Christianity came, the Coptic Church and the Church in Ethiopia were long established there (Mbiti 1969).

Mbiti's Argument

Mbiti's theological standpoint is best articulated in his article, "Some African Concepts of Christology" (1972). Mbiti suggests that for African theologians to achieve their task they have to take into account four sources. First, the Bible, as the scripture, contains the final authority on religious matters. Second, the Old Churches of Europe have a rich theology, scholarship, and traditions, which can be inherited. Third is traditional Africa that embraces the traditional thought forms and religious concerns within which our peoples live. Fourth is the Church in Africa that has seen significant numerical and spiritual growth. Of these four sources, I will concentrate on the third - the African world. Mbiti always emphasizes that the African world is the most important element for African theology. He argues that the African past remains the necessary "preparation for the Gospel", despite the negative attitudes expressed by colonial missionaries:

> It is my contention that, even though officially Christianity either disregarded African religion altogether, or treated it as an enemy, it was in fact African religion more than anything else, which laid down the foundation and prepared the ground for the eventual rapid accommodation of Christianity in Africa, and for the present rapid growth of the Church in our continent (Mbiti 1973:86).

African theology remains locked in a struggle for an African identity as a result of "colonial and imperial spiritualism" which came as a part of the whole colonial-imperial exercise to Africa. As Jean and John Comaroff note, "the final objective of generations of colonizers has been to colonize their (African) consciousness with the axioms and aesthetics of an alien culture" (Comaroff & Comaroff 1991:4). They go on to say that, though consciously colonized, Africans remained conscious of this colonization. African theology is one example of this consciousness. Mbiti, in agreement with the Comaroffs, argues that mission Christianity was colonial rule in disguise. Mbiti remains one of the people who became conscious of the fact that the stigma of colonialism made the mission Christianity fail to recognize and take time to understand the significance of African religions, hence the imposition of Western (and American) types of Christianity upon Africans. Mbiti argues that, though a new form of religion was imposed on the Africans, Christianity came to Africa and found Africans not "religiously illiterate". Africans were already prepared by their own African past to receive any gospel other than African gospels. At one point Mbiti asserts that Christianity in our continent has no great service to render other than to replace the existence of the religious people of Africa with the existence brought by the Christian gospel and Jesus Christ, so that all the peoples of Africa can proclaim Christ as Lord and King (Mbiti 1986).

Mbiti's understanding of John 1:14 is that the Incarnation was a direct invasion of God into the world of humanity and that Christ came to reveal all that religions had been previously ignorant about. For example, he argues that in Africa, as in Jewish traditions, it is said that God, because of his greatness, was considered a distant being, far away from his people - probably in "the Holy of Holies". But through Christ, God came and dwelt among his people. Mbiti argues that Christianity should not be presented as an enemy to African religions. Christianity and the African religions should not fight each other; they are complementary. For the Christian gospel to redeem Africans, it needs African religions as a background and a vehicle, claims Mbiti (1970a). In other words the gospel is meant to fulfill and not to destroy. If the Christian gospel does not fulfill its role well, Africans will always remain in a state of tension and a form of "religious schizophrenia" as Desmond Tutu (1978) has observed. Mbiti's arguments have become a very important help to many Africans faced with the dilemma created by the presentation of Christianity as an enemy to African religions, and who have been told that Africans lacked their own divine past and traditions.

Western cultures remain a stumbling block to establishing harmony between the Christian gospel and Africans. The African has remained a most puzzled person, because after making all the preparations - having done the donkey work, as Mbiti puts it - what he has done is despised, condemned and sabotaged (Mbiti 1970c). Those who brought the Christian gospel to Africa wanted to deny it the opportunity to fulfill and redeem, by promoting it as part of their own cultures. For example, Christian tradition confines God and the gospel to one culture and to a building generally entered once a week. But unless the gospel was and is presented through the medium of African religions, it will not take root in Africa and if it remains in Africa, it will remain meaningless and foreign. Had people like Mbiti and those in the African independent Churches failed to take sides with the Christian gospel, the gospel could have completely failed to develop strong roots in Africa. It is for this reason that people like Welbourn and Ogot have already declared the gospel a failure in Africa:

> In terms of the conversion of a people, the Church has failed ... partly ... because it has largely been unable to present to Africa more than a western image of its faith.... (The Church) can make men at home in a nation, or in the world, only if they have first learnt to be at home in local terms (Quoted by Mbiti 1969:237).

In his arguments, Mbiti has discussed many things that this chapter cannot cover. Instead, it will look specifically into his discussion on the religious literacy of the Africans, elements of African religions and African religious expressions. The chapter will conclude by examining the implications of Mbiti's argument on women.

Religious Literacy in Africa

Mbiti presents Africans as the most religious peoples ever seen: "Africans are notoriously religious" (Mbiti 1969:1). Africans become religious even before birth, they are born as already religious babies and remain religious even after death. Individuals as well as their societies remain religious and it is not a matter of choice that makes one religious but a matter of birth. In African societies, religion permeates all aspects of life - social, political, and economic. This makes Africans religious beings and there is little scope for being irreligious. To an African, life is a whole: there is no formal distinction between what other societies term the secular (profane) and the sacred. Mbiti concludes that because of lack of this distinction, many African languages do not have a term for "religion". This conclusion might be correct because even when I examine the Setswana language for a word that refers to religion I fail to find one, except ones for tradition, faith, or life. It is still a problem, even for most Batswana students of religion, to define the term religion unless it is within their context, which comprehends religion as a way of life. From an African point of view, religion has nothing to do with place, time or a founder: one is born already religious hence many Africans would understand their religion as also God-given.

Mbiti argues that if the presentation of the Christian gospel to Africa overlooks the fact that Africa is religious enough to nurture the Christian gospel, the latter will achieve little in Africa. In other words, he is agreeing with what Welbourn and Ogot (quoted by Mbiti, 1969) have already said. Mission Christianity has not penetrated sufficiently deep into African religiosity (Mbiti 1969), because as compared to the African religious past, it (mission Christianity) was not religious enough, as it does not fill the whole life of Africans and their understanding of the universe. Mission Christianity has only brought into African religions rules to observe, promises to expect, and the Book, without paying attention to the African spiritual outlook. I remember what one of my university teachers said about one missionary among the Ngoni in what is now Malawi. He said, "The missionary reported that, 'At noon I got up and called them to the tent door.... I showed them a Bible and told them it was this that made our nation rich and powerful.'"

Mbiti invites Christianity to take advantage of African religious milieu and not to remain only spiritual and abstract but to be involved practically in the lives of Africans. Christianity should be seen in all African activities like agriculture, politics, and social rites of passage. In this way the Christian gospel will be acknowledging the fact that the ground was already prepared by African religions. If Christianity hides in a church building, it will remain a stranger in Africa.

Elements of Religion

Mbiti identifies some elements found in Christian and African religions: divinities, gods, spirits, and many others. This illustrates that Africa is as religious as any other place. It does not need any other religion to help her nurture the Christian gospel. There is no enmity as Christians seem to believe. Most religions claim knowledge of God, and when Christianity was brought to Africa Africans already knew God. In his *Concepts of God in Africa* (1970b), Mbiti gives a wider picture of the knowledge of God among the Africans by looking into several African groups' concepts of the transcendent: the Akan in West Africa, the Zulu in Southern Africa and the Banyarwanda in East Africa. Mbiti claims that all these groups acknowledge that God is omniscient, omnipresent, omnipotent, transcendent, and immanent. Like the African religions, the Christian religion cannot be complete without speaking about God, spirits, and divinities. Mbiti wondered as to why Christianity had and has to introduce new Gods, new spirits, new divinities and new everything to the Africans, a process which he sees as creating unnecessary antagonism. Christians should have utilized the existing known religious concepts to convey the Christian gospel. To Mbiti, it is a grave mistake to dismiss African religious background without studying it first with a view to utilizing it for evangelical ends.

Religious Expressions

Mbiti (1970c) discusses beliefs or doctrines, practices, personnel, and religious objects and places as ways through which we can understand the religiousness of Africans. These concepts or aspects have religious connotations, and can be used to communicate and explain Christian ideas to and by Africans.

Beliefs of Christianity and African Religions

Christianity and African religions should be studied and compared without any one religion adopting an aggressive approach to the other. It is at this juncture that Mbiti (1970c) calls for what he terms "a religious dialogue". He says dialogue between Christianity and African religions would be an advantage, as African beliefs and religiosity would enrich Christianity. This would, in turn, mean that Christianity would no longer destroy traditional religions but would enhance them. New spiritual dimensions would be brought in which would complement the old beliefs. These would not necessarily oppose what is not already in the traditional religiosity.

Religious Practices

Mbiti has already emphasized that Africans hardly distinguish between the secular and the sacred. Africans do not need any systematic formula to calculate that religion equals life. Mbiti argues that the African concept of community is a vital point for the Church in Africa to use. It is an overriding factor in all aspects of life in Africa. "The individual says: 'I am because we are and, since we are, therefore I am.' He is conscious of himself only in terms of the corporate group. This is the context within which the individual discovers himself in the traditional solidarity of African community" (Mbiti 1972:61).

It would be an advantage for the Church in Africa if conversion takes place within the cultural framework of the community concept. The community concept in Africa embraces the home, the society, and the rest of nature. African Christians have to remain conscious of themselves in terms of other members of the corporate group and the environment around them. This would enrich the African Church as a community of believers in Christ. Africans cannot survive long outside their own community. The African community is an interdependent community. Mbiti suggests that the Christian church should maintain the old community set-up. It should not break the old set-up just for the sake of establishing new foreign structures. For example, the breaking-up of African traditional communities and replacing them with parish churches is a blunder. African communities consider the home as the center of nurture and education. Mbiti argues that it must continue to be so for Christian families because church buildings are not the most suitable places for communicating and experiencing a real sense of faith (Mbiti 1977). If this were taken into account, the Church in Africa would be celebrating the wholeness of life where there is no compartmentalization. In Africa, Mbiti argues, Christianity cannot afford a merely private life. From their homes, Africans should not be expected to take their faith to a church building only, but to all spheres of life, and even beyond that to their departed relatives. A Christianity, which is based in a church building, leaves Africans in a vacuum - uprooted, frustrated, and unsatisfied. Mbiti argues that if African peoples are "saved" without their cultures, history, and environment, their salvation will be lacking.

Mbiti thinks that salvation for God's whole creation would be another great contribution from African religions. Had Christianity not been aggressive, the African world-view would have made a wonderful contribution to the prevention of the current ecological crisis that, at times, Christianity is blamed for. For example, Lynn White's (1965) article, "Historical Roots of Our Sociological Crises", blames the Christian faith for rejecting nature as a candidate for salvation, hence nature has been misused in the name of God. Christianity is blamed for being only anthropocentric and for having established "polar-dualism" between humanity and nature, and for its insistence that it is God's will that man uses, and misuses, nature (and women) for his own ends. Whenever Christianity spread to places like Africa, in contrast to what the Africans believe about nature, it denied divinity in nature - rivers, mountains and trees were no longer sacred. White argues that our science and technology have grown out of Christian attitudes. One would argue that the view on nature of African religions corresponds very well with that of the writer of the book of Genesis: God saw that everything He created was good.

Though humanity was given dominion, it was a guardian dominion over a sacred nature.

The Availability of Personnel

Mbiti wonders why mission Christianity was, and still is, concerned with bringing and using people from abroad, and training new local people for their mission purpose, when there are many experienced and religiously prepared people from African religions to do this work. This is a curious argument from someone like Mbiti who has worked outside Africa for many years. He also says that Western Christianity came to Africa to find that there were already priests, *dingaka* or healers who could have been utilized, but were rejected as heathens, witches, barbarians, savages and demonic individuals instead. These were the people who understood African world-views better than the missionaries and everyone else. Almost all Africans remained adamant and unconvinced that their own healing systems were in error (Katz, Biesele & Denis, 1997), and that their ancestors were idols. Whether the Christianity that was imposed did or did not accept African personnel as part of the preparation for the Christian gospel, Africans continued to consult African religious personnel: their priests, healers and many others. Because of this situation African Independent Churches later received strong backing as they established themselves as institutions independent of Western personnel and financial assistance.

Religious Objects and Places

According to Mbiti, one of the fundamental mistakes made by mission Christianity was to reject African art and symbols as means of communicating the Christian gospel. African objects and places of worship, like African personnel, were dismissed as superstitious, satanic, devilish, and hellish: in short, "masterpieces of hell's invention" (Gairdner, 1910). Our sacred African environment (trees, mountains, rivers) was deemed secular. Instead, new sacred places called "churches" were built and were considered superior and civilized. Then Mbiti (1977) questions how effective conversion could be if not done within the peoples' context and understanding. He stresses that it is sin that God wants Africans to reject, not their culture. Indeed, the Gospel should be transmitted, disseminated and accepted through the medium of the culture.

Without their cultures, Africans would not understand themselves and others. Mbiti further argues that as the Christian gospel moved from Palestine into all parts of the world it was carried on the wings of culture. African cultures too, like other cultures, should be given the opportunity to carry the Christian gospel, at least and especially to its own people. African peoples have their own mouths to sing, musical instruments to play, talents to express, hearts to contemplate, intellectuals to theologize, feet to carry and language to communicate the Christian Gospel (Mbiti 1973). To Mbiti, the African religious past has enough tools to evolve a viable Christianity for Africa. Africans do not need the missionary cultural heritage in order to understand, articulate, and propagate the Gospel.

John Mbiti's elements of religion reflect the dimensions of religion used by Ninian Smart (1989) to characterize religion. Smart has worked out these dimensions on the assumption that any tradition that has most of these dimensions qualifies to be classified as religion. These dimensions can be used to describe rather than to define religion, as most of its definitions are inadequate because they are narrow, exclusive, and judgmental (Hick 1989).

Evaluation of Mbiti's Argument

We see Mbiti (1970a) dismissing the theory that African beliefs, practices, personnel, objects and places are devilish as inadmissible. However, he admits that though largely valuable, the African religious heritage is not entirely compatible with the Christian gospel. He argues that unacceptable features of traditional religions, such as sorcery, witchcraft, magic and even divination, are not compatible with Christianity because they are not elements of it.

I wonder what Mbiti means by magic, witchcraft, sorcery and divination. It seems the criterion he has used to isolate the above African concepts is Western and Christian-oriented, especially in that he does not define these concepts to help us understand how they are used. To Mbiti, whatever he sees as not compatible with Christianity hinders the Christian gospel and has to be eliminated by the power of the same Christian gospel. It is on these grounds that he says African religiosity is a *praeparatio evangelica*, which the Christian gospel has to penetrate, redeem, and fulfill (Mbiti, 1970a). In other words, Mbiti suggests that African religions are not complete and need the gospel. However, at times Mbiti contradicts himself by using the words gospel and Christianity interchangeably, in spite of the distinction he has attempted to draw between the two. According to Mbiti, the Christian gospel is to judge, evaluate, and transform the African religions because (African) cultures are sinful (though at the same time he claims the cultures are God-given) because they were created by "man". God created the Christian gospel. In short, Mbiti strongly emphasizes that African religions are only a preparation, which cannot achieve fulfillment in itself.

Mbiti argues his point thoroughly by backing it with examples from broad aspects of African religions: concepts of god, eschatology, prayers and spirituality. He employs these to rebuild that "bridge of continuity" and communication between African traditions and the bridge, which was destroyed by the mission, colonial, imperial Christian tradition. But the other side of Mbiti's argument is that without the Christian gospel, African religions could not have been redeemed. In this way, he is saying African religions are inadequate in themselves. This is both a dilemma and a paradox in the sense that the God-given African traditions still need to be fulfilled! What for! What kind of God is this that decides to give Africans partial knowledge and make them suffer until they accept foreign civilizations and salvation? By accepting salvation or fulfillment from foreign sources, then whatever partial knowledge they had before becomes confused and destroyed.   In so doing African people lose their identity and independence, their power and their humanity.

Historically, Mbiti started this kind of an argument at the time when the spirit of African nationalism had reached its peak - at the time when Africa was struggling against Western colonial oppression. As the politicians were rising against political colonialism, the theologians were not left behind, and we see Mbiti as one example of this. In other words, Mbiti's argument is a response to "religious colonialism".   Contrary to the colonial Christian mission that dismissed all aspects of African religions as absolutely devilish, Mbiti has argued that African religions prepared the ground for the Christian gospel. In other words, Mbiti argues that there is no contradiction between African religions with Christian gospel. This is a rejection of the colonial Christian mission's claim. But one would like to know the extent to which Mbiti's argument is relevant to the so-called post-colonial Africa. It is relevant in the sense that it allows us to see how colonized he was. He tries to defend African religions but could not overcome the colonial framework, which puts the Christian gospel above non-Christian religions. Mbiti fails to grant that African religions are complete on their own and that they have a right of their own to exist.

What was presented to Africa as the Christian gospel was a colonial package "which has shown itself on the African scene in many forms: (colonial), ecclesiastical, social, theological, cultural and administrative" (quoted by Bediako 1992:35). Agreeing with Mbiti, Desmond Tutu says that most of what is subsumed under the heading "African Theology" is resistance against cultural and ecclesiastical colonialism (Tutu 1978).   It is this colonial package that forces people like Mbiti to struggle and draw a distinction between what he terms "the Gospel" and "Christianity". The distinction helps us understand what Mbiti is trying to say: he is trying to say that the colonial package was not all that unworthy.   To Mbiti there was something worthy in the package and probably that is what he terms the Gospel. Tracing Mbiti's argument one would conclude that though he is rejecting the colonial package, at the same time he is trying to snatch something from it - what he refers to as the Gospel. Because of what Mbiti identifies as the Gospel, we find him preferring not to harp on the ills and mistakes caused by the missionaries: instead, he disassociates himself from the debate on missionary errors. But then Mbiti subscribes to the colonizing approach by defining African religions as *praeparatio evangelica*. This implies that African religions are not complete on their own.

Time and again Mbiti mentions Europe and North America, areas whose colonial and imperial relations with Africa are very evident. At this juncture we can now identify colonialism and the struggle for independence as major factors that generated African theology and made it necessary and inevitable. But Mbiti has been blamed by some who argue from an African perspective, such as p'Bitek, of "smuggling" foreign ideas in to hellenize African traditions (Westerlund 1985). On the other hand, conservative African Christian scholars have criticized him for demonizing Christianity (Kato 1975). In spite of all these arguments, Mbiti's work cannot be dismissed out of hand. It is a starting point or a stepping-stone to a wider and probably a better understanding of African religions and their struggle against being dismissed during the colonial and even post-colonial period.

It has to be appreciated that Mbiti has, to a certain extent, brought forth the value of the African cultures and traditions, including religions. At times he fails to take his arguments to their logical conclusions and ends up cutting the ground from beneath his own feet. He still sees "the Old Churches" of Europe as one of his major theological pillars in Africa. Like the eighteenth-nineteenth century European anthropologists, scientists, and missionaries, he is struggling to find a better place for his culture in "the now-invisible Great Chain of Being". But we must not overlook the fact that the same Mbiti who is struggling to secure a place for his culture has become what some people would term a "Westernized" African scholar. His dilemma is attested by his ambivalence in claiming African identity, and at the same time classifying African religions as secondary to Christianity – a *praeparatio evangelica*. This shows us how difficult and sometimes impossible it is to pluck the Christian Gospel from the colonial package without pulling on the strings to which it is attached. Mbiti failed to resolve his dilemma.

Mbiti's theological standpoint suggests that he accepted not only the Christian Gospel but also the colonial Christian tradition. He is influenced by the Christian Western gospel. Mbiti is also a Christian New Testament scholar, one who studied within Western structures of education. As a Christian scholar his interpretative key is determined by his own theological commitment, which is Western Christian (Bediako, 1992). Mbiti received and grew up in this type of Christianity, which he is trying to take into account in his struggle for African identity. This wider inheritance has influenced and shaped Mbiti's line of thought. Westerlund, confirms this when he says the study of African religions in Africa and by Africans has a strong Christian base:

> These (Christian) theological motives also guide African scholars of religion in determining what should be the main issues in the study of African religion.... The tendency of some scholars to "Christianise" African religion more than other scholars would like should partly be attributed to the fact that the two groups subscribe to different theologies of continuity. (Westerlund 1985:56)

Implication of Mbiti's Argument for African Women

Mbiti's arguments raise a major question. This is: Does Mbiti's presentation of African religions as *praeparatio evangelica* help the status of women in religion at all? To Mbiti, African religions are *praeparatio evangelica* just because they do not have the concepts of Jesus Christ as we see it in the Christian tradition – a male Nazarethian. Perhaps looking into Elizabeth Amoah and Mercy Oduyoye's (1988) attempt to find out whether traditional christological constructions take into account women's experience of life can answer the question raised. Amoah and Oduyoye see traditional christologies as male dominated for they always portray Christ as male. In their article, "The Christ for African Women", the two women attempt to take into account African women's experience of life in christological constructions. Their argument is that in many African societies, figures whose acts have led to more life and wholesome relations are not always male. For instance, Amoah and Oduyoye identified two issues to support their argument. First, as they reflect on the "Fante Gospel", they relate how the woman Eku saved her people by drinking the water of the pool. After drinking and being saved, people started praising Eku by saying, "Eku aso" meaning that "Eku has tasted on our behalf, we can now drink without fear of death." Secondly, Amoah and Oduyoye reflect on the christology of ancestors, which many traditional theologians failed to present as neutral or as both female and male. In many African societies ancestor qualifications do not recognize the sexuality of a person but take into account ungendered issues like parenthood (Fortes & Dieterlen 1965), good morals (Newell 1976), death (Ntloedibe 1993) and other aspects.

Amoah and Oduyoye help us to answer the question raised above. However, after identifying a Christ-figure from the Fante Gospel they weaken their argument by naming Jesus of Nazareth as a higher and universal Christ for Africans as well as Fante women. Their conclusion takes us back into John Mbiti's theological framework, which still sees African Christs as *praeparatio evangelica* for the Christian Christ and tradition. Thus we see African women theologians still operating within the colonial walls or frameworks. In justification for their assertion, the two women say that, as Christians, the Christian theology of "no other name" places them under an obligation to name Jesus of Nazareth as the Christ above all others Christs in non-Christian traditions.

This is a manifestation of the oppression to African women, as women as well as Africans. As much as they have to struggle for equal recognition between women and men they also have to struggle for the same equal recognition between Africans and other identities and traditions. While

African women were indeed oppressed in African religions, they were not eliminated from the official structures as was and is the case in the new Western Christian texts and institutions. Ife Amadiume, in her book, *Male Daughters, Female Husbands: Gender and Sex in an African Society* (1987), reminds us how the first mission Christian lessons in Africa focused on condemnation of African beliefs and the imposition of Western Christian patterns on African thoughts. For instance, she explains how a male image of God (and his only begotten son) was used to condemn the Nnobi goddess religion in West Africa. In a short space of time the condemnation of African goddesses shattered the focal symbol of African women's self-esteem (Amadiume 1987).

As new structures were put in place to disempower African women, they continued on their own to struggle for empowerment. For example women in Southern African religions could become healers: *dingaka, amasangoma,* prophets, *wosana.* When their African religions were condemned as incomplete, their position as spiritual leaders in the community was taken over and utilized by women in the African Independent Churches. There are many Batswana women working as "prophet healers" in African Independent Churches, who have claimed *bongaka* (healing) as a woman's role as well. Showing their creativity in the development of *bongaka,* healers in African Independent Churches use the Bible as a tool for divination (Merriweather 1992), because according to Batswana beliefs it is divination that makes a healer complete and powerful (Krige & Krige 1942). One might argue that African women found African Independent Churches as fulfilling and empowering because that is where they could become leaders and prophets of religious institutions, unlike in most European-founded Churches. In Africa women had a role to play in religious institutions:

> Apparently, when Christianity was first introduced in
> Nnobi, it was not seen as a thing for the masses....
> Women do not seem to have been involved at this stage....
> The fact that their lives were centred on the service of
> the goddess would have made it impossible for them to

welcome the new religion.... Indeed the earliest recorded mass protest movement by Igbo women was the Nwaobiala – the dancing women's movement of 1925. The basic demand of the movement, which was dominated by elderly women, was the rejection of Christianity and a return to traditional customs. (Amadiume 1987:120-121)

The time has come for African scholars, and especially theologians, to go beyond the colonial paradigms of preparation, which still present Africa as incomplete and powerless. African traditions have to set themselves free from other religious traditions and define their contexts, patterns, dimensions, and theologies. By so doing the African traditions will be in a position to present their unique identities and compete with other world traditions. Giving the study of religion independent African images of faith will empower African women not only against patriarchy but also against colonialism and globalization. When they have this independence, African women can create new and wider paradigms, from what Mbiti suggests, and move beyond Amoah and Oduyoye's frameworks for African identities, autonomy, and survival.

In conclusion, Mbiti's argument for a theology of continuity is well grounded. But, as I have said, his framework should be used as a starting point to subscribe to different theological frameworks, which might take African religions/theologies beyond preparation. Mbiti's claim that African religions are only a preparation with the Christian Gospel as their fulfillment needs further investigation. When one examines Mbiti's argument, one sees that Mbiti's perspective reflects a trend that is taken by mission and colonial Christianity, which influences many African scholars, including women. Most African theologians adopted Mbiti's standpoint, though to different degrees depending on their different contexts and backgrounds. However, I would like to take the "minority position"[1] and argue that African religions are salvific in their own right. Therefore, the African traditions need to be left independent to define their completeness, contexts, patterns, dimensions, and Christs for their own identity, autonomy, and survival.

Further, African religions give more power to women as attested by the spiritual position of leadership they hold in Southern Africa, as *amasangoma* among the Nguni, *wosana* among the Kalanga-Shona, and *dingaka* among Batswana. This is also attested by the fact that African Independent Churches, who fully utilize African religions, have women as central players in their institutions. But African Independent Churches, unlike Mbiti, use African traditions and religions not as a *praeparatio evangelica*, but as an equal partner to Christian tradition.

Endnotes

1. This position is minority because it is questioning the definite normativity of the Christian tradition, which has become popular. The position asserts that there are other religious ways of leading an authentic human life, other than the Christian way (Knitter, 1985).

References

Amadiume, I. (1987). *Male Daughters, Female Husbands: Gender and Sex in an African Society.* London: Zed Books.

Amoah, E., & Oduyoye, M. A. (1988). "The Christ for African Women" in V. M. M. Fabella, & M. A. Oduyoye (eds.), *With Passion and Compassion: Third World Women Doing Theology.* New York, Maryknoll: Orbis Books, 35-46.

Bediako, K. (1992). *Theology and Identity: The Impact of Culture upon Christian Thought in the Second Century and Modern Africa.* Oxford: Regnum Books.

Comaroff, J., & Comaroff, J. (1991). *Of Revelation and Revolution: Christianity, Colonialism and Consciousness in South Africa.* Chicago: University of Chicago Press (Vol. 1).

Curtin, P. (1964). *The Image of Africa: British Ideas and Action 1780-1850.* Madison: University of Madison Press.

Fortes, M., & Dieterlen, G. (1965). *African Systems of Thought.* London: Oxford University Press.

Gairdner, H. T. (1910). *Edinburgh 1910: An Account and Interpretation of the World Missionary Conference.* London: Oliphant and Ferrier.

Hick, J. (1989). *An Interpretation of Religion.* London: Macmillan.

Kato, B. H. (1975). *Theological Pitfalls in Africa* Kisumu: Evangelical Publishing House.

Knitter, P. F. (1985). *No Other Name: A Critical Survey of Christian Attitudes Towards World Religions.* New York: Orbis Books.

Krige, E. J., & Krige, J. D. (1942). *The Realm of a Rain-queen: A Study of the Pattern of Lovedu Society.* London: Oxford University Press.

Mbiti, J. S. (1969). *African Religions and Philosophy.* London: Heinemann.

Mbiti, J. S. (1970a). "Christianity and Traditional Religions in Africa" in *International Review of Mission.* Geneva: WCC Publications,*59*(236), 430-440.

Mbiti, J. S. (1970b). *Concepts of God in Africa.* London: SPCK.

Mbiti, J. S. (1970c). "The Future of Christianity - 1970-2000" in *Communio Viatorum: Theological Quarterly,* 13(1-2), 19-38.

Mbiti, J. S. (1972). "Some African Concepts of Christology" in G. F. Vicedom (Ed.), *Christ and The Young Churches.* London: SPCK, 51-62 .

Mbiti, J. S. (1973). "African Indigenous Culture in Relation to Evangelism and Church Development" in R. P. Beaver (Ed.), *The Gospel and Frontier Peoples.* Pasadena: William Carey Library, 79-95.

Mbiti, J. S. (1977). "Christianity and African Culture" in *Journal of Theology for Southern Africa,* 20, 26-60.

Mbiti, J. S. (1986). "Christianity and East African Culture and Religion" in *Dini na Mila: Revealed Religion and Traditional Custom,* 3(1), 1-6.

Merriweather, A. M. (1992). *Medical Phrasebook and Dictionary: English and Setswana.* Gaborone: Pula Press.

Moffat, R. (1842). *Missionary Labour and Scenes in Southern Africa.* London: John Snow.

Newell, W. H. (Ed.). (1976*). Ancestors.* The Hague: Mouton.

Ntloedibe, G. S. (1993). "Ancestors Qualifications and Functions with Special Reference to the Ashanti Speaking Akan of West Africa." Unpublished essay.

Seaver, G. (1957). *David Livingstone: His Life and Letters*. London: Lutterworth.

Smart, N. (1989). *World's Religions*. London: Cambridge University Press.

Smith, E.W. (September 1926). "The Christian Mission in Africa" in *A Study Based on the Work of the International Conference at Le Zoute*, Belgium, London: Edinburgh House Press, 14-21.

Tutu, D. (1978). "Whither African Theology" in L. Fashole (Ed.), *Christianity in Independent Africa*. London: Rex Collings, 364-369.

Tylor, E. B. (1930). *Anthropology: An Introduction to the Study of Man and Civilisation*. London: Watts.

Westerlund, D. (1985). *African Religion in African Scholarship*. Stockholm: Almquist and Miksell.

Westermann, D. (1937). *Africa and Christianity*. London: Oxford University Press.

Douglas, M. (1966). *Purity and Danger*. London: Routledge.

McGuire, M. (1997). *Religion: The Social Context*. Belmont: Wadsworth.

Smart, N. (1997). *Dimensions of The Sacred*. London: Harper Collins.

Stanley, B. (1990). *The Bible and The Flag: Protestant Missions and British Imperialism in the Nineteenth and Twentieth Centuries*. Leicester: Apollos.

Rethinking Sin and Grace: An African Evangelical Feminist Response to Niebuhr

Esther E. Acolatse

A Personal Reflection

I am an evangelical Christian from Ghana, West Africa. My growth towards feminism has been tentative and slow. My first few brushes with feminism, notably as it was portrayed in some Christian feminist theologies, left me with the distinct impression that Christianity was the major cause of oppressive measures against women, whether directly or indirectly. The result is that I felt all writings, especially biblical narratives, were to be read with suspicion. Unfortunately this hermeneutics of suspicion carried the message that Christianity as it is, was no longer good for us. But my experiences as an African Christian belied this assessment. Christianity was good for us, and for some women, who would have otherwise been nonentities in our culture. Thus it is the source of status to some degree. One just has to visit churches, especially the Independent African Churches, for this evidence. Most of these have been founded by women. They are the matriarchs and the prophetesses, and they wield an enormous degree of power. My conclusion from all this evidence was that feminism, and especially feminists' voices, only offered criticism.

I then began to hear of concerns that I had missed, due largely to my own preconceived ideas and partly to my upbringing. I was oblivious to the inherent gender discrimination found in attitudes and actions. But they were there all along, in worse forms than I had ever imagined. It goes beyond such incidents as a primary school teacher taking the boys to task for letting a girl take the first position in class tests. It is also captured by the Akan man's question at the birth of an infant, who asks: "Did you have a human being or a girl?" This sums it all up. There are human beings, and there are women. What feminism is really about is women asking to be allowed to be human.

When it comes to understanding and explicating biblical texts my own evangelical stance, with its belief in the errancy of scripture, caused me to assume the automatic subordination of female to male. But I would always wonder why justification, and especially sanctification, was divided along gender lines. If all who are called to follow Christ are also called to be transformed into the image of Christ by the power of the Holy Spirit, why is humility "a quiet and gentle spirit"? Why is submission and other manifestations of this spirit expected more from women than men? Does the Holy Spirit sanctify us on gender lines? These questions and more have lingered in my mind over the years. Recently, I was given the opportunity to explore what I began to see as the theological underpinnings of this state of affairs.[1]

Introduction

Feminists have recently called attention to the male bias in anthropological studies. They contend that these speak from and to the powerful male experience.[2] Much of the literature from such studies speaks largely from the male experience and emphasizes a dichotomy between the two genders. It also helps to perpetuate the stereotyping of the sexes. Roles are assigned based on this stereotyping and, in what is obviously circular reasoning, the stereotyping is said to derive from the roles, which are then seen to be biologically determined. The norm is to see the male as active and the female as passive and receptive. An understanding of the differences between the two genders is taken for granted, and this is reflected in current literature. An example of gendered reasoning can be seen in the work of Freud in the field of psychoanalysis. He points out that the differences between men and women have emerged as civilization developed. He asserts that women have a passive role, as he sees them as incapable of the sublimation required for shaping civilization that is built on industry.

It is men who spearhead the industrial process while women stay at home. What is forgotten is that she is home because it is the course of civilization has kept her there. Again, Erikson, who seems to be more sensitive to women's issues, nevertheless sees female maturing as growth that helps others fulfill themselves. As he says "A true moratorium must have a term and a conclusion: womanhood arrives when attractiveness and experience have succeeded in selecting what is to be admitted to the custody of inner space for keeps" (Erikson 1967:6).

The assumption is, therefore, that a woman does not define or create any space for she herself, but only for the future husband and any possible children. It is almost as if she is never fully a person – a self – without reference to those who define her, and who name her wife and mother. Traditionally, the tendency is to shun and look down upon a woman and it is my pastoral experience that more women tend to lament the lack of a spouse and children than do men.

Not only is this passivity expected and endorsed, it is affirmed and reinforced so that most women expect it of themselves. For instance in her book, *Sixpence in her Shoe*, Phyllis McKinley (as cited in Niebuhr & Tillick, 1980) has not only assumed this passivity on the part of all women, but has also made it the moral imperative for them. She calls on women to see themselves as the "sacrificers, the givers, not the eaters-up of life" (McKinley 47). In short, women are to be self-denying for the good of the created order, no matter what it costs. The picture painted is that it is good and right to assume the passive role, sacrificing ourselves for the good of the husband and children, as our ordained place in society requires of us.

The role of religion in perpetuating this centuries old stereotyping, which re-enforces the dichotomy between the genders, is what most feminist theologians are speaking out against. Much of this has been blamed on the scriptures and their inherent male bias, but much more on the way these scriptures have been interpreted in the past. A classic example in the Christian faith, which has recently come to receive attention, is the understanding of one basic human characteristic – sin. Somehow, even this human "leveler" seems to have been dichotomized along gender lines, not so much through any inherent features of the phenomenon itself, but as the way the two genders are perceived to relate to it in the works of some theologians.

In this chapter I will trace the historic-biblical understanding of sin and grace as explored by a neo-orthodox and influential western theologian. I will try to show that the definitions of sin and grace, as we have come to understand them, are narrow and therefore do not deal with our real sin and sinfulness. Emphasis will be given to their inherent male bias, showing the harmful effect this perception has not only on our inter-personal, but also our intra-personal relationships. Following other feminist theologians, I will then draw upon our common human experience, but especially the experience of African women. In particular I wish to show that the classical definition is not only too narrow but prevents us from seeing sin in its reality. Speaking from an African evangelical feminist perspective, I will draw on some familiar scriptures and point out ways in which erroneous interpretations of them are used to reinforce certain harmful tendencies and how these tendencies can be arrested and corrected. I will also show how positive patterns can be fostered in their place through a reorientation of our understanding of sin and grace.

It might seem a little strange to base a chapter, which is intended to speak to our African experience, on theories from western theologians. But, speaking from a Christian perspective, much of our basic theological understanding until recently has been largely derived from western theologians. This is due to the fact that they were the principal missionaries of the gospel to our lands. Moreover, most Christianity in sub-Saharan Africa is Mission Christianity.

Theologies that speak to and from our experience sometimes require the rethinking of earlier theologies. This involves critical dialogue, and this is undertaken in order to come up with a viable understanding of scripture for our context. I am aware that this may sound as though we are unable to formulate theologies of our own without recourse to other theologies, especially western ones. But this kind of thinking may only serve to entrench in us an "ours" and "theirs" mentality, which is antithetical to our basic belief in "us" and "we". I also think it is our Christian responsibility to break down the walls and divisions set up between us and the west as a result of our colonial past. To take as the point of departure the issues of sin and grace, seem to me a very appropriate starting point because these issues underscore our common humanity. This includes our common states of impairment and healing, that have for so long been the medium of suppression and oppression of the weak and the poor, the majority of these being women. Thus all humanity can readily identify with the weak and the poor. When we are set free from sin, which I have increasingly come to believe as the refusal of the self to be the self it was meant to be, we are enabled to be what we were made to be. This concept will be further elaborated on in this chapter.

Sin and Grace: The Classical Perspective

Most theologians and theological anthropologists who have dealt with sin have followed the Pauline/Augustinian lines in depicting sin primarily as pride, and secondarily as sensuality, which is often linked with pride. Since sin is seen as pride and extreme self-love, the antidote – grace – is automatically conceived of in terms of a shattering of the self, seen mainly through self-sacrifice. But a shattering of the self and self sacrifice are what women do ordinarily, and so making self sacrifice and the shattering of the self an antidote for pride does not speak to and from the experience of women, and is therefore a partial story of sin and grace for all humankind. It is this anomaly in the understanding of sin and grace that has prompted some feminist theologians, such as Judith Plaskow (1980) and Carol Lakey Hess (1993), to challenge the basic doctrines of both sin and grace as they have been formulated in the past. Reinhold Nierbuhr's formulation of sin has been the main focus of their discussions and this also serves as a point of departure for this paper.

In his two-volume book *The Nature and Destiny of Man* (1941; 1943) Niebuhr sets forth his ideas about sin and grace. He believes that human nature can be properly understood and interpreted through the revelation of God's will at both the individual and socio-historical levels of experience.

Both levels of revelation are dependent on each other for credibility and validity. Individual revelation relies on historical revelation for definition and control while historical revelation depends on individual revelation for its credibility. It is only when revelation is worked out in individual experience that revelation can be perceived as authentic.

Niebuhr, following his understanding of the relationship between revelation and experience, draws heavily on experience to formulate his doctrine on sin and grace. But it is questionable as to whether he follows his own reasoning through with regards to the doctrine of sin and grace. His definitions and arguments seem very one-sided, and he speaks primarily with reference to a particular experience. In spite of this somewhat narrow focus he claims that his aim is to relate the biblical conception of sin as pride and self-love to the observable behavior of humankind.

For Niebuhr, human experience is important since it is the locus of individual revelation as well as the point at which general revelation is validated. Following his intention to speak from human experience, and using philosophical comment, Niebuhr sees human beings as self-transcendent and "egocentric" subjects. Human beings, he says, have the capacity to stand outside themselves, and to scrutinize themselves as well as their world. In reaching beyond themselves in a religious vein, human beings are seen to eventually come in contact with the ultimate reality. Three things result from this contact – a sense of dependence that comes with acknowledging a creator, a moral obligation that is felt as laid on one from outside, and a longing for forgiveness. Sin and grace belong to the latter two.

Four elements can be identified in Niebuhr's doctrine of sin. First is the "occasion" for sin, which he sees as present in the nature of human beings as both finite and infinite, and as both bound and free. Second, there is the "precondition" for sin, which stems out of the anxiety one feels in the presence of one's finitude and a feeling of being bound. Thirdly, he posits that the actual character of sin has two dimensions, the moral/ethical and the religious.[3] The religious character of sin shows up in rebellion against God and in usurping God's place. Here the ego is at the center, subordinating all else to it. The fourth aspect, the direction of sin, manifests itself in pride and sensuality. In the first instance, the self identifies itself with the "beyond" it apprehends, that is pride. In the second, it identifies itself with natural vitality, thus denying its freedom – sensuality. Thus the self escapes the anxiety of its unlimited freedom in the light of its finitude by falling into sin. For the purposes of this chapter I will focus on the dimensions and directions of sin in order to point out how far removed it is from all human experience; I will do so by identifying the inconsistencies within Niebuhr's own thoughts on the issue of sin and thus grace.

Taking the premise that all human beings are predisposed to sin, and that all commit sin (even if in varying degrees) thereby missing the mark of their true calling in God, Niebuhr posits that the basic sin of humanity is pride. It is pride and inordinate self-love that is the driving force of man.

Though he recognizes another expression of sin – sensuality - it is completely subsumed under pride or self-centeredness. Pride is seen in three forms namely power, knowledge and virtue. In pride as power the ego either assumes its independence, as is seen often in powerful people, or lusts for power, as depicted by insecure people. The worst, he thinks, is the pride of virtue – moral pride – that makes virtue a vehicle of sin, making the moral self the standard of judgment. He points out that it assumes its worst forms in institutions that claim to be serving God. In this I think Niebuhr is correct.

In sensuality, one hides one's freedom and loses the self, becoming embroiled in unlimited devotion to limited values. These limited values, according to Niebuhr, find expression in gratifying the impulses within the self in a way that recalls the sins of the flesh portrayed in the Pauline epistle to the Galatians. Though Niebuhr recognizes sensuality as deriving from one's inability to appropriate one's God-given-freedom, he focuses on the symptoms and the acts, rather than the cause, that is the loss of self as a result of inability to use freedom appropriately. This is where I think Niebuhr's doctrine of sin and grace fails to address the whole of human experience. My contention is that in both the understanding of sin primarily as pride, and in the narrower definition of sensuality largely in terms of gratification of sensual appetites, Niebuhr speaks primarily to men.

In our common human experience, it is generally men who are in the position of power and authority, whether self imposed or incorporated in patriarchal societal structures. These structures place the male population in the dominant position, subordinating the female to them. The result is that the male feels inherently superior to females, and expects subservience from them. It is in this regard that sin as pride, self-assertion and the expression of inordinate self, in expecting others to serve and not serving others, that pride as depicted by Niebuhr describes male sin rather than sin generally. It is in the light of this understanding of sin that Niebuhr sees grace in terms of a shattering of the self, self-sacrifice, and love of others. Using the story of "The Giving Tree" by Shel Silverstein, Carol Hess (1993) has illustrated Niebuhr's point. The following is a short synopsis for those who may not know the story.

This story, which is often used as the epitome of sacrificial love, begins with an idyllic picture of a relationship between a little boy and a flourishing apple tree. They would play together often, the boy gives company to the tree and the tree in turn would let him swing on her branches and provide shade and recreation. Over time the boy grows up and rejects the tree for the company of girls and travel beyond the world of this immovable tree. Each time the boy returns, always dissatisfied with his travels, the tree would give of her best to his increasing demands. First, it was her apples that he demanded, then the branches to build a house, and then her trunk, to build a boat to sail the seas. The tree is distressed because she no longer has anything to offer. But all that the boy needed was a place to rest, and this, the tree "in her sacrificed state", could offer. She straightens herself up as best she could so that the boy could sit and rest. She is happy once more. This is her crown and glory, the opportunity to be of service to the boy.

Obviously the boy represents the powerful, usually the man, and the tree represents the woman in most marital relationship. All cultures, in varying degrees and, until recently, without question, seem to affirm, expect, and impose this as the norm for marital relationships. It is particularly so in our African cultures. It takes on a different turn, however, when the scriptures upon which one's faith is built are also interpreted in such a way that this unjust system is sanctified as a way of grace, especially for women. Moreover, if what women do ordinarily is what constitutes grace for men, what constitutes sin and hence grace for women?

Feminist Critiques

Generally, the feminist theologians, such as Plaskow (1980) and Hess (1993) who have spoken out against Niebuhr's doctrine of sin are agreed on the fact that his analysis speaks to and from the male experience. This needs to be qualified, as both feminists and Niebuhr himself notes, because these are the experiences of the rich and powerful. But the powerful male is the norm. Apart from the fact that this understanding of pride speaks primarily to the omnipotent males, I think that Niebuhr's employment of the narrower definition of sensuality also seems to leave women out. He focuses on aspects of sensuality that are linked to pride, which boil down to inordinate self love and shows up mostly in physical gratification, normally of a sexual nature. Here he follows closely Paul's outline in Romans 1. It is thought by many that the basic need for men is sex, hence they are more prone to look for physical sexual gratification, and are thus more likely to fall into the sin of sensuality that Niebuhr describes. Yet the erroneous assumption that the female seeks physical gratification primarily from a sexual union has persisted, and this is reflected in various forms of repressive measures to curb any such tendencies.[4]

The kind of self-sacrifice that has become the norm for women is one without integrity. Drawing an analogy from marriage, the relationship becomes one in which the powerful partner is not made to be aware of his lack of humanity. Living in the right relationship with the wife suggests a relationship in which the wife is not free to be the self she was made to be. Full humanity is achieved by neither party. Neither becomes the self they were made to be.

The African understanding of sin as pride and sensuality in this narrow form does not apply to women, and thus its antidote, which is intended to be a way of grace to overcome the sin of pride and sensuality, does little to help women. Our various experiences affirm this.

Consider the case of the typical African woman, whose day starts long before breakfast. She not only works at home but is also in the market place until sundown, selling her wares and taking care of her children at the same time. Often the husband is out to work in a job that is organized and follows a pattern, and involves the kind of work that may not demand much effort and gives little stress. After work he will probably visit a drinking place to wind down before returning home to a cooked meal. If the meal is not prepared by the already exhausted wife, it is often prepared by another woman, an older daughter or a maid. Not only does the wife labor at home, she is also a breadwinner.

In urban centers, women with careers comparable to their spouse's tell the same tale. They need to give everything to their careers because their marketability depends on it: at the same time they also try to give everything to their families.[5] Apart from the high level of stress associated with this dual role, society often frowns on her because she is a successful woman in what they consider to be a man's world. Habitually, however, women's careers take a back seat to their families and their marketability goes down. This adversely affects their capacity to support themselves and numerous children should a husband's contribution be absent through death or divorce or unemployment.

If what women do ordinarily, whether voluntarily or obligatorily, is the source of grace for men what then is woman's sin and what is the antidote, her source of grace? Does it mean that woman is sinless if neither pride nor sensuality can be attributed to her?[6] In this I am not claiming that women are blameless. In fact, because society affirms her self-giving as virtue, pride in a form other than descried by Niebuhr can set in. Moreover, as Hess (1993) points out, to talk of sin and virtue separately "is to miss the important relationality of life" (Hess 1993:356). Sin and grace are often intertwined. Giving heedlessly (as the tree and hence women do), tends to affirm the boy or the other's selfishness, rather than to do the other any good. Moreover, self-immolation for the sake of the other is equally a sin. It is a greater sin than self-assertion, which is sometimes a virtue when it is done for the sake of the other. This is because self-sacrifice, just for the sake of self-sacrifice, can easily become individualistic and very self-centered.

The validity of the feminist critiques leveled against the Niebuhrian conception of sin and grace is borne out by experience. Yet these critics only point out the differences between the genders. They thereby leave the inherent dichotomy between the sexes in place, since it sees pride as the primary sin but points out that the antidote for pride is the sin of the woman. In this final part of the chapter I propose to offer a new perspective on the understanding of sin, one that ties in with Niebuhr's own formulations as well as with African conceptions of sin.

Sin Reconsidered

A broader definition of sensuality, one found within Niebuhr's own theology on sin and grace, that he subsumes under pride, speaks directly not only to woman's sin but also to our common sin as human beings. In this I see neo-orthodox themes, as indicated in the ideas of both Niebuhr and his sources, as means of addressing the critique that feminist have brought against male bias in the understanding of sin.

Within the broader definition of sensuality, which is the attempt to solve the problem of ones finiteness amidst limitless freedom, by denying freedom, Niebuhr is closer to the truth of sensuality and woman's sin. This definition of sensuality is very much in line with Kierkegaard's (1941) definition of sin as the failure of the self to be a self, and to live grounded in the one who posited the self. Sin is the failure to realize that one is a self, so that one merely vegetates instead of existing before the living God. Moreover, I think that in this definition, pride ought to be subjugated to sensuality, and sensuality becomes the ultimate sin of humanity, rather than the other way round. These are Neibuhr's own words:

> Man contradicts himself within the terms of his true essence. His essence is free-self determination. His sin is the wrong use of his freedom and its consequent destruction. (Neibuhr 1941:6)

Thus in pride, the refusal of the self to be a self takes the form of fanciful flights of grandiosity, a form of gratification of the false self, and in sensuality, narrowly defined, the fanciful escapes are focused on bodily gratification.

In the first place, if sensuality is identified as the self's refusal to be a self, to appropriate the God given right of freedom, why is this not seen as the primary sin of man from which all other sins emanate?[7] If the essence of human beings is "free-self determination" then any deviation from that, detracts from his humanness. This then becomes the ultimate sin, the lessening of full humanity. Kierkegaard (1941) puts it succinctly when he declares that, aside from God, becoming a self is the next important thing. As one of the early Church Fathers said "the glory of God is the fully alive human being."

If who we are, and who we are to become, is left to go to waste, and we live subhuman lives, then we are, in effect, throwing the gift we have been given in God's face. (If sin was classified, I cannot imagine a worse sin than this.) In this regard, rather than make a virtue of the self-immolation that women have been told is self sacrifice, they should instead be chided for not "becoming a self" that they can share with God, themselves and with others. Surely the powerful, such as men, can be censured to abnegate excessive self-love, which is linked to pride, but in the light of women's experience, to do the same to them would be to perpetuate their sin. In the light of this discussion, the way to grace for women is by having a greater degree of assertiveness, and a journey towards selfhood, a coming into themselves, and even feeling more self-love. But do such thoughts agree with our concept of sin as Africans who also live by the Jewish-Christian tradition?

The African Concept of Sin

Many African societies normally make distinctions between what one would call wrongdoing, with its ethical moral dimensions, and sin, which upsets the equilibrium of social and personal relationships.[8] The effects of sin extend to the whole cosmic order, and unless appropriate expiation is made, whole villages are wiped out. In spite of these distinctions, the relational character of sin is always in the foreground. This understanding of sin as primarily relational ties in with the Jewish-Christian understandings of sin. The Decalogue, which offers a classic example of the understanding of sin in the Hebrew Bible, shows that every offense is directed against God, oneself and the rest of the community. Sometimes an individual's action affects the whole of the nation.[9]

Though both sensuality and pride have relational components, sensuality as the refusal of the self to be a self, seems to fit well into a relational understanding of sin in a way that pride does not. Emphasis on pride makes sin too individualistic, whereas there is a corporate and communal aspect to sensuality. Consider, for example, the gains for the earth and humankind if each were allowed to be the self they were meant to be. Think also of the oppressive measures that prevent people from being who they were made to be. We are all culpable and we participate in each other's sin either by commission or omission. What are the practical implications of a doctrine of sin that focuses on the refusal of the self to be a self, and calls for a greater degree of self-assertion, especially for women at this point in history?

As an evangelical, I believe in the inerrancy of scripture, but I also know how oppressive a dogmatic adherence to inerrancy of scripture can be, and how it continues to be used to make those whom Christ has freed even more bound. This is often the result of a narrow reading of a few select verses, a reading that ignores the broader context. Sometimes the grace in the gospels slips back into law in the epistles. It is almost as if it were easier for us to live by the law rather than by grace. It was as if we were still afraid to use our God given freedom, even when it has been repurchased for us at such high cost. Descriptions of situations and prescriptions given for dealing with and healing those situations become general prescriptions for all time. The epistles can only convey the grace of God – which is the way of freedom for all – if they are read in the light of the gospels and Jesus' interaction with all peoples. In the gospels it is clear that Jesus abolishes and stands against all oppressive hierarchical structures.

The issue of the submission of wives to their husbands, a code of conduct that has been extended to submissive behavior in the presence of all men is, I believe, one such grace that has slipped into law and has become a way of bondage for women. This is especially so for twentieth-century women who rub shoulders with men in every sphere of life. In many African societies this expectation, which is said to be sanctioned by scripture, reinforces an already overly oppressive system. This is because we are a very religious people, and adherence to religious norms is our way of life, and thus we readily accept and live by them. But I believe that the issue of submission of wives to husbands (which always comes to mind when we are called upon to re-examine biblical understandings of relationality) is one such misunderstood and misappropriated scripture.

The issue of marriage, and the submission of wives to husbands, is addressed in the Christian Testament. It must be borne in mind, however, that the matter was examined against the background of the first century, when the implications were different to what they are today. The passage often alluded to is Ephesians 5:21-33, which is a part of the instructions on how the Christian household should operate as part of the body of Christ, of which he is the head. In fact it is actually a call to live so that all are accorded their full humanity. The initial call is for all to be subject to one another out of reverence for Christ. In the same way that Christ was God, equal in every way to God but who chose to walk in obedience to God, so each one of us should live that way. Thus this is primarily a call to equals, not a call to super-ordinate and subordinate. Again, the call for wives to submit to their husbands is redundant in a culture in which they counted for nothing and were virtually enslaved to their husbands. The only way a call to submission makes sense within the context is that there was an acknowledgment of the freedom that Christ brought to them, thus according them full humanity and therefore making them moral agents. This was a status denied women and slaves in the Hellenistic world. Only moral agents, full persons, had rights that allowed them to make choices. Submission is a choice that only a free moral agent can make, for otherwise it is plain servitude. If service is not rendered in freedom, a freedom that is both physical and spiritual, such service is of little consequence.

Again within that cultural setting a call to love one's wife in the way that Christ loved the church requires greater submission and discipline. The purpose of submission, like any other spiritual discipline, is freedom, freedom to be all that we were meant to be. It is a means of attaining full humanity in our own unique way. If freedom of body, spirit, and soul is not the outcome it is not of God. Moreover, it is not an act of the flesh, it is not what we try to do, but rather it is what the Holy Spirit works in us as part of the sanctification process. We are obligated to make a distinction between an attitude of submission fostered by socialization and temperament, and what is the fruit of the

Holy Spirit of Truth, who works God's purpose in our lives. A quiet and gentle attitude in a woman could easily be a laid-back temperament, mere acquiescence or genuine submission. By the same token assertiveness and outspokenness in a woman is not necessarily lack of submission. To base all judgment on external acts is to miss the message of the Gospels and, in fact, the whole Bible: God searches the heart, and it is not the action that is significant it is the motive.

Some Practical Considerations

The foregoing discussion calls for the need for taking some practical steps towards living together within the household of God in a way that edifies all who belong to the community. This means that men, women, and children live together in such a way that full humanity is accorded to all participants in the *oikos* of God. It entails a living towards self and towards others in such a way that in the *oikonomia*, the economy of God, nothing is lost or wasted, either through pride in which one feels one is the only one able to do all things, or through sensuality, broadly defined, in which one squanders potential choice, or through societal norms imposed by those in power. We must begin by admitting that the understanding of masculinity and femininity we have is a distorted one, and this distortion is due to our fallen nature. Suggesting that the fall and its consequences, as described in Genesis 3, sanctions male domination of women goes only to prove the point that the present state of affairs is not what the Creator originally intended. Rather than see this as a justification for the male/female relationship for all time, it ought to be seen only as a description of an incident in time.

Moreover, the harmony and standing of the equal partnership that existed before the fall has been reinstated, as with all things, by the second Adam, Jesus Christ. In all our relationships we should be aiming towards working out what he has worked for in the same way that we "work out our salvation in fear and trembling", and this requires willingness on our part, as well as God's grace and strength.

Conclusion

In the light of the discussion of sin and grace presented in this chapter, a call for self-sacrifice on the part of men as well as women at this point in our history is unnecessary and not warranted. Women ought to move towards greater self-assertion and the fulfilling of themselves; only thus will we be enabled to speak of sin and grace in relation to all humanity. But until the structures are changed the present dichotomy between the sexes will remain in place. This will remain so unless we learn to live in mutual reciprocity with one another. This chapter is not a call to balance the equation by weighing things in favor of women. What I have intended is to provide guidance to help us move from the present dichotomous position towards one which stresses full human status for all - females and males.

We are called to abundant living in Christ, who is the Prince of Peace, and who calls us to live so that we can be at peace with God, with others and with ourselves. Jesus began his public ministry by promising deliverance to all those who are oppressed. This deliverance is not only spiritual. It is also aimed at the body, soul and spirit, as was made clear in his public ministry. The purpose was to usher in "the year of the Lord's favour" (Luke. 4:18-19), the year of jubilee, of justice for all. For there can be no peace without justice. For real peace, we must live justly with God, with each other, and with ourselves. To achieve and sustain such a state entails resisting anything that reduces us as full human beings, whether the will to achieve it comes from within ourselves or from others. Anything less than this would lead us into sin – thereby missing the potential of our full humanity.

Endnotes

1. I owe this new insight to understanding sin and grace to a doctoral seminar I took with Carol Hess in the spring of 1994. Most of this paper is based on issues raised in that class as well as those that the class raised for me.

2.   Consider, for example, the fact that psychological theories upon which psychotherapies are based are derived largely from observation of the male population. And yet these became the norm against which the behavior of both genders was judged for normalcy or deviancy. See Gilligan, C. (1981). *In a Different a Voice.* Cambridge: Harvard University Press, for further elaboration of this idea.

3.   It is difficult to understand why Niebuhr would make a distinction between the religious and moral dimensions of the character of sin. One would assume that the religious entails the moral aspect, which he identifies with injustice. It is interesting to note the distinction Niebuhr makes between the religious and ethical components of sin: for me it explains why religious institutions could live with gross injustice and not be bothered by it.

4.   Consider for instance the issue of female circumcision, which goes on in different parts of the world, and the age-old use of the chastity belt. It seems as though its purpose is to keep marital fidelity, at least from the woman's side, by reducing sexual gratification, which for most men is usually linked to the genitalia. But on the whole, sexual gratification for women is not so much based on orgasm as it is on the warmth of a loving relationship. Thinking the same is the case for women is clearly male projection.

5.   For more detailed discussion and statistical findings see Moller–Okin, S. (1989). *Justice, Gender and the Family.* New York: Basic Books.

6.   This is not an agenda to find woman's sin. I am aware of the guilt a woman carries because she is made to feel guilty about everything, both good and bad. If she is intelligent and articulate, especially in the presence of men, she feels guilty. If the children do not turn out the way that society expects, then it is her fault. But much of this guilt is imposed by the cultural structures from without, and thus can easily become a source of neurosis. My intention is to call our attention to what constitutes sin in actuality so we can seek the grace which will free us and set us on the way to becoming all we were made to be. As a pastoral counselor, I know that this is not easy, but that is what we need grace for in our time of need.

7.   This is not just an attempt to stratify sin and to be competitive about whose sin is the greatest. But if sin constitutes missing the mark of our true humanity, and we are serious about

corrective measures to bring us to full humanity, then we are better for naming it and finding healing for it.

8. Normally different words are used for these two concepts that the vernacular Bibles translate with the same word. The Eve of Ghana, for instance use *nuv* and *busu* respectively but the Bible translates all sin as *nuv*.

9. Consider for example the story of Achan in Joshua Chapter 7.

References

Erikson, E. (1967). "Inner and Outer Space: Reflections on Womanhood" in R. Lifton (Ed.), *The Woman in America*. Boston: Beacon Press (pp.).

Hess, C. L. (1993). "Gender, Sin and Learning: A Response to Reinhold Niebuhr" in *Religious Education* 88, 350-376.

Kierkegaard, S. (1941). *The Sickness unto Death*. Princeton: Princeton University Press.

Niebuhr, R. (1941; 1943). *The Nature and Destiny of Man* (Vols. 1 & 2). New York: Charles Scribner's Sons.

Moller-Okin, S. (1989). *Justice, Gender and the Family*. New York: Basic Books.

Plaskow, Judith (1980) *Sex, Sin and Grace: Women's Experience and the Theologies of Reinhold Niebuhr and Paul Tillich*. Washington: University Press of America.

Rediscovering
Ataa Naa Nyonmo -
The Father Mother God

Rose Teteki Abbey

Introduction

For many centuries, the Christian image of God as male has been accepted almost without question. Pauline Webb, a lay preacher of the Methodist Church, U.K, tells of a Sunday school class preparing for a nativity play. As part of the preparation, the teacher asked the children what they thought Mary would be doing as she prepared for the birth of her child - Jesus. One of the children suggested she might be knitting. Hearing that, another child asked why God did not make clothes for the baby. Whereupon a little girl retorted sharply: "Don't be silly. God is a man, he cannot knit!"(Webb 1979:1).

In that short sentence, the little girl had made two statements. First, that God is male and second, that knitting is a woman's job. It is the first part of her sentence, the masculinity of God, that will be dealt with in this chapter. The idea of God as female is nothing but a joke to some people. For some others, it is more serious than a joke: it borders on heresy. However, for an ever-increasing number of people, the femininity of God is neither a joke nor heresy. Many people are concerned and are asking if God really is a man. Feminist theologians, comprising both men and women, are wondering if the masculine and "macho" image we have of God really gives a true "picture" of God. Such people believe there is more to God than being almighty, transcendent and omnipotent. They are searching for the other qualities of God, the feminine, motherly side of God. As Elisabeth Yoihuam-Wendel says:

> The idea of God is conceived mainly in masculine terms: male leadership roles are used to describe what God does – He reigns, judges, governs; what God is corresponds to what men would like to be – judge, king, ruler, army commander. In the process, women's experiences of Jesus have been forgotten – Jesus as a friend who shares their life, and is ever near them, a friend who offers them warmth and tenderness in their loneliness and powerlessness. (Yoihuam-Wendel 1986:164)

Among the Ga people of southeastern Ghana, God is traditionally known as Ataa Naa Nyonmo. This name not only means Father Mother God, it also implies and stresses the maleness and femaleness of God. Seeing God as Father and Mother emphasizes the creative power of God as opposed to the macho image, which gives the idea of controlling power. Although Ga Christians have adopted and use this name, its etymology has little impact on their image of God.

Ataa and naa mean father or grandfather and mother or grandmother respectively. It must be noted that the terms, father and mother used here do not necessarily mean one who has directly borne children. They are terms usually used for adults. Referring to someone as an aunt, for instance, does not have to mean one is related to that person. It is in the same sense that Ataa Naa is used for God. Calling God "Mother" is an attempt to emphasize God's femininity rather than to isolate childless women. To rediscover the motherhood of God is to make Christianity more relevant to all Christians in general and Ghanaian women in particular.

This chapter is an attempt to join the many people who are not satisfied with the one-sided image of God that currently exists. In order to conduct this search, we will take a look at the contemporary, biblical as well as traditional Ghanaian metaphors of God. We will also take a brief look at the roots of African Christianity in an attempt to find out how and or why the true meaning of Ataa Naa Nyonmo has been watered down in Christian theology.

Biblical Metaphors of God

The Hebrew word *adam* (the earth creature) is used to denote male/female or humanity. This section will look at some metaphors of God from contemporary Christian and biblical points of view. Talking about the "capturing of Christianity" by patriarchy, Louise Tappa says:

> God is presented in masculine terms and God's functions are reduced to male power roles. He reigns, he judges, he governs. He is almighty, fiercely jealous and possessive. He has none of the so-called feminine traits such as gentleness, tenderness, sensitivity etc. Christianity has turned God into a prison warder. God is not different from the macho, usually absent from home yet served and feared, irascible and vindictive when he thinks he has been wronged. How can this picture reflect the God who "so loved the world that he gave his only son" and for whom the only commandment is love? (Tappa 1986:101).

One of the main criticisms made by feminist theologians is the use of language. The language of the Christian community as a whole – be it in worship or about God – is male. This, according to Oduyoye (1986) is made worse by assuming the linguistic assertion that the term "man" includes women. The issue, she says is complicated further when they confused the specific human being called Adam who was a man, with the partner of Eve.

The problem is even more evident when we talk of the Supreme Being. God is characterized by strength and might, and as a warrior, fighting our battles. As Tappa (1986) rightly says, titles like King of kings, Lord of lords, heavenly Father and so on are frequent in Christian liturgy creating the impression of a distant God. Hell and brimstone preachers who present God solely as a judge coming at the end of time to punish the wicked have not helped in this. In the words of Tappa, "Patriarchy has created God in man's image" (Tappa 1986:101). The fact that the Hebrew word for the Holy Spirit, "*ruach*" is feminine has also been overlooked in translations. The English pronoun for the

Holy Spirit is "He". In German, the Holy Spirit is *der Heilige Geist*; again the masculine definite article is used.

Although the metaphors mentioned above used to describe God are biblical, they present an incomplete view of God, who is also described in the Bible in motherly terms. One of the attributes of God is compassion. In Hosea, chapter 1, one of the children born to the harlot is to be called "Not Loved" or "Not Pitied". This name is explained as Yahweh taking away His compassion from Israel. Later on in Hosea 2:21, God says He will have compassion on "Not Loved". The word compassion is said to come from the Hebrew word *rehem*, which means womb or uterus – an obviously feminine word.

Referring to the idolatry and injustice of Israel in Isaiah 42:14, God is depicted as a woman in labor, gasping and panting. Virginia Mollenkott says, "... out of this (God's) travail, comes a new world in which the blind are safely led, their darkness turning to light" (Mollenkott 1987:15). Other feminine biblical metaphors of God include God as a Mother who has carried her children since infancy (Isaiah 46:3-4) and as the One who wipes away our tears. In Isaiah 66:13, God will comfort Israel as a mother stills her child.

It is obvious from these texts that the concept of God as a mother is biblical. However this does not often stand out in our theology because very often our perception is determined by what we search for. For instance, in order to legitimize patriarchy and the domination of women, theologians and Christians often "see" Genesis 3 where Eve is cursed with the domination of Adam. They repeatedly "forget" about Genesis 1, which records the creation of *adam*, that is, humankind – both male and female – in the image of God. The fallen order is preferred to the perfect one. In the same way, the motherhood of God is overlooked because it challenges the patriarchal nature of our societies.

Some African Concepts of God

Contrary to popular belief that Africans only worship idols, they do believe in a Supreme God who is above all. John Mbiti says:

> African peoples do not consider God to be a man, but in order to express certain concepts, they use anthropomorphic terms and images about him as an aid to their conceptualization of him whom they have not seen and about whom they confess to know little or nothing. (Mbiti 1970:9).

African concepts of God are embedded in the meanings of the names given to God. To be able to get a picture of some of these concepts, we will take a look at some of the names, appellations and metaphors attributed to God. Sometimes, names given to children also reveal how God is perceived.

There are many names that describe God's omnipresence, love and justice as well as being the Creator. *Maudzingua*, a popular name amongst Krobos in Ghana denotes the greatness of God. Similarly, there are other names that describe God's omnipresence, love and justice as well as being the Creator. One of the important attributes of *Mau* (the Krobo word for God) is *Kpetekplenye*, meaning mother of all big or wonderful things. This is almost always associated with *Mimidzolo*, that is, the One with the soft or cool stomach. Amongst the Akans, *Onyankopong* (the mighty One) is also *Obosuo* (Creator of water) and *Obowia* (Creator of sun). God is also known to them as *Onyame*, that is, the One who gives satisfaction or when you have Him you are satisfied. The most popular attribute that goes with *Onyame* is Obaatanpa meaning good mother.

Apart from the above, God is portrayed as father amongst other Africans including the Akans, the Bemba of Zambia and the Banyoro of Uganda. Amongst the Nuba of Sudan, the Ndebele and the Shona both of Zimbabwe, God is portrayed as a Mother (Mbiti, 1970). Ataa Naa Nyonmo, the Ga name for God, which forms the title of this paper, is perhaps the most significant as far a balanced and holistic concept of God is concerned. For it speaks of God neither exclusively as Father nor as Mother, but it takes the whole of humanity into account.

Christianity and Patriarchy

If, as we have seen, the Bible has both male and female metaphors of God, and if African Traditional Religion has female as well as male concepts of God, why is it that the one sided, male view of God prevails in African Christianity too?

Patriarchy

The major reason that accounts for this absence is the patriarchal nature, not only of the ancient Israelite community, but also of our present societies. Ancient Jewish society was particularly patriarchal that every day, a Jewish man allegedly thanked God for not creating him, amongst other things, a woman. It is therefore doubtful whether any metaphor of God that is not male would be taken seriously. When Matthew reports the miraculous feeding of the five thousand (Matthew 14:13-21), he writes that there were 5,000 men, "to say nothing of the women and children". This leads one to wonder how many more references to women and feminine metaphors of God have not been recorded in the Bible. It is, in fact, surprising that some have survived at all.

For centuries, women have been denied ordination, and the study and practice of theology has been dominated almost entirely by men. This may have contributed to the repression of the few mother images of God in the Bible. For some theologians and preachers, this repression has been unconscious. They have inadvertently used only those metaphors that they can identify with. However, for some, the femininity of God might have been deliberately repressed out of fear. Such people seem to accept as true and operate on Mary Daly's radical statement that: "If God is male, then male is God" (Daly 1973:19). Having consciously or unconsciously got this premise in their minds, it is very frightening for them to think of God in female terms. For, to them, it would then mean: "If God is female then female is God." The femininity of God then becomes a threatening thing to be fought against at all costs. This may be an additional element that would account for the absence of a feminine God from our pulpits.

But, one would ask, if the Motherhood of God was accepted in African Traditional Religion – as in the case of the Ga people – why hasn't it influenced Ghanaian Christian theology? The answers would be much the same as the reasons given above, except for one additional factor – the Christian mission and colonialism.

Mission and Colonialism

The missionaries to Africa in the 19th century, to use the words of Peter Kodjo, "came not only with their various cultural values ... but also with the identifiable ideology of their age – colonialism" (Kodjo1992:2). According to Kwame Bediako their overriding image of Africans was that they "... were not only savage and uncivilized, they were also in the very depths of ignorant superstition" (Bediako 1992:227). He also quotes Dr. Adrian Hastings as saying that:

> In fact, neither in the nineteenth nor in the early twentieth centuries did the missionaries give much thought in advance to what they would find in Africa. What struck them undoubtedly was the darkness of the continent; "its lack of religion and sound morals", its ignorance, its general pitiful condition made worse by the barbarity of the slave trade. (Bediako 1992:225)

Bediako goes on to say:

> It is not surprising that, as a result of this perception of Africa, the European missionary approach tended to "treat everything pre-Christian in Africa as either harmful or at best valueless, and to consider the African once converted from paganism as a sort of *tabula rasa* on which

a wholly new religious psychology was somehow to be imprinted. (Bediako 1992:225)

What Bediako, in quoting Hastings, was putting across was the fact that the cultures of Africa were not taken seriously by the early missionaries. It was for them inconceivable that Africa would have anything to contribute to the enrichment of Christianity. All African ideas were thought to be so irreligious and superstitious that for Christianity to flourish, these ideas had to be put to rest.

But, one may still ask, why was it so easy for the missionaries to prevent the usage of traditional concepts of God in Christian worship? This question may be partly answered by a Krobo proverb: "*wotse le le e wonya ba*". This literally means: "It is the owner of an idol who best knows how to worship that idol."[1] The missionaries did not present God as one already known to the Africans. The Christian God was not *Onyankopong Tweadeampong*, that is, God Almighty.[2] The Christian God was presented as a new and foreign God. Converts had to renounce their traditional forms and concepts of worship and prayer and learn new ones; so much so that, for instance, even though priestesses were a common occurrence in Traditional Religion, African Churches also barred women from ordination until the "owners" of the Christian God started ordaining them.[3] To use the concept of the Motherhood of God in Christianity, therefore, would be unacceptable if its sole basis is the fact that God was (and is) traditionally Ataa Naa Nyonmo.

A look at the traditional social structure of the Ga people might help explain why their "image" of God is so gender balanced. The Gas, traditionally, had a unique social structure. Women and men lived separately. Each family had a *hii amli* (men's quarters) and a *yei amli* (women's quarters). A marriage ceremony, for instance, took place in the women's quarters and no man was allowed to take any part in the proceedings, not even the bridegroom. It was the women's affair and they decided on and received the bride price. The bride then moves into the female quarters of her husband's house. When they had children, these children would stay with their mothers until the adolescent period when the boys would join their fathers. It is probably this balanced view of society that influenced their theology.

This, however, is not to say that patriarchy is foreign to Africans. Most, if not all, African societies are patriarchal. As Oduyoye rightly says, "Matriliny may give the impression of the structural dominance of women in certain parts of Africa, but ... no real power resides in the hands of women. As to political power, even the matrilineal, matrilocal Asante are not matriarchal" (Oduyoye 1986:123).

From the above, it is clear that the argument is not about a women's utopia in traditional times. Rather it is to point out that since the message of Christianity is to liberate, if there are concepts of God in African Traditional Religion that are biblical and make the message of God more relevant, attention must be paid to them. In any case, it is ironic that missionaries failed to recognize and make use of the feminine names of God from African societies, because even though they considered Africans pagans, most of the names given to the Christian God were from the traditional names for God – but the dominant ones were always the male and macho-oriented names. One wonders the reason for this selective memory.

Effects of a One Sided Theology

Is God female?

In view of the arguments put forward concerning the validity of the motherhood of God, a vital question is: Is God a woman? No, God is not a woman. But then, neither is God a man. The anthropocentric images of God are there to help our conception of the Supreme Being especially in regard to how God relates to us. It is essential that Christians in general and theologians in particular bear this in mind. The metaphors that we have of God have nothing to do with the form of God. Because we only know "personhood" in terms of male and female, we think if God is personal, then God must be either female or male. Neither is it a question of allowing God's femininity to supersede as His masculinity has done. The need for a balanced view of God cannot be overemphasized.

For a feminine imagery of God to be possible, it is necessary to understand the root metaphor of Christianity as a relationship, rather than a state of affairs between God and human beings. As a relationship, many models from many experiences are not only appropriate but also necessary. That is to say all images of god are analogies. This idea that God is not a man (or a woman for that matter) seems to have been forgotten and many Christians and theologians have almost taken the metaphors of God to mean not God's characteristics but the physical image. The commandment "not to make any graven images" is forgotten and Christianity has gone on to make pictures of God. In the words of Rosemary Ruether,

> Christian sculpture and painting represent God as a powerful old man with a white beard, even crowned and robed in the insignia of human kings or the triple tiara of the pope. (Ruether 1983:66).

The Supreme Being who defies description and refuses to be named, saying only I AM WHO I AM or I WILL BE WHO I WILL BE, has become an idol created in the image of man.

The metaphor "Father" has lost its meaning of the one who creates – the Source of all being. It has taken on a literal meaning that, as has been pointed out already, has led to the assertion that God is male and not female. Many people have stretched this further to prevent women's ordination. Such people argue that since pastors and priests are God's representatives on earth, women cannot be ordained because they could not be true representations.[4]

The implication of a "male-God" is not only disastrous for women who want to be ordained. It destroys the faith of many Christians who, from experience, have almost no positive images about their earthly fathers. The Mission Department of the Protestant Church organized a seminar in Germany, on the theme "Rediscovering our Faith", for

Christians who no longer believed in God. Participants were to share their religious experiences and why they stopped going to Church and or believing in God. During the keynote address, one man suddenly interrupted the speaker in the middle of a sentence about the love of God. "I do not know this God you are proclaiming" the man shouted:

> This God who loves and cares is alien to me. The God I know is that almighty, all-knowing, all-seeing, invisible Being who follows me everywhere with a big note book recording all the evil I do. He is a bigger version of my father; eager to punish me as if to emphasize the physical difference between us. It is a God who only notices me when I am wrong. **From Children's Service till I stopped going to Church, this is the God that has been presented to me. The loving and caring God you are talking about is foreign to me.**

Somewhere in this tirade, the man stopped and said hastily: "I am Catholic, you see." It was a predominantly Protestant group and it seemed he was anxious to let the group know that if what he was saying sounded foolish, it is because he comes from a different theological background. However, many Protestants quickly assured him that their picture of God was no different.

It is true that not all earthly fathers maltreat their children. It is equally true that not all mothers are loving and supportive. There are examples of women who abuse their children and maltreat their domestic helps. But that is beside the point. And, in any case, God is the ideal of all we have. A bad father or mother does not make God bad. Nevertheless, the fact is that in presenting the image of God, we must present a true and total picture. And our picture of God can only be true when it presents not only the masculine but also the feminine aspects of God. It must be remembered that in God's transcendence God is immanent. In God's justice, God is loving. Over-stressing one, at the expense of the other, results in an unbalanced and incorrect idea of God. It is equally important to recognize that God is also variously described by such terms as wind, rock and elephant. These do not mean that God is wind, rock, man or woman. They are only there to help us fathom God. And we need the humility to admit that as human beings we can never presume a complete "revelation" of God. For as John Mbiti says:

> May God forgive for attempting to describe him and for doing it so poorly. Even if I am presenting here the wisdom and reflections of many African people, it is at best only an expression of a creature about the Creator. As such it is limited, inadequate and ridiculously anthropocentric. God is still beyond our imagination, understanding and expression. Here then is only one scene of man's groping after his Creator; the voice of the stammering child calling on to the parent. (Mbiti 1970:ix)

The humility Mbiti expresses is essential for all of us if we are to rediscover Ataa Naa Nyonmo – the Father Mother God.

What about Christ?

One of the arguments used against the idea of a feminine God is Jesus Christ. People argue that Jesus Christ, the incarnation of God is male and therefore God must surely be male! Commenting on this type of argument, Anne Nasimiyu-Wasike says:

> All the theological references for defining Christ were defined in male-centred or androcentric ways. This reinforced the assumption that God was male.... The term *logos* was all-inclusive for the divine identity for Christ and pointed the whole of humanity to the true foundation of its being, but the term was overshadowed by the cultural realities of the time. (Nasimiyu-Wasike 1992:76)

By that, Nasiyimu-Wasike is saying that Jesus Christ points to humanity and not to man. I would add to that by saying that Jesus was a man, a masculine being; but as the Messiah, Christ supersedes humanity.

Preaching on the "maleness" of Jesus Christ, the Reverend Nick Cuthbert said, God incarnated as a man to challenge the traditions of the time, that is, patriarchy. He said, God came to earth as One who serves. In the patriarchal society of Israel, it would not have made much difference if Jesus had been born as a woman who serves. Washing the feet of the disciples (John 13:1-17) and cooking for them after the resurrection (John 21:9) would just have supported the so-called "role of women" if Jesus had been a woman. In Luke 10:41, Jesus told Martha to come and sit at His feet to be taught instead of worrying about cooking. In saying that Jesus Christ was challenging the *status quo* that put women in the kitchen and men at the feet of rabbis. One of the deepest theological discussions held by Christ was with the Samaritan woman at the well (John 4:1-42). In doing that, Christ was asserting the worth of a human being regardless of race (she was a Samaritan), sex (she was a woman) and morals.

In other words, God did incarnate in the male form not to show that God is male but rather in order to change society's attitude to the oppressed – the poor, the sick and women – through His own attitude to them.   When we hang on to the maleness of Christ, we miss the point. Christ lived as God wants us to live. Christ's life on earth is meant to give us a lesson on ideal humanity. His maleness shows us that He was real; after all, human beings are either male or female.   Christ's divinity, however, obviously embodies both the male and the female and even transcends them both.

Just as with theology, Christology is very male oriented. In Africa this is compounded. Jesus is not only very masculine He is white. In most pictures Jesus has blond hair and blue eyes. And yet, looking at the gospels, we realize that Christ uses female imagery as well as male ones. The Kingdom of God is compared to a woman looking for her lost coin or a woman putting yeast into dough and kneading it. Jesus talks of longing to gather Israel as a hen gathers her chicks (Luke 13:34). In laying down His life for us all, Jesus acted as a typical woman; for as Anselm, Archbishop of Canterbury is quoted as saying in 1093:

And Thou, Jesus, sweet Lord, art Thou not also a mother?
Truly, Thou art also a mother, the mother of all mothers, Who tasted death, in Thy desire to give life to Thy children. (Quoted by Robins 1986:160).

Conclusion: Vision for the Future

At a conference of African women theologians in Accra in 1989, Mercy Oduyoye said she looked forward to the time when "theology would be allowed to fly with two wings". In saying that, she was expressing the hope that the function of theology as an academic concern will no more be confined to men, but that women will also be recognized as having a vital part to play in it. I will stretch her sentence to embrace even more. Our theology – conversation about God – can only be said to have two wings when the Motherhood as well as the Fatherhood of God can be expressed freely by men and women undertaking the pursuit of theology. "Doing theology" here does not only mean the activities of trained theologians. It also includes the praises, fears, conversations, prayers, poems and hymns about God and about our faith; by men, women, girls and boys who call themselves Christians. For even though these prayers, poems etc. need theological investigation and "scientific" inquiry by trained theologians, it is the gathered community of faith that creates theology. As Oduyoye rightly says "The Church cannot (afford to) have specialists in the worship of God as the academy has specialists in law and astrophysics" (Oduyoye 1986:126).

To be able to do this, there is the need to reorient our thinking. Even though merely changing the language of our theology is not enough, it is a very important and crucial starting point. There is no denying the fact that there are many more masculine metaphors of God in the Bible than feminine ones. But this, Mollenkott (1987) says, should not discourage us. The mere fact that they are there at all should surprise, delight and challenge us. Referring to what she calls the "half-empty" theory, she says we should not be repelled that there are so few female metaphors of God in the Bible. Rather, we should see the few present as a triumph over patriarchal repression of the motherliness of God. It should delight us, but that should not be the end. If the femininity of God survived the patriarchal nature of biblical times, then it should challenge us into working for a theology with two wings.

The need for a theology that recognizes both the maleness as well as the femaleness of God cannot be overemphasized. The rediscovery of Ataa Naa Nyonmo (that is, God as both Father and Mother) is essential for the Ghanaian woman. It is essential for the rape victim whose image of men might have become one of brutality. It is necessary for the one who grew up with sexual abuse from men, as well as for those whose fathers walked out on the family leaving them to starve. The recognition of both the male and female metaphors of God is of crucial importance for the faith of all those who, for one reason or the other, have negative ideas about men. However, the urgent necessity to rediscover and relate to God as both father and mother, nay, as a Spirit beyond father and mother, goes beyond the above-mentioned people. Even for those of us who have excellent fathers, brothers and husbands, yes, even for men who have no problems with themselves and with other men, it is still of utmost importance to acknowledge this. For the transcendence of God will be incomplete without God's immanence. The justice of God will be no different from human justice without God's compassion. The picture or the image of Him as the warrior is misleading without a picture of Her as a woman in labor. Humankind is only complete as male and female and God is no less so.

Moreover, the motherhood of God does not merely portray the femaleness of God. More importantly, it portrays the nurturing, caring and sustaining aspect of God's nature. There are at least two things at stake here. Firstly, bringing out the motherhood of God helps to show the compassionate and loving side of Yahweh. Secondly, it helps to emphasize the nurturing aspect of Yahweh that is manifested in sustenance, continued creation and the maintenance of the created order. After all, it is mothers who go after wayward children. Ataa Naa helps us to capture the essence of ideal parenthood both in its male and female forms.

The task of Christian theology as it enters the twenty-first century is to allow God to be black as well as white, Gentile as well as Jew, poor as well as rich, crucified as well as risen, male as well as female. This will not only enhance our relationship with God, it will also change the way we relate to each other. It is when we can "see" God in these contradictions, these opposites that our theology will fly with two wings. This poem by Mary Ellen Gaylord captures it all:

> Many faces have I thought were you ...
> The judging father
> successful demanding
> expecting excellence
> asking that I earn approval
> that I deserve attention
> ... hoping for his love.
>
> Many faces have I thought were you ...
> The caring mother
> martyred and all giving
> self sacrificing
> always thinking of others
> her way the only way
> ... longing for her love.
>
> Many faces have I thought were you ...
> A comforting friend
> to be depended on
> nurturer and guide
> with me in the desert
> walking through the valleys
> and long forgotten paths
> ... seeking love together.
>
> Many faces have I thought were you ...
> the tragic human figure
> loving ... hurting
> angry ... sad
> not spared the death of a son
> but one with us in suffering
> ... needing to be loved.

Many faces have I thought were you ...
all of them ... and none.
(Quoted by Robins 1986:169-170).

Indeed, all these are the faces of God: all these - and
none; all these - and more!

Endnotes

1.   The practice of "buying" an idol from another area used to be
      quite common among the Krobos. Such a "buyer" had to
      learn the "dos" and "don'ts" of that idol and to abide by them.

2.   One cannot blame them when one considers that prior to
      Christianity, Europeans had no notion of the Supreme God.
      Thor, the god of thunder, Zeus, Apollo and others could in no
      way be compared to Onyankopon or Ataa Naa Nyongmo. The
      former refers to gods whilst the latter are names for the
      Supreme God. (Thor and Zeus could only be compared to
      Kotoklo or Nadu, gods of the Krobos). If pre-Christian Europe
      had no idea of a Supreme God, how could they expect Africans
      to have it?

3.   Although there were a few exceptions, for example in instances
      where Anglican Churches started ordaining women before
      the Church of England, on the whole "missionary" Churches
      waited for the "mother Churches" to start ordaining women
      before following suit.

4.   Whether a priest or minister is really supposed to represent
      God is another thing altogether.

References

Bediako, K. (1992) *Theology and Identity.* Oxford: Regnum Books.

Daly, M. (1973). *Beyond God the Father.* Boston: Beacon Press.

Kodjo, P. M. (1992). " The Confluence of Mission and Colonialism."
    Unpublished pamphlet.

Mbiti, J. S. (1970). *Concepts of God in Africa.* London: SPCK.

Mollenkott, V. R. (1987). *The Divine Feminine.* New York:
    Crossroad.

Nasiyimu-Wasike, A. (1992). "Christology and African Women's Experience" in R. Shreiter (Ed.), *Faces of Jesus in Africa*. London, SCM Press, 70-81.

Oduyoye, M. A. (1986). *Hearing and knowing: Theological Reflections on Christianity in Africa*. New York: Orbis Books.

Robins, W. (Ed.). (1986). *Through the Eyes of a Woman: Bible Studies on the Experience of Women*. Rushden, Northants: Britain: Stanley L. Hunt.

Ruether, R. R. (1983). *Sexism and God Talk*. London: SCM Press.

Tappa, L. K. (1986). "God in Man's Image" in J. S. Pobee, & B. von Wartenberg-Potter (Eds.), *New Eyes for Reading*. Geneva: World Council of Churches, 101-106.

Webb, P. (1979). *Where are the Women?* London: Epworth Press.

Engendered Communal Theology: African Women's Contribution to Theology in the 21st Century

Musimbi R. A. Kanyoro

The African Dilemma

Africa is a land wealthy in proverbs. One of my favorites relates the dilemma of the hyena. The hyena was following the general direction of the aroma of barbecuing meat. He wanted a share of this enticing and mouth-watering meat. Suddenly his path forked into two. He was not sure which one would lead him to the meat. In his uncertainty, he put his legs astride the two paths and tried to walk along both but the poor hyena split in the middle.

The African Christian often walks with one foot in African religion and culture and another in the Church and western culture. While the former is seen as tradition and must disappear with time, the latter is presented as progress and encouraged. The dilemma of the African Christian cannot simply be wished away, especially today when it seems as if the center does not hold and things are falling apart (Achebe 1958). Christian women of Africa are part of these two worlds. Often at times, they feel the strain of splitting apart when trying to correlate the pull of the culture on the one hand and that of the church on the other. The tension between the notion that it is possible and desirable to live by the gospel without culture is a belief that is wishful thinking. Reality tells a different story.

In the African indigenous thought system, culture and religion are not distinct from each other. Therefore, culture and religion in Africa embrace all areas of one's total life. There is no sphere of existence that is excluded from the double grip of culture and religion. The presence or absence of rain, the well-being of the community, sexuality, marriage, birthing, naming children, success or failure, the place and form of one's burial, all these and others come within the scope of religion and culture. It is, therefore, great threats to communal security to be critical of culture, for there are elements in these cultures that are the very roots through which the solidarity of communities are nurtured.

However no culture or religion can ever be static. Hence, culture and religion in Africa today, while bearing a direct link to the past, have had contact with other cultures through colonial occupation, trade, religious encounters and other diverse links. Change today is made even faster and easier by communication networks and its technological artifacts, travel and the globalization of western education.

In addition, African religions and cultures have had to contend with new political realities, the formation of new identities, and interaction with the surrounding and new contact cultures and religions. Despite such encounters, it amazes both Africans and foreigners alike to see how cultural practices in Africa are alive and well, and remain intact despite their exposure to new encounters.

The African Woman's Dilemma

Women in Africa are the custodians of cultural practices. For generations, African women have guarded cultural prescriptions that are strictly governed by the fear of breaking taboos. Many aspects that diminish women continue to be practiced to various degrees, often making women objects of cultural preservation. Harmful traditional practices are passed on as "cultural values" and therefore are not to be discussed, challenged or changed. In the guise of culture, harmful practices and traditions are perpetuated. Practices such as female genital mutilation (Efua 1994)[1], early betrothals[2] and marriages, and the stigmatization of single women, barren women and widows hinder the liberating of women. Yet, in fact, it is women who sustain these practices. Such a state of affairs illustrates the reality of women's powerlessness and vulnerability in the face of cultural prescriptions.

When trained women theologians begin to make connections between what happens at home and in church with a view to suggesting change in the name of justice, they have to be cautious about disturbing the set order. It takes time and extended discussions with other women in order to establish the trust that is necessary before beginning to advocate change. It would be easier just to pursue the study of academic theology, that is, reading, reflecting and writing. But for us in Africa, it does not matter how much we write about our theology in books, the big test before us is whether we can bring change into our societies. This is a tall order and we agonize about it.

A majority of African Christian women have been raised in very evangelical and conservative churches. We therefore often find ourselves struggling with our history and our present personal change that has developed through theological studies, ecumenical exposure, and encounter with the analysis of women's global issues. Sometimes being at this crossroad leaves us in great pain as Nyambura Njoroge suggested in the presentation of her paper Groaning and languishing in labour pains: But for how long Lord? to the Circle meeting in Nairobi in 1994[3]. Njoroge, a woman pastor raised in a Presbyterian home and church, laments that her training as a pastor never equipped her to deal with social or gender issues. Instead, she was trained to see people as souls without bodies, a perspective that made her ministerial work narrow and limited, if not impossible.

Whether in the pews, or among theologically trained women, there is only a handful that are comfortable with challenging the text of the Bible by subjecting the hermeneutics of critical analysis to the Biblical text, as theologian Schüssler Fiorenza (1985) has suggested in her framework of feminist hermeneutical theory. At this point, one of the immediate tasks before us is to gain confidence to face the dilemmas and contradictions that are part of our history and present. When we advocate that women be included in the ordained ministries of the Churches in Africa, we are hoping that these women pastors will be strong pillars for establishing relationships of trust and mutuality with women in the congregations. We are hoping that women pastors will be willing to talk about the reality of women's experiences in their sermons, and therefore be able to make connections between church, home and society. That in itself is a possibility for women to be included in the telling of the story of faith to the community of faith. We also trust that the body language of women and men working together in ministry will show men and women sharing leadership and responsibility. Such a possibility can have a far-reaching impact in other areas, including the home. However, we have come to find out that it is not enough to have trained and ordained women: the kind of training is even more important if change is to come to our societies.

The African continent's history of colonialism and Western imperialism causes a dilemma for African women theologians and activists at large. There is always a struggle as to how to relate to Western culture, indigenous culture and religious culture, coupled with the daily need to support life despite all odds. The quest for justice for women is trivialized in favor of "larger" issues such as national liberation, famine, disease, war and poverty. Acts of individual resistance to injustice and inequality in the Church are seen as immoral rather than scriptural. Women who subject recent and current church practice to analysis are accused of being in pursuit of the western ideals of feminist liberation rather than African and Christian ones. This often makes women vulnerable.

There are also many issues on which women do not agree. We are especially at odds on issues concerning culture. For instance, there are huge differences about how to regard cultural practices such as female circumcision (genital mutilation), *lobola* (the giving of bride price), polygamy, the dominantly male right to inheritance of land, and numerous other practices. Some perceive these practices as the essence of our culture, and therefore the center of our identity. In other words, some believe that these practices help to underpin who we are and therefore they give us a stable base and a uniform community. Yet for some among us, many of these practices are acts of injustice to women and they need to change. These practices are harmful, oppressive and they reduce women to mere instruments of men and culture in general. These dilemmas continue to divide us, but the stage has been reached whereby diversity of opinion will ensure that the women of Africa will not remain silent.

Gender as a Concept of Theological Analysis

Theological engagement with gender issues seeks to expose harm and injustices that are in society and are extended to Scripture and the teachings and practices of the Church through culture. Today, most women's scholarship globally recognizes the web of oppression, which even leads women to oppress other women. Gender analysis seeks to identify such injustices and to suggest societal correction is warranted. African women have benefited from the theological work being done by women globally. African women are part of the trend whereby women now study theology. African women's theology places prior emphasis on women's humanity and as beings also created in the image of God. Its roots and its responses relate to the dilemmas and celebrations of God's people on the African continent. It also requires that the African world-view be taken into account in analysis. Nevertheless, African theology does not embrace the assumption that the African world-view or feminist view is universal, or that there is only one mode of interpretation.

If African women today are able to name some of the oppressive aspects of African cultures, such a stance has not come easily. Telling these stories of dehumanizing cultural practices is still rare and involves struggle. There are still many women who would not speak of their own experiences either as victims, perpetrators or even sympathizers. African women theologians who have encountered feminist analysis do not quickly jump to condemn women for being custodians of dehumanizing cultural practices. It is appreciated that even women's actions may be deeply rooted in patriarchal socialization, and, therefore, the analysis of women's oppression has to be undertaken in the context of gender analysis.[4] Using gender analysis for our theological explorations, we seek to search and understand how our societies are organized, and how power is used by different groups of people, by men and women, by young and old, and by people of varying economic means. Who benefits from a particular interpretation of culture and how is the system kept in place? We strive to clarify for ourselves ways in which roles, attitudes, values and relationships regarding women and men are constructed in our societies and, indeed, by all societies all over the world. The concepts and practices of equality and discrimination as determined by social, economical, religious and cultural factors lie at the heart of the theology of women in Africa in this new millennium.

The task confronting women theologians, in Africa, is how to incorporate discussions on culture in our African communities so that women find it safe to speak about issues that harm their well-being. The Biblical conviction that men and women are created in God's image in itself demands that women too must live in dignity. Any pattern of discrimination, domination or oppression is contrary to God's justice.

Cultural Hermeneutics as a Key to the Liberation of Women in Africa

In 1994 I first clearly saw the need for analyzing culture as a process for seeking out liberation for African women. I made the following preliminary remarks:

> The complexities inherent in cultural debate require space and a safe environment of mutual trust and mutual vulnerability in order for dialogue to take place.... A new aspect of feminist analyses has been brought to theology mainly by studies of women from Africa. This new thing deserves its rightful place in the theological paradigms. It could be called "Cultural Hermeneutics".[5]

I suggested that cultural hermeneutics is an important first step towards an African Women's liberation theology. All questions regarding the welfare and status of women in Africa are explained within the framework of culture. Women cannot inherit land or own property because it is not culturally "right". Women may not participate in the leadership because it is culturally the domain of men. Whether the subject is politics, economics, religion or social issues, in Africa, none of these are safe from all-pervading culture. However, it is not enough simply to analyze culture without reference to the people who maintain the culture and on whom the culture impacts. Here is where the need arises for a gender sensitive cultural hermeneutics because it performs two functions as it addresses issues of culture, while being critical of that culture from a gender perspective.

The church is part and parcel of the subject of analysis. It is in the Church that the dilemma of how Africans should live as Christians and people of a culture persists. The status of women within their church is a microcosm of their status within the society of which the church is a part. Even when the rights of women are enshrined in law, custom, and tradition, popular attitudes and values lag far behind and continue to oppress women. Since the Bible forms the base and informs the African Christian on what they can validate or not validate in their culture, I have since 1982 been working from the framework of reading the Bible with African women's cultural eyes. It was through reading the Bible with women in my village for a very long time that I came to a realization of the importance of culture in people's lives and the consequent influence of that culture on the interpretation of the Bible. I stay with the Bible as the source of my own research, while acknowledging that cultural hermeneutics could also be done from a different standpoint.[6] It is important to understand how the Bible is understood in order to locate the accountability of the Church in regards to gender issues in church and in society. Cultural hermeneutics seeks to find ways to raise questions of accountability of the society and the church to women, and the accountability of women in taking responsibility for their lives.

I have presented my work to seminars in Africa and abroad and tested various hypotheses with other African women from different disciplines. Three years ago, I began to develop a theory based on previous hypotheses, and my long time encounter with the text of the Bible in Africa and the various interpretations of it by preachers, translators and Bible study groups. My theory is that the culture of the reader in Africa has more influence on the way the Biblical text is understood and used in communities than the historical culture of the text. In stating this I suggest that not knowing the nuances of the culture within which the Bible is read or preached has much wider-reaching repercussions to the exegesis of the texts than is often acknowledged by Biblical scholars and preachers alike. I further argue that cultural hermeneutics is a necessary tool for those who teach homiletics and pastoral work in seminaries and other institutions for training clergy. More important, though, I claim that it is a prerequisite for understanding African women's liberation theology.

I base much of my theory on the experiences gained by reading the Bible with communities of African rural women between 1982 and 1996. The lessons gained from such readings underscored for me the urgency of affirming the concepts of social and cultural hermeneutics that have been dealt with so well by many authors (Gottwald & Horsley 1993; Segovia & Tolbert 1995; Tiffany & Ringe 1996). I contend that we have to analyze both personal and communal experiences in religion and culture. The stories of African women unmask sins of oppression and injustice and call for collective repentance and change from society as a whole.

A Context of Much Suffering

Theological study in Africa today has to take place amidst a people who have suffered greatly. There is so much death on our continent that reality makes a mockery of the suffering of Job, the Biblical figure associated with tribulations. As if illnesses and diseases were not enough, in Africa there are successive and simmering wars. Then there are repressive government regimes all over the continent, which only receive world attention when their actions are the subject of global media coverage. This coverage includes recent atrocious events in Liberia, Somalia, Rwanda, Burundi, the Congo and Sierra Leone. Economic conflict has been aggravated by globalization, the aftermath of Structural Adjustment programs, corrupt leadership and bad management of national economies. All this affects women's lives, prompting prayers, liturgies, songs and poems as ways of theologizing issues on the continent. Much of the time our loud lamentations are only heard as tiny whimpers. At other times, we are simply unable to cry. We preserve our tears for mourning our dead. In such a difficult context, culture can be seen as the only constant element for communities. Challenging culture amidst such upheavals is no mean task, yet there is a need to address cultural questions and, when required, to dare challenge culture and much of what it stands for.

Cultural Nationalism

In pre-independence years, African nationalists sought the re-establishment of coherence and integrity in African life through programs of cultural retrieval. These efforts in literature resulted in works characterized as "cultural nationalism" which debunked European culture and extolled African traditions. Novelists such as Camara Laye (1959) and Chinua Achebe (1958), in addition to anthropologists such as Jomo Kenyatta (1938), paid attention to the wholesome dignity of African traditions and institutions.

In the wake of liberation movements seeking independence from European colonialists, African politicians such as Kwameh Nkrumah of Ghana, Jomo Kenyatta of Kenya and others also claimed cultural identity as a badge of African solidarity as well as uniqueness. The white government in South Africa interpreted the cultural uniqueness of Africans as one reason for asserting that cultures must develop separately. They introduced the evil system of apartheid, the demolition of which has been stained by the blood of many people. Scholars of African religions stated categorically that there are no boundaries between the sacred and the secular in African cultural and religious life. It was stated repeatedly that in the African religions, the "sacred" and the "profane" are on the same level of experience and not cut off from one another (Evans-Pritchard 1965).

African theologians of the last three decades, in reaction to the colonial mentality of the Church in its interpretation of Christianity to Africans, posited a theology of inculturation, various aspects of which are presented by Maimela (1994), Mugambi (1990), Parratt (1995) and Pobee (1979). Inculturation theology attempts to "Africanize" in the sense of affirming African culture and positing it as the basis for developing African liberation theology.[7] The dominant participants in the theory of inculturation - whether they were novelists, politicians or theologians - were men, and were indeed perceived to be speaking for all African people.

Inculturation is not Sufficient

In coming late to the scene, African women theologians are caught in the dilemma of disagreeing with the presentation of inculturation as the basis for African liberation theology. While affirming the need for reclaiming culture through the theology of inculturation, we African women theologians make the claim that inculturation is not sufficient unless the cultures we reclaim are analyzed and are deemed worthy in terms of promoting justice and support for life and the dignity of women.

Undertaking such a theology of inculturation from a women's perspective requires that one draws wisdom from the methods used by both African and Feminist theologies of liberation. While drawing upon these theologies, method of analysis and systemization, we also employ an African method of story telling familiar to our African communities. In using this method, we seek to examine the cultural conditioning of African women's thinking in order to discover the roots of the belief system of which they are also a part. We choose feminist methodology because it challenges cultural socialization by rejecting the assumption that the roles of men and women have been fixed, either by the Creator or by culture. In addition, feminist theologians begin from the basis that existing stories, structures and beliefs do not tell the stories of women or that they have distorted the truth about women.

Both feminist and inculturation theologies are contextual. They are involved in the present state of the world and thus adapt a hermeneutic approach to the text. They base their power of analysis on the people's own named experiences. These factors are important for us as women of Africa as we begin to add our experiences to those of western feminists, African American "womanists", Latin American "*mujeristas*", as well as Asian and Latin American women's perspectives in theology. The choice of feminist methodology as a frame of analysis for pursuing African women's theology is useful because feminist theology has been tested and subjected to critiques by other women (Isasi-Diaz 1993; Cannon 1988; Williams 1994) and we can learn from its identified weakness.[8]

In recent years, African women have strongly suggested that liberation theology in Africa can only be credible if it also subjects culture to stringent exegesis. Using their lives as examples, African women question the premises, which celebrate all cultural practices regardless of their negative impact on women. "How can a theology of liberation be based on non liberating cultural practices?" they ask (Oduyoye 1986; Oduyoye 1995; Oduyoye & Kanyoro 1992). As Christian women in Africa, we see the need to take responsibility for ourselves to illustrate the consequences of reading the Bible with cultural lenses by bringing our own experiences to bear on the texts of the Bible. In so doing, we address the place of women in the story of faith.

Engendered Communal Theology

The issues we address in our theological work are African: they are both religious and cultural at the same time, but they affect women differently from the way they affect men. Labeling this method of undertaking theology, that analyzes culture as "cultural hermeneutics", seemed sufficient in 1994 (Ortega 1995). At the present time, I do not see that as an appropriately distinctive name to label the struggles of African women. Hence, I have moved on and I would now elect to refer to this method as "engendering cultural hermeneutics". This term reflects and captures the challenges that African women bring to the theology of inculturation by examining culture with women's eyes. Thus, pursuing a theology of inculturation from a gender and feminist perspective is a new step forward. The process of breaking a long held silence is very difficult. It requires a safe place to discover and build solidarity with the others in the community. In Africa, commitment to the changing of oppressive systems has to be done within the community, otherwise its validity will be questioned. It is for this reason that I would prefer to refer to theology currently being done by women in Africa as "engendered communal theology".

A method of theology that gives us African women our own voice and space is timely. The result of personal experience is the creation of new literature in which truths about women of Africa will be told. The new literature from women provides light to new ways of reading the Bible.

African Women Undertaking Engendered Communal Theology

The Circle of Concerned African Women Theologians: A Safe Place to Speak for Ourselves

In 1989 we founded our African women's theological community, the Circle of Concerned African Women Theologians (hereafter, "the Circle"). In 1992 our first continental volume, *The Will to Arise: Women, Tradition and Church in Africa*, was published by Orbis Books (Oduyoye & Kanyoro 1992). We have never gone back to sleep again. We are writing, speaking, preaching and studying the Bible and meeting to reject the dehumanization of African women. Today, the Circle has a membership scattered all over the continent. Women write papers and then meet to present these papers to each other for joint critiques. Some end up in books, while others appear in journals and yet others in the media. More than nine books have been produced since the launching in 1989.

The Circle has become for many of us a circle of solidarity. Talking about various research projects in the company of the Circle is important so that African women can help eradicate the dearth of literature that represents women's perspectives from the continent. The professional "death" of trained scholars in Africa is the norm and this particularly affects African women (Dube 1996).[9] With a membership of about four hundred women from all over Africa, extending from Cairo to Cape Town, the Circle members are pursuing theology in the context of their own setting. Currently, we are divided into four study commissions, namely:

1. Cultural and Biblical Hermeneutics

2. Women in Culture and Religion

3. History of Women

4. Ministry and Theological Education and Formation.

Each Commission has a team of two people, trained in the appropriate discipline, to coordinate the study. The coordination involves designing the nature of studies and inviting several members from different parts of Africa to carry out relevant field research on the topics identified, and then writing about them. Currently most of the writings of the Circle are in the form of articles and books. The importance of the Circle's theology is that we want to contribute something new to theology by bringing in the voices of women in Africa. Actions, such as returning to our villages to do theological work with our communities, make our task exciting. We do not stop at simply asking for some issues from our communities as subjects for research, as has been done in the past. We stay with the issues, slowly discovering with the communities what the Word of God or our culture is sending us to do. We examine these with feminist hermeneutical keys and then we engage ourselves practically in some form of change.

It is for this reason that women who belong to the Circle believe that the study of theology from the women's perspective is a gift to the church and a gift to women. It is a gift to the church because it calls the Church to repentance for its role in the subordination of women. It is a gift to women because it has opened our eyes to the fact that the future of society and the future of women depend on our placing our trust in the message of God rather than the message of men. We can read and interpret the Bible by ourselves and we can count on God's word that says God created men and women in God's own image (Genesis 1:27). The study of theology by women is the proverbial equivalent of the lion learning to write.

The Circle's vision is to encourage African women to write and publish their works. The goal of the Circle is to promote the well being of African women and all women through theological analysis and the study of the Bible. This, in turn, commits us to social action. The discovery of women's theology has provided for us a renewal and a reformation not yet realized or acknowledged by the Church. It is a renewal that we wish for all women in Africa and for the whole Church in Africa. Since its birth in Ghana in 1989, African women have found, through membership of the Circle, a safe place in which they can dare speak and write about many subjects considered as "taboo" in the African culture. The most courageous move has been to talk openly about sexuality. The Circle women talk of sexuality as much as they talk about anything else. Bernadette Mbuy Beya, a Roman Catholic religious sister from Congo (formerly Zaire), pinpoints this cultural taboo in categorical terms:

> The implications of sexuality in our culture make it anything but comfortable for us to address this topic. In our culture, the subject is a taboo. Despite the

difficulties, however, some of us African women determined to study this matter in depth. After all, sexuality is a prime factor in the determination of behavioral reality, both of human beings in general and of women in particular. (Mbuy Beya 1992:55)

It is remarkable that in almost all of the writings of the Circle, women have something to say on sexuality even if it is only by implication. Sexuality is defined in very broad terms as an expression of our identity, and a means by which we express our relationships with each other in our communities. Thus, for us in Africa, relationships are at the heart of sexuality. Bernadette Mbuy Beya provides an African definition of sexuality as: "...the ensemble of activities by which human beings seek and attain satisfaction of their sexual inclination. Our traditional behavior and customs include a whole series of sexual initiatory practices" (Mbuy Beya 1992:156).

Beya goes on to explore sexuality in categories such as marriage, fidelity, prostitution and single life. Other African women address sexuality through discussion of polygamy, clitoridectomy, secret societies, barrenness, child marriages and sex in societies. Behind all of these practices there are certain implications for sexuality in the society.

I have singled out sexuality because it is the foundation for engendering cultural hermeneutics. Many cultural behaviors that are detrimental to women's health are closely linked to sexuality. Sexuality and fertility are one issue. A whole string of factors are attached to fertility such as the value of children, the impact of AIDS, female circumcision and polygamy. Many women in Africa testify to the Church's fears and suspicions of "women's sexuality". Sexuality is given as an excuse for denying ordination to women. Not only are women's bodies seen as symbols of sexuality, but also, and because of that, women are seen to be unacceptable as church leaders. It is interesting to me that the African society, which is very hospitable to new life, has not provided a theology that affirms the woman through whom new life finds the possibility for growth.

Polygamy is another issue closely connected to sexuality. Here the church, too, has found itself in a dilemma. Until recently, the subject of polygamy has appeared in Christian debates mainly as a moral issue relating to marriage. Convinced that the Scriptures advocate monogamy through texts such as the creation of Adam and Eve (Genesis 2: 23-25), the Christian Church has taken pains to condemn those cultures in which polygamy is a form of accepted matrimony. Polygamy is deemed immoral, and the Church considers all those involved in it as sinners, so the Church has proceeded not to accept men, women and children in polygamous families as members. Often men were asked to choose one wife and to leave the others in order to be accepted in the Church. The Christian Church is also in contention with Islam, which legally stipulates that a man may have up to four wives. Recent studies by Bahemuka (1992), Nasimiyu-Wasike (1992), Kanyoro(1992), Fanusie(1992) and Mbuy Beya (1992) perceive polygamy as an institution oppressive to women. Polygamy thrives in patriarchal cultures that uphold the superiority of male persons. In such societies men may own not only property; they may also own women and their productive powers as well. Polygamy has been the basis of the exploitation of women and children's labor because polygamy is justified as a means of enhancing the productivity of property for the man. Polygamy also depicts women as weak and in need of the constant protection of men. It reduces women's capacity to cope with circumstances of their body such as barrenness. Both in the Bible and in African cultures, women who do not give birth or who give birth only to girl children are degraded to a degree, and this helps to perpetuate polygamy.

The Church is often in a dilemma about polygamy because on the one hand it finds evidence in the Scriptures, which seems to advocate monogamy, and yet there is no direct condemnation of polygamy. African feminists argue that the case for monogamy should be based on the dignity of women, rather than on moral judgments or the "advantages" of one form of marriage over another. Failure to teach true equality of the sexes, is failure to instill into society that the superiority of man over woman is contrary to God's intention for human beings. Today, however, there are books and articles by African women theologians, published locally and internationally, that are a resource that give fresh new gender perspectives to these lasting issues.

Learning to Accommodate Diversity in Communitarian Contexts

Often detractors choose to perceive the efforts of African women to promote the perspectives of women as foreign and Western, and not in accord with our African values and religious beliefs, especially when we struggle to be come to terms with our differences. These people want African women theologians to be silent and submissive in the face of injustice and oppression. They condemn us when we do not sing in unison on all issues affecting women. Differences of opinion amongst women on any issue is taken as weakness on the part of the women. This denigration takes its toll on women and threatens many women who genuinely seek the way of justice. To choose to move forward, despite these criticisms, is the privilege of only the few women who have other support systems, such as families who understand, or have economic and social self-reliance. This defines the social location of those women who chose to actively protest against the status of women either through theology, the legal systems, political activism or any other possible means.

These issues weigh heavily on women who have received theological education. Many simply do not have time to sit and write long papers with footnotes and quotations from numerous other scholars. Many cannot take time for academic study and pursuits. Many do not have access to books and libraries, and money is short and theological books are expensive. Those who judge African women as people who lack theological expression and reflection need to hear, read and respect our choked silence. In some instances the seeming silence may well be the expression of a strategy of protest. But it may also be an expression of despair, anger, overloaded daily lives and other circumstances that continually weigh us down. The reality is that African women live daily in vulnerable situations, and whether by talking about it or remaining silent, they are engaged in a daily struggle to transcend their reality.

Illiteracy as a Marginalizing Factor

The practice of theology in Africa today has to take into account rural non-literate women. This is a question of method not content. Many women on our continent cannot read and write but they sing, they dance and they speak. However, when it comes to the written Scriptures as the basis for belief, they will always depend on other people interpreting the Scriptures for them. Thus, the image of whom they are in the story of faith largely depends on the teaching they receive.

For a long time, print media has marginalized the voices of African women. African rural women are singing songs; they are also creating poetry, proverbs and dirges. Their reflections should challenge us to undertake theology in a different way. We who can write must explore new areas and new avenues for the works of our sisters to be heard beyond the confines of our borders. We must not repeat the theft by other researchers who have often taken these works without credit being given to the original owners. Sitting in comfortable offices producing complete manuscripts in dominant languages will leave out so many of our own sisters from participating in theological reflection. When we African women cry for inclusion and participation we cannot at the same time opt for struggle by and for individuals. Our success depends entirely on our ability to make our theology a communal theology. While maintaining global sisterhood with other women, we must seek to establish our own methodology. Illiteracy on our continent will not determine our access to the grace of God, but it has to be a factor for those pursuing theology in Africa. My own experience of taking part in Bible studies with rural women in Africa, and more specifically with those in my village, shows that it is possible to work with illiterate communities and that inclusion should be a matter of justice, not simply one of choice.

Prophetic Engagement

Finally, we must ask what the consequences of incorporating women's perspectives and methods in theology will be for the Church in Africa. I see foremost the possibilities in awakening the Church to the fact that Biblical history did not stop at the end of the first century of the Common Era. It is important for the Christian Church in Africa to realize that the power of God, which enabled the Hebrew people to preserve their history by telling stories about their encounters with each other and with God, is the same power that led early Christians to tell their stories and by so doing relating the powerful story of Jesus. That same power of God still lives with us for whom the promise of the Holy Spirit was given and fulfilled at Pentecost.

I see our work as only one of the beginning parts of a long journey for African women and the African church as a whole. It is a journey that could lead towards envisioning a new beginning for women in Africa and for the Church in Africa. The experience of a faith that holds itself aloof from people seeking to escape marginalization poses serious risk to the future of the Church and the church of the future in Africa. In order to safeguard the prophetic witness of the Church, action is needed now, for justice delayed is justice denied.

Speaking up on issues that diminish life has been the most difficult part of our self-understanding as individuals and churches. Speaking out is a prophetic task and therefore we, the African women engaged in theology, are participating in a prophetic mission. It involves some very serious risks. In our situation, where democracy is thought to be a luxury, speaking up involves foremost risking the wrath of the powerful. Those who have dared to speak out despite all the risks involved are the prophets that our continent badly needs today. During the World Council of Churches (WCC) Ecumenical Decade, 1988-1998, many women in the churches of Africa spoke up (Phiri 1995). Some were reprimanded, others excommunicated by the churches and others have lost their positions in the Church.[10] I yearn for a time when the men in the churches of Africa will be prophetic about the things that adversely affect the lives of African women!

Women of Africa are asking the Church to be credible as we link our theological analysis to cultural hermeneutics. We give credibility to the Church when we make it aware of its own shortcomings and the need for repentance. Perhaps, with the knowledge that other women have gone courageously before us, we as African women can refuse to be victims of history and claim our share of the right to be God's dignified persons.

We must also listen to each other. To seek justice is to break the boundaries of injustice. The European theologian Dorothee Sölle says: "The question posed by feminist liberation theology is not 'Is there God?' but, 'Does God happen among us, too?'"(Sölle 1991:49). Engendered communal theology is about God happening among us as African women who are daughters of God and daughters of Anowa (Oduyoye 1995).

Endnotes

1. Female Genital Mutilation. Female circumcision is the cultural term used for cutting parts of the female genital organ to mark the coming of age of a woman or to reduce her sexual pleasure with the view of curbing her need for sex. In the recent past, Human Rights groups have renamed this practice as "Female Genital Mutilation (FMG)". It is argued that removing a healthy organ or deforming it to an irremediable shape cannot be anything other than mutilation.

2. Early Betrothals - a common practice in parts of Africa. Basically it involves parents promising their girl child in marriage to another family. A girl child can be betrothed soon after birth Dowry may be paid for her at the time of the betrothal. That means in reality that she is bonded and will be forced, when she grows up, to marry into the family that her parents arranged. She may marry a younger man in the family or even an old man fit to be her great grandfather.

3. Nyambura J. Njoroge presented a paper entitled, Groaning and languishing in labour pains: But for how long Lord?, to the Circle of African Women Theologians, Nairobi, Kenya, January 1994, and published in Kanyoro, M. R. A., &. Njoroge,

N. J. (Eds.). (1996). *Groaning in Faith: African Women in the Household of God* (pp.3-15). Nairobi: Acton Publishers.

4. For feminists, patriarchy does not just mean the rule of the father, or the rule of males for that matter, but it carries with it connotations of an unjust hierarchical and dualistic ordering of life which discriminates against women. Patriarchy should not be seen as the opposite of matriarchy. For further reading, see Ruether, R. R. (1996). Patriarchy. In L. M. Russell, & J. S. Clarkson (Eds.), *The Dictionary of Feminist Theologies.* (pp. 205-206). Louisville: Westminster/John Knox Press.

5. See the report of the United Nations on the fourth world conference on women: Beijing Declaration and the Platform for Action, 1995, United Nations Information Center, New York.

6. In her book, *Daughters of Anowa: African Women and Patriarchy,* Mercy Amba Oduyoye presents the best example of engendered cultural hermeneutics available today. She does not use the terminology because her book is about content and starts from analyzing oral literature. This work starts from analyzing the reading of the Bible in a cultural context and seeks to name the theologies of African feminists. The Akan people understand themselves as "children of Anowa" (a legendary Akan woman who represents Africa in contemporary Ghanaian creative literature), and women are her "daughters".

7. See the bibliography for book resources on African theology of inculturation.

8. Womanist and Muherista theologians have provided the most significant critique to feminist theology.

9. Musa Dube points out that professional death comes to third world people because they are trained in methods that stifle their own questions.

10. The Presbyterian Church, Blantyre Synod in Malawi, for example, fired women church-workers and penalized Dr. Isabel Phiri when the women in the church talked about injustice towards women in the Church and society.

References

Achebe, C. (1958). *Things Fall Apart.* London: Heinemann.

Achebe, C. (1964). *Arrow of God.* London: Heinemann.

Cannon, K. G. (1988). *Black Womanist Ethics.* Atlanta: Scholars Press.

Bahemuka, J. M. (1992). "Social Changes and Women's Attitudes Toward Marriage in East Africa" in M. A. Oduyoye, & M. R. A. Kanyoro (Eds.), *The Will to Arise: Women, Tradition, and the Church in Africa.* New York: Orbis Books, 119-134.

Beya, B. M. (1992). "Human Sexuality, Marriage and Prostitution" in M. A. Oduyoye, & M. R. A. Kanyoro (Eds.), *The Will to Arise: Women, Tradition, and the Church in Africa.* New York: Orbis Books, 155-178.

Dube, M. (1996). *An Introduction: How We Come to Read with.* Semeia, 73, 10-15.

Efua, D. (1994). *The Cutting of a Rose - Female Genital Mutilation, the Practice and its Preventation.* London: Minority Rights.

Evans-Pritchard, E. E. (1965). *Theories of Primitive Religion.* London: Oxford University Press.

Fanusie, L. (1992). "Sexuality and Women in African Culture" in M. A. Oduyoye, & M. R. A. Kanyoro (Eds.), *The Will to Arise: Women, Tradition, and the Church in Africa.* New York: Orbis Books, 135-154.

Gottwald, N. K., & Horsely, R. A. (Eds.). (1993). *The Bible and Liberation - Political and Social Hermeneutics.* New York: Orbis Books.

Isasi-Diaz, A. M. (1993). *En la Lucha: In the Struggle: A Hispanic Women's Liberation Theology.* Minneapolis: Fortress Press.

Kanyoro, M. R. A. (1992). "Interpreting Old Testament Polygamy Through African Eyes" in M. A. Oduyoye, & M. R. A. Kanyoro (Eds.), *The Will to Arise: Women, Tradition, and the Church in Africa.* New York: Orbis Books, 87-100.

Kanyoro, M. R. A., &. Njoroge, N. J. (Eds.). (1996). *Groaning in Faith: African Women in the Household of God.* Nairobi: Acton Publishers.

Kenyatta, J. (1938). *Facing Mount Kenya: The Traditional Life of the Gikuyu.* Britain: Martin Secker, Warburg LMT.

Laye, C. (1959). *The African Child.* London: Fontana.

Maimela, S. S. (1994). *Culture, Religion and Liberation.* Pretoria: Penrose Books.

Mugambi, J. (1990). *African Heritage and Contemporary Christianity.* Nairobi: Longman.

Nasimiyu-Wasike, A. (1992). Polygamy: "A Feminist Critique" in M. A. Oduyoye, & M. R. A. Kanyoro (Eds.), *The Will to Arise: Women, Tradition, and the Church in Africa.* New York: Orbis Books, 101-118.

Njoroge, N. (1996). "Groaning and Languishing in Labour Pains: But for How Long Lord? in M. R. A. Kanyoro, & N. J. Njoroge (Eds.), *Groaning in Faith.* Nairobi: Acton Publishers, 3-15.

Oduyoye, M. A. (1986). *Hearing and Knowing.* New York: Orbis Books.

Oduyoye, M. A. (1995). *Daughters of Anowa: African Women and Patriarchy.* New York: Orbis Books.

Oduyoye, M. A., & Kanyoro, M. R. A. (Eds.). (1992). *The Will to Arise: Women, Tradition and the Church in Africa.* New York: Orbis Books.

Ortega, O. (1995). *Women's Visions: Theological Reflection, Celebration, Action.* Geneva: World Council of Churches.

Parratt, J. (1995). *Reinventing Christianity: African Theology Today.* Grand Rapids: Wm. B. Eerdmans.

Phiri, I. A. (1995). "Women, Church and Theological Identity" *in Ministerial Formation, Geneva.* World Council of Churches Publications, 71, (39-43).

Pobee, J. S. (1979). *Towards an African Theology.* Nashville: Abingdon Press.

Russell, L. M., & Clarkson J. S. (Eds.) (1996). *Dictionary of Feminist Theologies.* Louisville: Westminster/John Knox Press.

Schüssler Fiorenza, E. (1985). *Bread Not Stone.* Boston: Beacon Press.

Segovia, F. F., & Tolbert, M. A. (Eds.). (1995). *Reading from this Place. Vol. 2 - Social Location and Biblical Interpretation in Global Perspectives.* Minneapolis: Fortress Press.

Sölle, D. (1991). "Liberating Our God-Talk" in U. King (Ed.) *Liberating Woman Conference Reader.* Bristol: University of Bristol, 42-52.

Tiffany, F. C., & Ringe, S. H. (1996). *Biblical Interpretation - A Road Map.* Nashville: Abingdon Press.

Williams, D. S. (1993). *Sisters in the Wilderness - The Challenge of Womanist God-talk.* New York: Orbis Books.

Circle Transformation
of Society and Church

Women in the Church in Africa: Possibilities for Presence and Promises

Bernadette Mbuy Beya

Introduction

This chapter deals with how African women have been living their experience of God and how they have expressed this experience at various ecumenical meetings, whether local, national, or international. In this chapter, we will speak of churches in plural, since Africa contains many cultures and many forms of church.

We operate on the premise that the churches of Africa are committing themselves more and more to the struggle for justice and freedom. They are even involved in the current process of democratization. It is then all the more surprising that these churches are silent – if not compliant – when it comes to the question of women. And yet, the plight of women in African societies does not present a pretty picture.

The Circle of African Women Theologians[1] has already condemned the deplorable situation of women. The group has been working tirelessly toward the goal that each woman and each man might be recognised as a child of God; it has worked for the human dignity of everyone. But these women do not lead this fight alone; more and more people are supporting them. Moreover, these women are not fighting for the notion that women are the same as men. Rather, they want to be fully "women" in society as well as in the church. Personally, let me note that the Circle of African Women Theologians has provided us with a footing for our fieldwork. For we firmly hope that as a result of the African

Synod in the Roman Catholic Church, all our churches will enter a new phase, will come to maturity, and will then begin to act boldly. That is, they will demonstrate their capacity for self-management and for responsibility, particularly with respect to Christian marriage and the role of women in church communities.

In this regard, in his letter on the dignity and vocation of woman, the Holy Father, John Paul II has already sounded the alarm. He takes up the message of Vatican II to women, a message that makes a strong call to our churches in these words:

> The moment is coming, the moment has come, when woman's vocation is fully realised; the moment when woman takes on in the world an influence, a radiance, a power until now unattained. That is why at this time when humanity is undergoing so many changes women filled with the spirit of the Gospel can do so much to help humanity not to fail.[2]

In the light of the Holy Father's words, we shall in this paper call upon the consciences of all the churches of Africa to bring about a radical change of mentality and a redefinition of the man-woman relationship in the church. Furthermore, we hope that this appeal will be the good news that the African Synod brings to African women.

In what follows we shall touch upon three points: the place of women in Africa; the presence of women in the churches; and finally, recommendations for the near future.

The Place of Women in African Society

We find it impossible to approach the question of woman in the church without first examining the indignity that she experiences in society. For it is from this background that she commits herself in the church that, for its part, does not perceive her any differently from the society at large. That is to say, the church itself has not and does not escape the temptation to discriminate against women, although perhaps never quite so overtly as the rest of the society.

The Democratic Republic of Congo (henceforth referred to as DRC) section of the Circle of African Women Theologians has been at work for the past two years studying closely the violence of which African women are victims, so as to find non-violent ways of actively combating it.[3] The violence inflicted on women may be physical, psychological, or moral. We have noted ten types of physical violence that have an effect on women's health. We classify them according to the kind of damage they cause women. These are beatings and wounds; rape; venereal diseases; premarital pregnancy; abortion; too-frequent pregnancies; bodily disfiguration; genital mutilation; purification rites; and prostitution. For each item we have worked out an analysis based on the following questions:

What?	The nature of the damage
By whom?	An individual or society
Against whom?	The victim – women in general, the young, the elderly
Why?	The situations leading to violence
Consequences?	Effects on persons and on society
What to do?	Outline of solutions
By whom?	Who is responsible for change?
When?	Time frame to achieve specific objectives

This analysis has brought us to the conclusion that the woman is the victim of violence from all sides and in her many roles: first in her family as a child; next as a young woman; then in her marriage as wife and mother; finally; in her social environment as worker or colleague. She suffers violence at the hands of a man or because of a man when there is a gap between the aspiration of society and individual drives which are badly controlled or uncontrolled. This violence affects both her body and her spirit. As a remedy, society must rethink ways in which the individual can be properly socialised.

As for psychological and mental violence, we have defined them as acts against a woman by another person, which alter or deprive her of her thought, her will, or her behaviour. They range from insults to the complete negation of a woman's personality. Considering the nature and form of such violence, we have noted six types of acts: insulting or humiliating words; taboos and prohibitions; infidelity of the husband (accepted by tradition); incest; repudiation of the wife; and refusal of her right to child custody. Such forms of emotional violence bring serious harm upon a woman because they destroy her inner well being, shatter her personality, and throw her life off balance. Responsibility for such violence falls upon African society as a whole, for that is where the violence originates. This state of affairs cries out to our collective conscience and requires a redefinition of our cultural and social values.

During the DRC's Sovereign National Conference, the Circle of Concerned African Women Theologians addressed a letter to the Conference's chairman, Archbishop Monsengwo, in which it raised its voice against what it called the systematic destruction of the family.[4] Here are a few of the sad observations made in the letter:

> Prostitution has become virtually institutionalised since the Second Republic. No law either prohibits debauchery or takes any measures to protect the population from this curse, which spares no family.
>
> Every young child has been tainted by moral, material, and intellectual corruption.
>
> The concentration of wealth in the hands of an affluent minority plunges the rest of the population into misery and gives rise to a class of merchant women whose children are left to the streets.
>
> The harmful intrusion of the extended family into the affairs of the nuclear family is a source of conflict and separation whose principal victims are wives and children.
>
> The dowry has become a source of important income, to the detriment of woman's dignity.
>
> Tribalism has been chosen as a strategy of resistance to democracy, producing ethnic conflicts that plunge DRC into a senseless bloodbath, and it is the children who suffer most.

The confiscation of the media by the ruling powers favours misinformation and estranges the people from the management of the commonwealth.

The deterioration of schools and health facilities severely compromises the future of our children.

While not exhaustive, this list of social ills is a useful barometer indicating the state of health of the DRC society: but it can be generalised to apply to most African societies today. The list above reveals the social world of the African woman. But an issue that must be raised is that of the role women play in the church in Africa, as well as the role she could play if the churches were to agree to work for her liberation.

Woman in the Church

Possibilities for Presence

Are women truly present in the church in Africa? Sister Justine Kahungu answers this question by saying that women are indeed present in God's church in DRC. Her activity is seen in the liturgy; she devotes her talents to the choir; she directs and guides the young; she proclaims the Word of God; and at the offertory, alongside a man, she offers to God "the fruit of the earth and the work of human hands". Sister Kanwungu speaks also of the women involved in Catholic Action movements, in the Charismatic Renewal as shepherdesses, and finally as leaders of "living ecclesial communities (CEV)", or as the wives of "Bakambi", the lay parish administrators. She notes also the increasing number of religious women who are taking on the duties of assistant pastors in parishes.[5]

We have met some of these women, and here are their testimonies. Mama Emerence Mbuyi is 54 years old, and a widowed mother of several children. She has sung in the Cathedral's Swahili choir for many years. Here is what she told us:

I love to sing for the Lord, and I've been doing it since
the age of nine. I was married to a man who loved the
Lord and who accepted my vocation in the church. In
the choir I come into contact with a great many young
people whom I help in preparation for marriage or as a
guide on the path of a priestly or religious vocation. My
vocation includes lots of joy but also pain. I have seen
many young people whom I thought were self-rooted in
Christ turn to the sects. The Christian community is
my second family. It strongly supported me when I lost
my husband a few years ago.

Mama Regine, Mama Prudence and Mama Rose run a
nutritional program in their parish. This is their way of
participating in the development of their CEV.

We started with forty-seven malnourished children, who
were examined by a nutritional specialist. They received
a ration of soya-bean porridge every day. The number
grew steadily as more children were recommended by
the leaders of the CEVs of the different neighbourhoods.
At the time of the second visit by the nutritionist, 19
August 1993, seventy children were examined: she noted
among them thirty-seven cases to be fed every day, and
thirty-three to be treated three times a week. Most of
the children began by being treated for worms; in one
case special medical care was needed. We watch over
attendance by the children; visit the homes in case of
illness or prolonged absence, and nutritional advice to
parents. We're very happy to come together each morning
and do this work for God.

In view of the serious economic crisis that the DRC is
experiencing, these women play an important role in the
CEVs.

Mama Leonie Kaj is a catechist in their parish, and she
simply shared her experience with us as follows:

I am the mother of two children, but I have seven at
home. I am in the magnificent community as "a woman
alone with Jesus", a movement for single women. I am
a math teacher at Maadini Institute, a school of the
Gecamines (the local mining company). In the parish of
St. John in Kamalndo I've been in charge of the religious
education program for both children and adults for five

years. My first term has just ended: it has, however, been renewed. As a catechist, in my CEV I work with catechumens and sometimes with First Communicants. My work as a teacher overflows into my work as a catechist. In each case it's a matter of deepening both the human and the spiritual. As a mother I'm thrilled by this work.

What time do I give to religious education? In the evening at about 5 o'clock, I'm at the parish. Before Christmas and Easter we prepare the catechumens or the First Communicant more intensively for the sacraments of Baptism, reconciliation, or the Eucharist. It's demanding, but for God nothing is too much!

When I was put in charge of the catechetical ministry the Christian community accepted me and helped me to improve. Comments about my Christian life came out of the woodwork and there were some investigations, but I wasn't shaken. Because my responsibility puts me in the limelight, from now on I have no right to make a mistake.

The priests of my parish have accepted me, despite differences about ways of admitting people to the sacraments. The catechists teach and try to explain Christian doctrines. Our priests take little interest in our catechetics. They don't know how, what, or where we teach. They're there to administer the sacraments, and sometimes we have to beg them to do that. The biggest problem in my parish involves the issue of children and young people being admitted to the sacrament of Reconciliation. Our priests prefer communal penance. But then when will our children and young people overcome their fear of confession?

Religious education is at the heart of parish life, and contact with our priests has to be ongoing to deepen the Christian knowledge of the catechists. All too often one gets the idea that catechism is the affair of the laity alone.

As a woman involved in the church at the parish level, I feel at ease since I participate in committee meetings and parish council meetings where decisions about the running of the parish are made. I also participate once a month in a "sector" meeting which bring several parishes together.

Mama Leonie concludes by noting that while women are very often involved in catechetical ministry, very few of them are engaged in pastoral ministry. She believes women are afraid of working face to face with adults, particularly men. She would like to see them undertaking greater involvement in pastoral ministry.

Mama Marie-Louise Kasongo Mujinga Kinyembo is in charge of the Charismatic Renewal in the Archdiocese. She is married and the mother of six children. She recounts her adventure with God as a series of calls at different moments of her life. Mama Marie-Louise has known joyful times, but has also suffered a great deal, feeling not accepted because she is a woman.

> The first call from God came to me when I was twelve, after my Confirmation. In the silence of my soul I felt God's passing and I realised that I was a Christian and saw that my life was changing: I loved to attend the Eucharistic celebration every time, to receive communion, to contemplate and to meditate. I heard the second call at the age of thirteen. Without knowing that another way was to open up before me, I thought of not consecrating myself in religious life. It wasn't hard for me to give up the idea of religious life and consecrate myself in marriage at the age of nineteen. However, the Lord has helped me through the trials of married life and in times of sickness. I've been sick and had to be operated nine times. The Lord has never stopped showing me his love and his hand is upon me.
>
> I was filled with the Holy Spirit in 1979 when the Lord chose me for his service. Guided by my Bishop, on 1 August 1981 I started prayer groups called "Light of the World". Things went well and the members used their gifts to answer the appeals of God's people through prayer and healing. My husband encouraged me in this new ministry, and my children prayed with me, especially the older girls, who still continue to be very active.
>
> In 1984 my pastor asked me to co-ordinate the groups' activities in the parish and to belong to the parish council. This indeed brought lots of challenges from (for) my male brethren. Although the pastor had entrusted the organisation of the entire group to me, my brothers could not accept his decision and clearly showed their preference to be guided by a man and not a woman. I was deeply hurt. Even now it is impossible to find unanimity in these groups and to provide any kind of

real organisation. I'm not ready to resign and I still trust the Lord.

In 1985 the Lord gave me another sign and called me to visit prisoners to share the word of God with them, and be to them a sign of His presence. We go regularly to the very large Kasapa prison, bringing with us food, which we cook there, administer first aid for those in need, and also to conduct prayer sessions with our brothers and sisters in detention.

In 1991 I was elected chairperson of the Charismatic Renewal in the Archdiocese. The first woman named to the post, I found it no small task. In this position I had to organise the first Congress of Charismatic Renewal. The Congress was a success, but the editing of the minutes was assigned to some male intellectuals who never did it, in spite of numerous reminders. Is this a way of protesting against my nomination? In any case it shows that we have a long way to go to be converted. As I've already told you, I keep struggling in prayer for wisdom. The Bishop and his Vicar General continue to encourage me, advising me to be patient. I'm not looking for glory, but as a mother I'd like to keep giving life in the church through a ministry of prayer and reconciliation. The Lord has done great things for me. I have witnessed the most unexpected conversions. How I wish for my whole life to praise! As long as the Lord needs me, I'm there and available.

Mama Veronique Kyabu Kabila, married and the mother of seven children, devotes herself fully to the "children of Light" (Bilenge ya Mwinda). With emotion she shares with us her great devotion to the Virgin Mary. She speaks of her "Marian devotion" in her family as she regrets the attitude of certain charismatic groups, which for the sake of hospitality towards our Protestant brethren, say leave Mary aside in favour of Jesus. But she says "Mary helped me find Jesus: its she who gave me to Jesus." Mama Veronique tells us that it was in 1981 that she felt the deep desire to serve the Lord, following Mary's example.

> I wanted to be handmaid of the Lord, to bring Jesus into the world through works that manifest him (John 4:21-23), be converted and helped others to be converted. This deep desire was for me a call, which I had to answer

> with an unconditional yes. Ever since, I've been
> working to serve the Lord my Creator anywhere he
> wants to use me.

Currently Mama Veronique is a member of the Youth Commission of her CEV and is a very active member of the Circle of African Women Theologians. She remains a mother to young people. Her motherhood has taken on a new meaning because of all the children her ministry has brought to the church.

Mama Veronique would like the clergy to trust and allow a greater freedom to the laity involved in the church. The Spirit breathes on them and on the whole Church community as well. She says we must be able to feel at home in the church. Of course, one has to count on common sense and the spirit of discernment of committed lay people, which unfortunately is not always self-evident, since they are not trained. However, the laity is not solely responsible for its own training.

In conclusion, Mama Veronique says she would like to pray for unity within the church before we go to meet with sister communities of other churches. "That they may be one as we are one" (John 17:21).

Sister Generose is a daughter of St. Paul in the DRC. Her religious vocation has something miraculous about it, given the milieu in which she was born and brought up. She calls us to share her joy as a consecrated woman.

> Those in the military are the first victims of the drop in
> standard of living that the DRC has been living through.
> For example, a DRC soldier – if and when paid – earns
> less than 100 Belgian Francs ($3) a month. However, a
> minimum of 1000 BF is required to meet essential
> monthly expenses. How in such conditions can one feed
> a family and pay for the children's schooling? In
> consequence, the military steals, pillages, etc. And even
> if they don't, public opinion automatically brands them
> as thieves.
>
> A lot of things happen in a military camp: robberies,
> rapes, rows among the wives, violence among the
> children, and so on. It's in this setting that I was born
> and grew up. My name is Generose Sibay and for several

years I've belonged to the Pauline family in the Congregation of the Daughters of St. Paul.

I have the good fortune to have as father a soldier who is a Christian and who understood the importance of education and good upbringing for his eleven children. My father tilled the soil very hard so as to raise us with dignity.

My vocation was born when I saw the enormity of ignorance in the military camps, especially among the girls, and when I saw old people accused and abused for sorcery. The Lord was calling me to be present in this milieu. I would have to announce the Good News and console his people. As we sing, "the Spirit of God has chosen me to extend the reign of Christ among the nations, we consoled the hearts worn down by suffering".

Today I am a consecrated woman in the church, and it's a great joy for me to be able to share all that the Lord has given me. Our congregation has made a preferential option for women, and we are working hard for the advancement of women in the mass media.

The liberation of the African woman is an urgent concern for our society and our church. Action must be quick if Africa is to be saved.

As a religious person I don't feel any complex as far as men are concerned. Our Mother Thecla (Merlo), co-founderess of our congregation, has taught me how to live complementarily so that the Word of God may spread quickly and be received with honour. (2 Thessalonians 3:1)

These few testimonies don't tell us all about the lives of women who are active in the churches, but they give us an idea of the different possibilities for their presence. They are a few rays of hope.

Promises

Ten years ago, at the opening of his diocese's synod, the Archbishop of Lubumbashi declared: "Africa needs a Gospel and a faith to save us from the sinful situations that make up our daily.... Let us then be prophets of Now and not cantors of a bourgeois gospel."[6]

But looking at the facts, we strongly fear that the situation of the woman is not considered as one of the situations of sin. Moreover, the minutes of the Synod make no reference to women, although women were invited to the Synod. In fact, among others, lay people and religious men and women were invited so as to widen the circle of priests around the Bishop during the Synod. I remember with great pleasure the evening when the lay people decided to leave the Synod because the church was making so little room for them and they were feeling like flies in the soup. As for the religious women, they could come up with a flood of tears to tell the Bishop that they too are full members of the church. In response, a moving Eucharist was celebrated to bring the Synod to an end.

Five years after the Synod, at Easter 1989, the Archbishop published a pastoral letter on women with the title "I am a Human and not your Doormat" that raised diverse reactions. It revealed an image that many still have of women – just a mat and not a human being.[7] In that letter, the Archbishop showed a deeper consciousness and denounced a situation that tends to ignore women: he challenged all to review their conduct. He noted that "she" (woman) appears like someone lost in the crowd, who is of no use to the church beyond giving birth in the sacrament of matrimony and being good mothers or – through a religious profession – "good sisters" as they are called. To belabour the facts is not very useful; we must join action to words and be perfectly consistent in our actions.

One rather encouraging sign took place in January 1992, during the Third General Assembly of Ecumenical Association of Third-World Theologians (EATWOT). It had been decided to have an outdoors ecumenical celebration. During the ceremony, we were called upon to ask pardon for the sins of our respective continents and to make a gesture of reparation for the benefit of the poor in Nairobi, where we were. One by one, Africa, Asia, Latin America, and the ethnic minorities of the USA each expressed repentance in his or her own way. Then, totally unexpectedly, a Catholic priest, a white Latin American, knelt down in the middle of the circle, inviting all the men to do likewise; then he began to ask the women to pardon the concrete sins that men had committed against them. A number of women present were overwhelmed, one woman was then designated to receive the demand for pardon and grant the pardon in the name of all others. She was an African religious woman, Superior General of her congregation. She knelt in an attitude of welcoming life and prayed to God that peace might come between men and women of the Third World.

Was it a logical chain of events? The next day at the five-year election, women were elected to four of the seven places on EATWOT's executive committee. Clearly, the men were ready to run the association together with the women, whereas at its foundation in 1976, one woman only had been admitted - as an observer.[8]

The African churches should fall into step with EATWOT's example, for women might just be "the stone the builders rejected" which could become the cornerstone of tomorrow's church.

The gifts of God are distributed without discrimination to all in the church, which needs all talents to be a credible sign of God's presence in the African world. Let us recall here Paul's message to the church at Corinth:

> I never stop thanking God for all the graces you have received through Jesus Christ. I thank him that you have been enriched in so many ways, especially in your teachers and preachers; the witness to Christ has been strong among you so that you will not be without any of the gifts of the Spirit while you are waiting for our Lord Jesus Christ to be revealed. (I Corinthians 1:4-8)

We must all then go beyond the Holy Father's beautiful meditation on the dignity and vocation of women in the church and in the world, and move to the effective recognition of this particular treasure through the sharing of ecclesial authority.

Vatican II in its Dogmatic Constitution on the Church, No. 32, says there is but one chosen people of God, having the same filial grace and the same vocation to perfection: one salvation, one hope, and one undivided charity. The

Council's declaration is very clear: in Christ and in the Church there is no inequality on the basis of race or nationality, social condition or sex. "For you are all one in Christ" (Galatians 3:28; Colossians 3:11).

Are our churches aware that they must lead the same fight against structures that oppress women as they lead against structures that oppress blacks in South Africa? We see it as one and the same struggle.

We have mentioned prostitution as a social evil, but we have not spoken explicitly of AIDS, which is decimating Africa. It is believed that there may soon be as many as ten million children orphaned by AIDS. Is it too much to ask the churches to take their people seriously and appeal vigorously to all consciences? It is not too late, for example, to issue a pastoral letter on AIDS, considering the extent of the plague and its grave consequences for the peoples of Africa.

Another evil to note concerns the women who say they are condemned to a secret life by certain priests who have taken them as wives. Rather than give a discourse on priestly celibacy – which we can leave to those concerned – we prefer to call the clergy to respect the dignity of women. At the same time, we equally condemn the equivocating or ambiguous attitudes of certain religious women and other women who are not sure as to who they are.

Love is a marvellous gift from the Lord. "As the Father has loved me, so I have loved you. Remain in my love.... Love one another as I have loved you" (John 15:9, 12). It is good to see the friends of the Lord love one another. "See how they love one another." The problem is to know how to manage affection, which is born of and grows in the church.

African Women and Theology

Theology developed by African women does exist. Since 1986, African women have been at work trying to express both the experiences they have had being discriminated against as women and the struggle they've led for the right to life and respect for their dignity. Among other publications, they have published *The Will to Arise: Women, Tradition and the Church in Africa,* a book that breaks the silence and speaks about their lives and their hopes.[9]

Women's theology in Africa concerns the whole life of every woman, regardless of education or social status, and it is contextual. Through it, women want to assert their belonging to the Church.

Africa is struggling to be freed from fear, hunger, racism, and oppression, be it economic, political, or religious. The answers won't come from a theological treatise on liberation. The Gospel – a message of liberation – will take root in African soil, thanks to women and men who aren't afraid of dirtying their hands in the earth and of risking their lives in the defence of the poor and helpless.

The difficulty for women's theology lies in the limitations imposed by poverty and all the demands of daily life. Its hard to think about writing with a baby on your back crying from hunger, or with a child having an attack from sickle cell anaemia, a disease which particularly affects blacks. We have papers collecting dust for want of funds to publish them. Such is the case with the Minutes of the Yaounde Colloquiumon, Theology from the Perspective of African Women, and the French translation of *The Will to Arise: Women, Tradition and the Church in Africa* (*Leve-toi, femme*), to cite but two instances. Another limitation, no less important, is the rate of illiteracy, which is rising in countries like the DRC, because of the destruction of the school system, or in countries like Angola, because of war. As a consequence, the gap in level of schooling between girls and boys continues to widen.

In Africa we are not hung up about God's gender. What women want is to live decently and to be able to express our experience of God in our human communities. Women do their theology in their own fashion. There are women such as Teresa Okure, Bette Ekeya, Teresa Hinga, Margaret Umeagudosu, to cite just a few, who should continue to work academically. However, our theological reflection is also based on wisdom and feeling: it is to be found not only in the head, but also in the heart and the gut.

In the Bible we meet women who – like ourselves – fought for the right to life, like the midwives at the time of Moses: women like Miriam, Deborah, Ruth, Esther, Judith, and, later, Mary the Mother of Jesus, the prophetess Anne, Martha and Mary. By their deeds these women were God's instruments.

However, women didn't always play only a positive role. Alas, the same is true today. That is why it is important that every woman has direct contact with the Word of God and has a personal encounter with the Lord Jesus Christ, as did the Samaritan woman at the well.[10]

At the present time, one group of women playing an important role in the church is religious women. The late Cardinal Malula, founder of the Sisters of St. Therese of the Child Jesus of Kinshasa, summed up his work in these words: "My whole effort can be summed up in three key words: from girls who are fully women, authentically African, and authentically religious."[11]

The consecrated life of women is a gift of God to the churches of Africa. Many international congregations have – with a view to survival – opened their doors to African girls, ever since the beginning of the second evangelization.[12] Many bishops have discovered for themselves the charisma of "Father Founder" in order to ensure a smoother collaboration with diocesan religious women. But often these religious women are treated like the personal housekeepers of the bishop and of the local clergy.

Even if religious women are ready to serve the church in the most humble of tasks, it remains clear that the meaning of consecrated life lies elsewhere. Called first of all "to be with the Lord" (Matthew 3:14), the African religious woman says yes to the Lord so that life may spring forth in Africa. For her the meaning of religious life is a question of fidelity to God and to the cultural values of life giving, of family solidarity, of responsibility, and of integration into the milieu.

Addressing an assembly of religious women, Oscar Bimwenyi, the well-known DRC theologian, asked this serious question: "Daughter of my people, are you good fortune or bad fortune for my people?" What does it mean to be "good fortune" for the peoples of Africa, crushed by all forms of misery: physical, moral, spiritual, and material?

In Shaba, a region of the DRC particularly infected with xenophobia, religious women have broken the silence, coming out of their convents to call upon those with political authority. They expressed themselves in this way:

> Governor,
>
> Those of us working in the field of health care deplore the lack of medicine, the lack of money, and the severity of illnesses whose principal cause is malnutrition. To go to the fields would be a solution.
>
> We have land and rain; however, many people have given up farming because of the insecurity.
>
> This is what we ask of you:
>
> That you make use of the media to encourage the people to farm;
>
> That you publicly ask the military and others at your service and who should be at the service of the population to help people farm in peace;
>
> We believe that you are hearing – through us – the cry of our people that we want to be heard and we are determined to continue until we are fully heard.
>
> As far as the agricultural campaign is concerned, we for our part are committing our efforts in the zones where we are present so as to organise collective work and do all that is within our power to make the project succeed.

While one group of religious women were meeting with the Governor, others were gathered in prayer in the Cathedral where they waited for their sisters. They were of many races and ethnic groups, coming from many parishes and different congregations.

One of the tasks of religious life in Africa is the christianising of various rites of passage affecting the lives of women: this is not an easy thing to do. Unfortunately, the tendency of African women to treat themselves as things does not spare the religious ones, who, in the name of holy obedience, might want to flee responsibility and the struggle for the dignity of women.

Thus, does the Circle of Concerned African Women Theologians aim for a new conception of the "feminine being" within current society? This new conception entails a change in mentality, which must take place first of all in the woman herself. She must first of all accept herself as a human being, loved and wanted, as she is by God himself (Genesis 1:27-28). She can no longer consider herself the dregs of humanity, and she should banish anything that tends to minimise her femininity. As such, the Archbishop of Lubumbashi points out that woman's identity is to be sought from God – it is in her relation with God her Creator – the relationship which safeguards her personality and which recognises her whole being.[13]

The Circle of Concerned African Women Theologians decided to undertake activities such as the following that are designed to equip women to raise their consciousness and be mobilised.

◈ Organise educational conferences with senior secondary schools. (This has already begun).

◈ Make it possible for women to become involved with the mass media for information and educational services. (This has been made possible through the Daughters of St. Paul).

◈ By means of a flier, launch a campaign to conscientize people concerning the rights of women, calling upon all of the powers that be. (This action has been made difficult by the current economic crisis).

◈ Use health care facilities to provide basic health education. (This was difficult to get started).

◈ Promote the participation of women in the CEVs. (This action is already going on).

◈ Promote and work for agricultural development. (This is difficult in practice because of insecurity).

◈ Arouse the consciousness of the people in order to protect the land of our ancestors, by fighting against deforestation and the dumping of toxic waste.

◈ Promote and work in the struggle against illiteracy. (This action is to be encouraged).

◆ Encourage the economic independence of women by the setting up of co-operatives (This has been difficult because of the current economic crisis).

The Archbishop of Lubumbashi, therefore, is right in asserting that it is not enough to pray or simply lament: women must be committed from now on to helping our people improve their lot.[14] Thus he calls upon women to give up wailing and to cease acting like defeated victims and to take full responsibility for their own lives. For the liberation of women is in the hands of women themselves and they must go forth to do this. The Roman Catholic Church in Africa must henceforth stop being a "masculine" church and become a church for both men and women. We know that many justifications are given for keeping women away from their real spiritual responsibilities. For instance, to demonstrate that women are incapable within the structure of the church, people usually select for office a woman of doubtful morality or one who is psychologically unstable. Men who show the same defects are, by and large, kept out of such office.

The priesthood of women is a difficult topic to address in the Roman Catholic Church, and this still more so in Africa! Yet it would be good to study it in the light of certain African traditions that have given women an important place in the life of the community.[15] It is not a matter of women becoming clerics. Male clericalism is itself bad enough: would female clericalism be any better?

The fact that so many women spontaneously emerge as "spiritual leaders" is a sign of the times that has to be reckoned with. The current proliferation of different kinds of spiritual life is a proof of the anguished searching of our people, who are hungry for God while crushed by suffering. These different forms of spiritual life pose a problem for, and are a challenge to, the structures of our institutional churches.[16] Many people marginalized by church law feel more at ease in prayer groups outside the churches. It is often women who, as shepherdesses, take on such welcoming ministries of thus show God's mercy.

Women's Ministries in the African Church

Before advocating an increase in the number of women ministers in the church, one must first work to guarantee to women the possibility of adequate theological training, so that they can effectively participate in the whole life of the church. In Africa, at least in the Roman Catholic Church, sacred studies are not seen as of great importance in the eyes of families. When it comes to girls, parents do not want to invest their money in such studies. It is therefore up to the religious congregations to see it as their duty to produce sisters who are capable and willing to be ministers, and who have a solid spiritual and theological foundation through appropriate training.

The struggle for the liberation of women must find strength in a great inner freedom acquired through prayer and through a spirit of sacrifice, in a deep and intimate relationship with Jesus Christ. This relationship can only be revealed to the woman herself, and this can help her prepare for the role of a mother, that is, giving and bearing life.

It must not be forgotten that we are invited all together, women and men, to seek a new way of forming the present-day church. Certain women – shepherdesses of prayer groups and religious women in parish or hospital ministries – have close contact with the life of the community and with people in search of God. It would be desirable for them to be able to take on certain sacramental ministries such as baptism, the sacrament of the sick, the sacrament of reconciliation, and the role of official church witness at weddings.[17] One need not even mention the roles of rector or homilist, which are also required. I myself have assumed the responsibilities of pastoral assistant in two different parishes.

Until now – in our diocese, at least – only religious women may distribute communion alongside the priest and laymen. We desire that any woman with a real responsibility in the church should be called to this task.

To conclude this chapter, we see it as our duty to offer several recommendations, which we think, could guide our reflections.

Recommendations

The churches of Africa have already devoted much effort to the education and advancement of women. To battle against the silence women bring upon themselves and the silence about the lives of women, we recommend that the churches encourage women to undertake sacred studies.

The churches of Africa have made great efforts in the liturgy so that God can dwell amidst his people. We recommend therefore that women especially be given the task of creating new symbols that touch the hearts of the faithful.

Because of increasingly high illiteracy rates, access to the media is a priority in Africa. Since virtually all Africans listen to the radio, we recommend that the churches encourage educational broadcasts hosted by women.

The struggle for the liberation of women and for the protection of creation concerns us all. Let the churches spare no effort to preach again and again against all forms of exploitation against women and children, and against the destruction of the environment.

"In the world and not of it": let the churches of Africa hold onto their freedom in the face of political power, let them defend the rights of the poor and the helpless, and let them protect the people from all forms of segregation.

"Arise, shine out, for your light has come": so let African women take their place in the Church without waiting for others to invite them. The concessions made to them could be a trap to keep them from taking real responsibility in important decision-making that affects the life of the community.

We are aware of major gaps in the formation and growth of our shepherdesses and in their cultivation. May the Church give them direction, and not sadden the Spirit of the Lord, which rests in them.

If on the one hand, women are asking the Church to recognise their feminine ministries, they must, on the other, show a spirit of enterprise and make bold strides in the vineyard.

To encourage greater solidarity among women of the Church, we recommend that the Democratic Republic of the Congo's Movement of Catholic Women be extended throughout Africa.

To conclude, we would like to express to all the faith we have in the African Synod for a better future in Africa, by citing this text from the Apocalypse:

> Then I saw a new heaven and a new earth; the first heaven and the first earth had disappeared now, and there was no longer any sea. I saw the holy city, and the New Jerusalem, coming down from God out of heaven, as beautiful as a bride all dressed for her husband. Then I heard a loud voice call from the throne "Do you see this city? Here God lives among men. He will make his home among them; they shall be his people, and he will be their God; his name is God-with-them. He will wipe away all tears from their eyes; there will be no more death, and no more mourning or sadness. The world of the past has gone." Then the one sitting on the throne spoke: "Now I am making the whole of creation new." (Apocalypse 21:1-5)

Endnotes

1. Le Cercle des Theologiennes Africaines a ete fonde en aout 1988 pa une equipe des theologiennes africaines reunies a Geneve au World Council of Churches sous la presidence de Mercy Amba Oduyoye. Il a ete inaugure a Accra en Sepembre 1989. Mercy Amba Oduyoye en est actuellement la presidente et Soeur M. Bernadette Mbuy Beya en est membre co-foundatrice.

2. Mullieris Dignitatem: Lettre Apostolique du Pape J.P. II sur la femme.

3. La femme-la societe-l'eglise. Mebu Dossiers Jounes, 37, 1-8.

4. Op. Cit. p. 6.

5. La femme dans l'eglise in Faire la theologies dans la perspective des femmes Africaines. Yaounde Aout 1986 (document non publie) par Soeur Justince Kahungu.

6. Voies Nouvelles pour l'Evangelisation: Actes di Synode de Luishia 19-29 Aout 1984. Archidiocese de Lubumbashii. p. 5.

7. Je suis un homme et pas votre natte: Lettre pastorale de Monseigneur Kabanga Paques, p. 89.

8. See p. 7 of A movement named EATWOT (1993) in V. Fabella, *Beyond Bonding: A Third World Women's Theological Journey* (pp.7-19). Publication of EATWOT and Institute of Women's studies.

9. See Oduyoye, M. A., & Kanyoro, M. R. A. (1992). *The Will to Arise: Women, Tradition and the Church in Africa.* New York: Orbis Books.

10. Faire la theologie dans la perspective des femmes Africaine. in Theologie Africains: Bilan et perspectives: Actes de la 17eme Semaine Theologuquie de Kinshasa par Sr. M. Bernadette Mbuy Beya p. 257.

11. Mets ton plus joli pagne. Preparè pour Global Forum on Religious Life; Manila 21-31 Aout 1993 par Sr. M. Bernadette Mbuy Beya.

12. Op. Cit.

13. Lettre pastorale sur la femme, p. 24.

14. Je suis un homme: Lettre Pastorale de Mgr Kabanga Careme 1976 dernier.

15. Op. Cit. voir note 11.

16. Experience feminine de Dieu dans le Renouveau Charismatique ‡ Lubumbashi in Faire la theologic dans la perspective des femmes Africaines. Younde Aout 1986 par Sr. M. Bernadette Mbuy Beya (non publie).

17. Op. Cit . voir note 11.

References

Actes du Colloque de Younde Aout 1986.

Actes de la 17eme Semaine Thologieque de Kinshasha Mars 6 Avril, 1989.

Actes du Synode Diocesain de Luishia Aout, 1984.

Bureau Diocesain de Catechese, *Mbegu Dossiers Jeunes Pour La Femme*, 17.

La femme - la Societe - l'Eglise, 37.

Oppression et Liebreation de la Lemme. Afrique, 6.

Concile Vatican II: *Constitution Dogmatique sur l'Eglise*

Ackermann, D., Draper, J. A., & Mashinini, E. (1991). *Women Hold up Half the Sky.* Pietermaritzburg: Cluster Publications.

Oduyoye, M. A., & Kanyoro, M. R. A. (1992). *The Will to Arise: Women, Tradition and Church in Africa.* New York: Orbis Books.

Fabella, V. (1993). *Beyond Bonding: A Third World Women's Theological Journey.* Publication of EATWOT and Institute of Women's studies.

Hebrad, M. (1984). *Les Femmes dans l'Eglise.* Le Centurion - Le Cerf.

Hourcade, J. (1986). *La Femme dans l'Eglise Tequi.* Paris: 82 Rue Bonaparte.

Jean Paul II, Paper: *Mulieris Dignitatem.*

Lettre Pastorale sur la Femme. Paques. 1989.

Lettre pastorale: *Je Suis un Homme.* Careme. 1976.

Sharing Power:
An Autobiographical View

Kabamba Kiboko

In her book, *Who Will Roll the Stone Away?: The Ecumenical Decade of the Churches in Solidarity with Women*, Mercy Oduyoye reported that during the decade, 1988 to 1998, regional and national gatherings were taking place around the world to confront oppressive structures which deny women full participation in church and community. She spoke of these efforts with hope and vision:

> In the decade 1988-1998 we seek justice for women, to dream bold dreams for a new community, and I hope the Decade will raise the awareness that a society's attitude towards women is directly related to its understanding of what it means to be authentically human and truly religious (Oduyoye 1990:68).

Women have answered this symbolic question, "Who will roll the stone away?" in many ways. Take, for instance, some women in the Democratic Republic of Congo (DRC), who have gone further. They ask the next question: "How do we roll the stone away?" Two cases of DRC women, living in two different social locations, will illustrate how "the stone" of long-established patriarchal ideologies and practices is being rolled away. These women are transforming power as they reach out to other women - irrespective of age or denomination. In both cases I know first hand of their power, because I have been a fortunate beneficiary of their work.

The first case is a group of United Methodist Women (UMW) - also called *Mama Kipendano*, which in the Swahili language means "loving women". This group started in 1942, with four women studying the Bible in their homes in the town of Lubumbashi. They grew in number until they had to move their meetings to their church building. By 1950, the group was recognized at the Annual Conference, and, as of July 1992 they numbered 750,000.

Ten years ago, these DRC United Methodist Women started reaching out to needy female university students, by providing room and board for those who could not afford it. (This act was partially a response to a world in which men with wealth were exploiting female students sexually). In 1979, when I entered the *Institute Superieur de Theologie* at Mulungwishi, these women heard of my enrolment as I was the first female student in the seminary from the Southern DRC Annual Conference, and they wanted to help make sure that I would remain emotionally, spiritually, and physically whole. They supported me financially and spiritually in more ways than I could possibly count. Today, even with all the turmoil that their country is experiencing, they continue to send love and support as I continue my PhD Studies in the US. To these women I owe a debt beyond anything I can express. Moreover, in addition to this wonderful outreach, these women today are rising up to take a stronger sense of ownership of their collective strength, and to shape their own vision - as the Spirit guides them. As they grow stronger, they are able more and more to reach out to the larger world as they reached out to me, and thus become models for all women who would walk in the Spirit.

The second group of women I want to tell you about is an informal group that formed themselves long ago in my Sanga home village of Dilambwe in the DRC. Like the UMW, the Dilambwe Women (DW) are today contributing much to the birthing of a new Africa. They are coming forth with bold dreams for a new and vital community that will recognize the full humanity of women. I believe that Jesus showed such recognition of the full humanity of women. Thus I want to tell you a remarkable story about how this group of village women and I came to understand just how he showed it, in his time and place, and how we are empowered by it today.

The Dilambwe village women of my childhood often gathered to attend to various socio-economic tasks, such as deciding in whose field they would work next, or to discuss how they might better guide their youth into the right paths. Whenever they gathered for the above reasons, they also made it a special event. Since none of them could read, and I was a little girl who had learned how to read in my Catholic school, they had often called me to read for them their mail and any other important items of interest. One hot summer day when I was about thirteen years old, my mother asked me to read a story from the Bible to the women. I chose at random, or so I thought, that story of Jesus where he met an unnamed Samaritan woman at the well (John 4:1-42). None of us could have predicted how dramatically that day's story would affect the lives of all the women in my home village, and perhaps beyond.

The story begins by providing the setting: Jesus comes to Sychar, a Samaritan city, and sits by the well at noon (John 4:1-6). When I read, "Meanwhile, a Samaritan woman came to draw water?" (John 4: 8) my mother interrupted the reading with a question, "What was wrong with the woman, that made her go to the well at noon?" The question was followed by a pregnant silence. I moved my eyes from the text and looked at the audience. On the women's faces I could see the movement of brows as they drew together in wrinkles that were shrinking down the eyes. Their expressions silently echoed the same question, "What could have been wrong with the woman, that made her go to the well so late in the day?"

You see, in my village, as in most villages in our country, women do not go to the well at noon. Every woman accomplishes this task early in the morning at the first call of a rooster, for several reasons. First, in the morning the well is full; it is easier to draw the water since one does not have to bend so far to reach it. Second, the earlier one goes to the well, the better chance there is that one can draw clear and clean water. Perhaps even more important is the fact that in the morning women get a chance to socialize as they walk to the well. Besides the social bond they experience through sharing in this common task, they also enjoy the wonders of nature. Water, for example, is regarded as a symbol of purification, and so they speak of water and spirits in the same way others speak of bees and honey.

The spirits are believed to speak in the singing of the birds, among other things. The singing of birds, furthermore, has extra significance because the Sanga people believe that wherever there is an ocean, river, lake, well, or any other body of water, there is the presence of spirits. So when the women of my village hear birds sing, they try to decode the message conveyed through the birds' song. For instance, the Sanga believe that the bird known as *mweni kintobyo* always sings to announce the imminent coming of a guest (and of course they have seen the prediction come true on many occasions!).

So, with this cultural background, it was natural for the Sanga women who were listening to me read that day to wonder "Could this unnamed Samaritan woman simply be lazy? Or was there a spirit that moved her to go to the well at this unusual time, perhaps to receive a special revelation?" And also, "Why would a man be at the well at noon? Could he be a spirit?" (You see, in their society, men never go to the well for any reason, because this task belongs to the females). "What was going to happen?" What an anticipation! After a long silence, one lady said: "Well, keep on reading! Let us hear what is going on!"

So I continued to read the story, as Jesus converses with this unnamed Samaritan woman who comes to the well at noon (John 4:7-15). First he asks her for a drink of water, and she replies, "How is it that you, a Jew, ask a drink of me, a Samaritan woman?" Her reaction speaks of the antagonism not only between Jews and Samaritans, but also reveals the tension between men and women. She is a Samaritan and a woman, she says. Thus she is showing her awareness of the fact that by initiating a dialogue with her, Jesus had already violated both the prevailing gender norms and the religious-ethnic barriers of that time and place. The woman's response, however, allowed Jesus to get to the point that we can imagine he wanted to make in the first place. He moved the conversation to a higher spiritual level when he said, "If you knew the gift of God, and who it is that is saying to you, 'Give me a drink'. You would have asked Him, and he would have given you living water" (John 4:10). But, the woman's next response remained on a literal level, as she wondered how Jesus would get this water, since he had no bucket and the well was deep.

She continued to question Jesus, perhaps in a challenging, derisive tone, asking whether he was "greater than our father Jacob who gave us the well". Jesus again differentiates between the water he gives from the water in Jacob's well. "All who drink from the well will thirst again", he says; but the living water he offers becomes, within the individual, a "spring of water welling up to eternal life" (John 4:14). This first part of the story closes with the woman's request: "Sir, give me this water, that I may not thirst, nor come here to draw" (John 4:15). (Perhaps the woman was at the point of understanding the metaphorical message that Jesus had for her, or perhaps she was continuing to mock him. We cannot tell from the printed page what her tone was.)

However, the Sanga women listening to this reading suggested that the woman was beginning to speak metaphorically in the same manner Jesus was doing. One of the women said, "Maybe she hated coming to the well at that unusual time, because it was a symbol of how isolated she was." Another objected: "She says she does not want to thirst again. She knows that naturally she will thirst again, and will have to come back to the well for water, so perhaps she is being sarcastic." Other women thought, "No, she is not being sarcastic; we sense that she has been hurt deeply, a hurt that no words can articulate. She resents the circumstances that force her to walk alone to the well at noon." However, along with the deep hurt exists her thirst for knowledge. There is the mystery that she senses in Jesus, this man who says he can provide "the living water that springs from within". As they talked further, these Sanga women concluded that the woman's talk about the drawing of the water reflected her own thirst for knowledge, which springs already within her. It is her own wisdom that leads her to squeeze from Jesus the hidden teaching that lies behind the literal words "living water".

We can see, of course, as students of the Bible, that the Sanga women by now were going beyond the words of the text. These are women's interpretations of what the text does not say. By this time in the reading and discussion, they had moved from an attitude of holding back from the strange woman who went to the well at noon, to a feeling of standing with her in the presence of Jesus, the giver of living water. They had come to forgive and champion this Samaritan woman. They were reaching out to her and empowering her in their imagination, just as they would wish someone to do for them in similar circumstances.

In a similar way, John tries to present the meaning of living water. It means Jesus' revelation to human beings, or the Spirit given by Jesus to humankind. Theologians have, in a systematic and formal sense, been dealing with this term as well. From medieval times, living water has been understood in Western theology as a symbol for "sanctifying grace" (Brown, 1966).

The Sanga women, however, were interpreting this biblical passage from within their own cultural traditions. In their native Sanga language, living water has been translated *as mena a bumi* and in their regional Swahili language it is *maji ya uzima*. In both languages it means "water of wholeness, wellness and life". This translation naturally sparked the women's imagination - helped, undoubtedly, by the fact that earlier that morning they had taken a spiritual walk in meditation. These Sanga women were thus seeking to experience the spiritual dimension of the story, and they decided to visit their own well at noon in order to see for themselves what the Samaritan woman might have experienced. After that short journey, I believe they were never quite the same again.

At the well, we went on reading. Now Jesus continued to reveal his knowledge of the woman's individual identity by asking her to go and bring back her husband. To the women in my village, this encounter with Jesus - "a Spirit" - must surely involve a process of drawing from the woman the most important truths about her life. So the request to bring her husband was simply a way of bringing those truths into the open.

The woman replies that she has no husband. Jesus agrees with her that she has no husband, and adds that she has had five husbands, and now she is with one who really is not her husband (John 4:18). Of course the Sanga women realized that Jesus was identifying her as a woman with unhealthy relationships. They nodded in understanding, as I read that the Samaritan woman realized that Jesus must be "a prophet". Otherwise, how could he know such things about her?

The dialogue continues to reveal more about the woman and about Jesus. The woman adds to the list of Jesus' attributes. In addition to being a man, a Jew, the giver of the living water and a prophet, she assumes that Jesus' Jewishness makes him one who believes that people should worship God only in Jerusalem, whereas Samaritans worship on "this mountain". She says, "Our fathers worshipped on this mountain" and "You say that Jerusalem is the place where men ought to worship" (John 4:20). Jesus presents to the woman a different way to worship, "neither in Jerusalem, nor on this mountain" but "in spirit and truth". He says further: "God is spirit, and those who worship God must worship in spirit and truth" (John 4:24). The woman does not disagree, but she suggests that such complex things would be cleared up by the coming Messiah, who would reveal everything - a belief Samaritans shared with the Jews. Jesus responded, "I am he" (John 4:26).

At this point in the reading, a 98-year-old lady in my group of listeners shouted, "She has a womb, the matrix of knowledge!" I knew what she meant by this, because my mother always told me that a woman thinks not only with her head and heart, but with her womb, too, which is the center of life. She always said that God surely thought that one needed to think from that center of life, because he chose it as the matrix capable of nurturing the Savior. This other woman of my village elaborated by suggesting that the Samaritan woman's statement about the shared belief in a Messiah could be her way of avoiding further argument or discussion of their differences. When Jesus affirmed that he is the Messiah, the woman immediately acts as though she believes him, and that gives evidence of her own ability to see beyond the literal and obvious - a "thinking with her womb".

Just as she had asked Jesus for the living water, apparently with the acceptance of the metaphorical spiritual message he was presenting, the Samaritan woman now responds by leaving behind her water jar, and going directly into the city to tell her people: "Come, see a man who told me all that I ever did. Can this be the Christ?" (John 4:29).

Obviously, the brief dialogue between Jesus and the Samaritan woman had opened up a new chapter in her life. Now the Sanga women began to understand why the woman had gone to the well at noon in the first place. They believed that the woman's lifestyle caused her to withdraw from the life of the community, which women customarily enjoy as they walk together to the well at dawn. They also believed that in the second part of the story, the Samaritan woman moves from a feeling of shame, despair, and embarrassment about her lifestyle, to a view of a life that can be full of hope and courage. The fact that she went back to her village, and told people of her experience with Jesus, was seen by the Sanga women as a ritual of purification. They saw her becoming an empowered woman, and in turn empowering others. They saw the Samaritan woman moving from a disintegrated life to an integrated one, and moving from her place of social and spiritual isolation back into a place of community.

The next part of the story deals with Jesus' dialogue with his disciples about food and harvest (John 4:30-42). I will not dwell on that part here, because I see the arrival of the disciples on the scene as interrupting the flow of the spiritual mood that the Samaritan woman and Jesus had been sharing. The woman chooses to continue in this spiritual mood by going to the city and expressing her belief that Jesus is the Messiah, which eventually results in a confession of belief by other Samaritans, based on the woman's testimony (John 4:39-42).

After I finished reading the story, the Sanga women reflected further on its teachings. They noted that the Samaritan woman had begun the process of revealing and identifying herself. Then Jesus helped her reveal herself even further and that led to her discovering her thirst for knowledge. Some of the Sanga women in the group suggested that each of us should search within herself and share whatever she finds, so that we too might bring forth the truth of our identities.

And so they began. Some identified themselves as widows who had chosen not to go through the levirate marriage, and consequently were looked upon as living with the spirit of their dead husbands. Because of this, the village also considered them "unclean", just as the Samaritan woman would have been considered unclean by the Jews, as well as by the other Samaritans. Others identified themselves as childless women, whose husbands and in-laws abused them verbally because of their infertility. Still others, although they were well-respected religious women, were abused by their husbands and were afraid to admit or complain about such treatment for fear of losing their status in the community. Some identified themselves as wives who endure abuse because the church teaches them that women were created to be at the service of men. Some also reluctantly identified themselves as oppressors: of their sisters-in-law or of the widows and childless women, or of others in the village who were seen as different from themselves. Eventually it became clear that there were two groups, oppressed women and oppressor women - or, put another way, powerless women and women with power. They then acknowledged that sometimes a woman could be both at the same time. The Sanga women decided that we should deal with this state of affairs immediately. An elderly woman spoke words of wisdom in the Sanga language, "*Muntu apa muntu apa mapankilo a nzala*", which means literally, "A person here, a person there, a way to overcome famine". This saying was a way of reminding us that there is power among us to overcome the worst that life presents, if we come together in unity. But we were further reminded that unless we really open our eyes and see each other as valued beings - regardless of our differences - that unity will never be.

The women of my village spoke more words of peace and reconciliation, and there was, unmistakably, a new feeling of unity among them. Their meeting could have ended right then, but this precious time of reflection, discussion, and reconciliation was not to be the end of that day's learning and transformation. Someone made a comment about the use of symbolic language, and they began discussing again. They spoke of the way Jesus had talked of spiritual things by reference to things in the material world. This is an everyday way of life among the Sanga, and not only in my village. Proverbs, riddles, and parables are tools that they, especially the elderly, have always used to convey wisdom. But these women wondered if that was changing in the urban areas. Since I went to school in the city, they asked me if I thought the women in urban areas would understand the story we had just read in the same way that they as village women understood it. I was unsure as to how to answer the question, but as they discussed the matter, most agreed that urban women had lost much of their ability to see the spiritual meaning in such stories. They were concerned about the loss of the culture and native languages in urban areas. So the women of my village decided to conclude their meeting with a litany against the plagues of modernization. They chanted:

> Our sisters in urban areas have turned their back on their culture;
> We speak against their neglecting the native languages;
> We speak against their cutting themselves off from us.

Back home that evening in my village, after spending such an enriching day with my mother and the "mamas", I reflected on the occasion. Even though this story of the Samaritan woman took place during the first century of the Common Era, it still spoke to the women in my village. I was intrigued by the intensity of their quest for wisdom. The most striking to me were those women who had wept as they identified themselves as oppressors of the widows during funerals. They wept as they realized that they had misused power to abuse their sisters instead of recognizing and accepting responsibility to reach out and comfort them. What power there is in the message of a simple story, I thought to myself, when the Spirit works through it. To painfully examine and transform one's own use of power is a difficult journey. Yet, that day I had witnessed such a painful yet joyous transformation.

The response of the Sanga women to the story of Jesus and the Samaritan woman has never ceased to amaze me. Their culture, language, and experience of reality became tools of interpretation. Although these women were illiterate and uneducated, isolated in their rural setting and inexperienced in the ways of the larger world, nevertheless they were - and are - powerful beings! The world needs their spirit and wisdom, perhaps today as never before.

These Sanga women had been transformed. They felt newly empowered, and - although they did not yet speak of it - they were ready to help transform others. As time went on, I was to become an instrument of their will and power to do that transforming. Their pride in me often gave me reason to keep going in school - to gather my courage as the only girl in a school of three hundreds boys. They would always remind me of that Samaritan woman at the well at noon. "Let the spring of living water continue to gush until it becomes an ocean", they would say to me. The spring of water gushing within these women of my village overflowed to water and to nourish me just as the spring of water within the Samaritan woman reached out to many Samaritans in her village. These women worked hard to collectively finance the best education available for me. At the time of harvest, they carried big loads balanced on their heads, with their babies on their backs. They worked in the fields under the burning sun of the equator to raise their crops, thrusting their hoes into the rock-hard ground, and they believed that their sweat was for a worthy cause. As they worked, they sang: "Thousands of women, with only one eye to protect". They saw me as the one eye they helped to train, to see for and with them. As I have become one of those who enjoy the benefits of urban modernization, I remember their litany against the "plague" whereby I might have allowed myself to become cut off from my culture of origin. I feel the responsibility of integrating my two worlds, and of providing leadership for others to do the same.

We are all mightily blessed by the work of women who helped to empower us. We must now ask, how many women have we empowered. My mother used to hold me on her lap when I was little. She would hold a cup of water and say to me: "I am giving you five seeds to drink, and they will grow into a big tree of wisdom." After these words, she would teach me the five vowels and have me take a bit of water after each one. My mother never learned to read, but she took what knowledge she had and used it to start me on the road to reading. Because of her, today I am able to read in thirteen languages and I am called to use this powerful tool of reading in the service of God and my people. "This is all I have", she said. "Build on it!" So we must also today take whatever we have, and build on it.

Today, I am a United Methodist minister, and I have witnessed many women who have journeyed as the Samaritan woman did. Their experience at "the well" has brought them a gushing spring of water. The Samaritan woman, like my mother, shared with her fellow Samaritans the only valuable thing she had - her experience with Jesus. Her encounter with Jesus led her to discover her own inner power: it was transformed, and she used the resulting energy to help transform others. We could even say that after encountering Jesus, she became the first missionary, because she drew many Samaritans to Jesus. Just as the Sanga women's interpretation of that gospel story challenged them, so we are called today to search within ourselves, to examine how we use our power - whatever kind it may be - before we point blaming fingers to others' misuse and abuse of power. I believe that both individually and collectively we are called to follow this path of introspection. As I have answered this call myself, I continue to gain new insights about myself and about the basic concepts of power and authority.

Authority translates as *kiselwa* in the Sanga language. This word *kiselwa* literally means "heaviness" or "boundness" - the condition of being bound or weighed-down. When one says in English, "I have the authority" it is usually said with a sense of power and pride: whereas when one says in the Sanga language, "*Andi na kiselwa*" it means literally, "I have the heaviness" implying that one trembles with the sense of responsibility that authority bestows. That overwhelming sense of responsibility that I feel when I must say "I have the burden" sends me straight back to that proverb of my people: "A person here, a person there, a way to overcome famine." Thereby, I am reminded that together we can carry heaviness, but heaviness borne alone can crush not only the carrier, but also the ones who fall under that authority.

"We want to transform power" as we say so fervently these days. But too often we are thinking only of transforming the way power is wielded by others, those whom we think of as more powerful than we are. As women, we are likely to think first of the dominant model of power in the world. It is impersonal, hierarchical, and basically a male concept. We call it patriarchy in English. The women in my village call it *aki belegi*, or colonialism, because we experienced it as practically synonymous with colonialism. Although it is said to be a male concept, women in power and authority also frequently conform to its tenets. We women who have reached certain levels of power and influence in a larger arena, a circumstance that was relatively rare in history until recently, have before us the choice of whether and how to share our power with other women. How many sisters have we brought to the place where they too can "eat at our table"? We must remember always that without the inner power that can transform our own lives and communities, we cannot hope to transform the outer power that oppresses.

What model or models are we going to follow in our process of transforming power in our beautiful Africa? We are painfully aware of how power can be abused, but I believe we must go beyond the negative role of stopping abuse and limiting oppression, as important as that role may be. I believe we must all work together to transform the patriarchal model into one of shared power - power that lifts up and strengthens others, not power that clings to keeping others down. We are called to become experts and leaders in that work, and to use all of our scholarly disciplines to flesh out the details of a model that shares power equitably. We must develop expertise in what has been called "the technology of participation", and we must help others to develop this same expertise. We must teach others what we learn, even while eagerly accepting the wisdom offered by the most uneducated among us. We must nurture every ounce of creativity that we possess among ourselves. Above all, we must keep to our spiritual path, walking hand in hand with the Spirit that gives us both the wings with which to soar and an anchor for surviving the worst of storms.

Specifically, in regard to our religious institutions, we have much work to do. The structures of our churches often make it virtually impossible for many women to reach out to their sisters of other denominations, yet we must somehow manage to communicate across those artificial barriers. We salute the spirit of ecumenism that hovers within the Church and draws the Protestant denominations together under the Federation des Femmes Protestantes (Federation of Protestant Women) - and one can hope that our non-Protestant sisters may be drawn to join with us as well. The ecumenical spirit enlightens these women, and helps them to know clearly what it is like to gather for the purpose of birthing a new community - as opposed to coming together in formal meetings, gatherings that perpetuate a stiff and lifeless structure and bring about little or no change. We salute denominations that acknowledge and honor women's call into ordained ministries. We encourage these denominations to facilitate the full participation of women ministers in ecumenical efforts, as well as in international efforts, because we urgently need to build a strong sense of sisterhood around the world. We can rejoice in the fact that for almost two decades the United Methodist Church in the DRC has been ordaining women, and that in the Central DRC Annual Conference of the UMC at least one clergy woman exercises executive leadership as a district superintendent. We look forward to the day when more women ministers will be able to exercise their leadership by holding executive positions in our churches and conferences. We look forward also to the day when it is not predetermined that the woman minister who marries another member of the clergy will automatically have to be a mere associate of her husband.

Along with this anticipation is my conviction that we are giving birth to a community in which loving equality will be natural and normal, not dependent mainly upon the structure provided by laws. The spring of gushing water within us is overflowing and gently pushing down the structural barriers, transforming them into bridges over which we are called to walk and to reach out, not only to our sisters, but to our brothers as well.

We of the Southern Congo, DRC, gathered in Nairobi in August 1996 for the purpose of seeking, in faith, ways in which African women could transform power. By doing so, we were answering the call and prayers of many sisters who still wondered, "Who will roll the stone away?" At this gathering we replied, "Here we are. We will roll the stone away! We will accept the 'heaviness' - the responsibility that can only be carried by all of us working together in love and in the Spirit. We will surround with our fire and love those hearts that seem made of stone. We will be God's instruments to open the tomb in which the full humanity of women has been kept for so long, just as we open our wombs to let life come forth! We will minister to each other, releasing the power of women into the world, that it may transform the way power is used on this planet. And so we will become conduits for that 'living water' that gushed forth in the Spirit of the risen Christ. We will strive to pass on to the next generation the very best of our ancient cultures, and we will fulfill our God-given task of creating new life and new culture - culture that cherishes the 'living water' within every human being."

So now I say, let us rise - the Sanga women, DRC United Methodist Women, the Circle of Concerned African Women Theologians and other women's groups. Let us take the metaphorical path to the well with the Samaritan woman. It is a path upon which once you walk, you will never be the same.

References

Oduyoye, M. A. (1990). *Who Will Roll the Stone Away?: The Ecumenical Decade of the Churches in Solidarity With Women.* Geneva: Risk Books.

Brown, R. E. (1966). *The Anchor Bible: The Gospel According to John I-XII.* New York: Doubleday.

Transforming Power: Paradigms from the Novels of Buchi Emecheta

Mercy Amba Oduyoye

Introduction: Transformation

The theme of the conference for which this chapter was written challenged African women to reflect on the issue of power. This conference, which was called by The Circle of Concerned African Women Theologians, focused on "Transforming Power: Women in the Household of God". Transforming and reconstructing have become key concepts in African theologies because people have come to realize that the situation in Africa calls for more than development and that change by itself is insufficient.

Power is a concept least associated with women but one that rules women's lives in all its aspects. It is also a word that the Christian Testament has called attention to and which has generated much theological discourse, especially as the Greek of the New Testament has two words for it, and both of them are used in the Christian Testament about the work of Christ. I am referring to the words, *exousia* and *dunamis*. It is therefore a word that African theologians have to seriously reflect upon. Some of the terms in which the concerns of the conference have been stated are formidable. They include: Transform, Power, Household, and Household of God, all of which seem to be pregnant with generative concepts.

If I were talking to my late grandmother, a staunch Christian of blessed memory who knew her Fantsi Bible, but did not operate with our theological vocabulary or in the English language, I would have a hard time getting across what we are trying to do in the conference. The greatest challenge would be the word "transform". Power would be rendered as *tumi*, the ability, skill and know-how, and the strength to do something or to make something happen. So I could start the conversation from there, for she was herself a "strong woman". If I were to tell her that to transform is to make marvelous things happen like turning water into wine, she would nod her wise head knowingly, for she was a woman who affected the life-style of the community in her time, making things happen because of who she was and what she did. Power is therefore, for the well being of the community. She would of course remind me that power is not always used for the good of others and the community. In this we would agree, for we both knew how power could be used to oppress. But the point would have been made, and both of us would know the various connotations of the word, for it is in our language and culture.

The *Asantehene,* the *primus inter pares* of the Asante monarchs, has the title *Otumfo. Otumfo* is also a word that appears regularly in Christian prayer and praise. God is addressed as *Otumfo Nyankopon.* God has power, God is able, God has the possibility to make things happen and God has the power to prevent things from happening. *Atumsem,* that is powerful deeds, has, however, a negative connotation. It is often applied to persons who attempt to wield power when they are not authorized to do so. Do women have power in the family, in the church and in the various communities to which they belong? Can women make things happen or prevent them from happening? In what domain of life do women exercise power? When and where can women wield power?

Power also carries the connotation of the opportunity to act, as well as the space within which to act. You may have the ability to read, but not the opportunity to read in Church if your church does not authorize you to do so. If the space is not provided in the liturgy for you to enter and to read, you will not exercise your capacity to read in church and you will be powerless, meaning without the power to read in church. What I would have to tell my grandmother then is that sometimes women do not participate because they do not have the requisite skills - they do not have the knowledge and the know-how - and that African women theologians are concerned with exposing and remedying this. I would go further, telling her that even when they have the capacity, sometimes they cannot act because they are not authorized. This means we have to find out who confers authority, why women do not participate in authorizing and how to get the "authorities" (the authorizers) to mend their ways. It is also the case sometimes that women who are "authorized" are prevented from participating by people who feel threatened by women in power, or are nervous about sharing work with women, or receiving services from women.

This exchange between us would, I hope, bring my grandmother and I to the understanding that power, authority, capacity, and opportunity are all related issues for our consideration. In the process she would have shared many life experiences to clarify the concepts. She would also have had a lot to say about changing things, leading to a mutual agreement that we would have to examine how power can be changed as well as how power changes people, their mindset and attitudes, their institutions, structures and systems. For both of us held or hold the belief that change is a norm in life and women have to participate in change in order to ensure that the outcome is life-giving to all. After all, the changes that transform us from girls into women are meant to make us the source of new life. That would be a typical African grandmother's vision of womanhood.

The phrase, "transforming power" has a dual meaning. First, it refers to that power which transforms, and second, to the notion of changing the meaning of the way power is conserved and applied. Jesus once said that, the one who would be great should operate as the servant (Mark 10:43). The words minister and ministry have the same connotation as servant and serving. A ministry of health is an organ of government that has the capacity and the authority of the state and people to serve the health needs of the nation. The church's ministry is to serve God's intentions for humanity. Those designated ministers by the church are authorized and sustained to serve the people in the church as well as of the nation and beyond. Many Christians are in God's ministry, but some do not depend on the church for their economic well-being. It is sometimes the case that the real experience people have of the ministers of both church and state is that they "lord it over" the people, thus acting like the wicked shepherds of Ezekiel. Jesus warns us that in the Household of God, such power and behavior is out of place.

Women and Power

Women and power are like oil and water in patriarchal societies. In many cases they cannot be put together and when they are mixed some onlookers become uneasy and seek ways of separating them. Attempting to locate the origin of this, I have come to suspect that traditions, mindsets, and attitudes going back generations, and reinforced by daily experiences, have to be the source of the fear, anxiety, and apprehension that power will get into the hands of women. Those who lord it over others are naturally nervous about other people having access to powerful positions. Such people's experience of power as a two-edged sword makes them feel safer if women are excluded from it. The life-giver must have no option but to concentrate on giving life and being occupied with general well-being. That is the way to ensure a generation's survival. In African culture, the voice of the ancestors and the voice of the elders reflect patriarchal concerns.

Women's power should be the capacity to serve, to live for others and, even more importantly, to do something for themselves: it is the power that transforms pain into pleasure, the threat of death into the state of life and hatred into love. As long as women wield power that produces this sort of transformation, they are hailed as "good women". But society needs other forms of transformation before it can approximate to what Jesus presents to us as the ethos of the Household of God, whose stones are living stones, and in which all have the opportunity and the capacity to participate: this is the Household in which there is sharing and healing, a welcoming place of peace. The theme of this conference points to women as full actors in ensuring the power that transforms, accepting that our churches and human communities are far from being communities in which God is the householder. The events that take place in many of the households that display the plaque "Christ is the head of this house" contradict this statement.

The aim of this chapter is to analyze the power available to African women within the parameters of African culture, and to attempt to discover its transforming agency in relation to church and society. This includes participating in the transformation of African attitudes towards women with the aim of empowering women to live as daughters of God in God's household. To illustrate the theme I shall present in some detail the writings of a contemporary woman seeking to discover her power and her views on women's power.

Buchi Emecheta: The Person and Her Characters

A contemporary model who illustrates the power of women is the Nigerian writer, Buchi Emecheta. She, in a manner of speaking, stripped herself to unveil the violence against women in her part of Nigeria and the racism that people of African descent suffer at the hands of Europeans. Having mastered sociology she has become a social critic and an advocate for the powerless and the exploited. In spite of the specificity of most of her numerous writings, which include more than eleven novels, many Africans can identify with her experiences. Her books are firmly lodged in social reality and offer us a mirror in which we see ourselves as African women. She has been condemned by some African men, and also by some women. This was not because the linen she has washed was not dirty but because she dared to wash it in public.

If your husband burnt the original and unduplicated manuscript of your first book length story, what would you do? The vulnerable Buchi survived this and improved her quality of life by sheer will power, tenacity and determination. In *Head above Water: An Autobiography* she writes about her own difficult marriage: "I kept hoping things would improve and that I would not have to make the bread" (Emecheta 1986:30). Helene Chukwuma, in reviewing Buchi's work, wrote that "what Emecheta has done is to create in fiction an aspect of African cultural heritage which most educated people pretend to be an illusion in public, but embrace in the privacy of their conscience" (Chukwuma 1989:2-17). By saying these things explicitly, she forced awareness upon us as well as pioneering and cultivating change in attitudes and beliefs. In Emecheta's novels one finds powerful statements that are also indicative of the vulnerability of African women: "You have already proved that you are a good daughter, but a good daughter must also be a good wife" (Emecheta 1979:155). "You see, only now with this son am I going to start loving this man. He has made me a real woman – all I want to be, a woman and a mother. So why should I hate him" (Emecheta 1979:52). "I am not going to play strike with my children's stomachs" (Emecheta, 1979:130). "They (women) will even sell their bodies if that is what it takes to safeguard the lives of their children" (Emecheta, 1981:207). There is no novel of Buchi Emecheta's that lacks the motif of marriage and children, the social reality that, more than anything else, defines the African woman.

In affirming marriage and motherhood, Buchi's characters also know how to empower themselves in their relationships with men (Chukwuma, 1989). They know it is a mistake to call men to settle a quarrel between women. They know that "men are just human", they make wrong decisions "but as long as no big calamity occurs we keep quiet to save their face" (Emecheta, 1983b:96). But when the occasion demands, a woman could use her tongue to move the toughest of men. Describing the power of the wife of a politician over men, the narrator states: "Even in their drunkenness, they fear her tongue" (Emecheta 1981:129).

It is also in Emecheta's novel, *Destination Biafra*, that Stella Ogedemgbe, a woman who was at first thought to have an opinion on nothing beyond her wardrobe, surprised her daughter with her view on Biafra, seen by many in the military in Africa as Utopia, but which was in reality a chimera. She said to her daughter, who, attracted by the ideals of such an Utopia, had joined the army, "You mark my words, go to the Biafra of your dreams and when you get there you'll find ordinary people. Not angels, just people" (Emecheta 1981:153). And it happened, just as she had predicted it would. We are yet to come to terms with the fact that the transformation of life in Africa is not to be achieved through the power of the barrel of a gun. Women know that when the gun helps to get rid of one set of oppressors, we are still left with the peace-making and the community building that the vulnerable always crave, and we are also left with the power of patriarchy firmly entrenched.

Women's Wisdom

In her novels Emecheta highlights the wisdom by which women live. Much of this seems to me to be anchored in the wisdom of accepting what one cannot change. A mother in *The Slave Girl* says to her son: "It boosts a woman's ego to think her consent is really sought in deciding her future" (Emecheta 1977:185). She had that experience herself. Why is she recommending that it be continued? Could it have been a delight to her to make people believe that she was naïve? Women know their lives are not in their own hands but they have to live it, so they suppress their real selves. They protect their inner beings from being violated. They lower their voices to speak when what they really want to do is to shout (Emecheta 1977).

Women protect themselves against being hurt by polygamy by saying to themselves "only a stupid woman would expect her husband to remain married to her alone" (Emecheta 1977:214). They shield themselves from getting hurt and the strong ones demand that if it is going to happen, then all the rules governing it must be observed (Emecheta 1983b). Most women go along with the popular assertion that "a man needs many wives, and a woman simply has to accept, Christianity or no Christianity" (Emecheta 1979:111-125). But when women accept the type of polygamy that obliges the whole household, children, wives and husband to share hearth and chamber, and even the same flat, as is reported from France, a situation of oppression has emerged and this results in the women developing a victim mentality. The urban polygamy that forces several hearth-holds into a single location is not traditional: it illustrates how the traditions that enabled women to hold to their human dignity have been eroded. Buchi demonstrates this in her writings.

In *The Slave Girl*, market women evoke a traditional norm to resist paying a tax introduced by the colonial powers. "Did you ever hear of a country where women are asked to pay for their existence? ... the custom requires that only our men should pay for their deeds, they own us" (Emecheta, 1977:163-164). Today women pay taxes but "bride price" is also demanded for a woman from a man before she can become a wife. Speaking of her mother Felicia Ekejuiba writes, "I also watched her and other women punish men who repeatedly battered their wives or who made disparaging comments about women and their reproductive anatomy ... bubbed *titi ikoli* with reference to Cameroonian women" (Ekejuiba 1995:48). In *The Rape of Shavi* (Emecheta 1983b) we are led into an understanding of why women give new meanings to situations in order to cope with circumstances that would otherwise have been devastating to their physical lives.

Women Strengthen Women

In Shavi, Buchi's fictional community, a visitor named Ronje, a white man, rapes a Shavi girl, a would-be queen mother. She, being young and inexperienced, was concerned with the rules of pollution, the demand for virginal blood on her nuptial bed, and so on. Sharing her anguish with her mother, her mother explains to her "You have not been violated. This Ronje is an animal" (Emecheta 1977: 91). So the event does not fit the rules. But the situation was not being treated lightly for "Rape ages any woman, young and old" comments the narrator (Emecheta 1983b: 91). Having comforted the girl, she and the older women set about avenging the vile crime. Like the market women in *The Slave Girl*, and those of Dubge market in Ibadan and other

West African cities and towns, the women of Shavi were too busy to go to court and certainly not to a court presided over by men. So they went to make sacrifices to Ogene the goddess, empowered by the knowledge that "The voice of women is the voice of Ogene" (Emecheta 1983b:108, 121). Women are energized when their offspring are in danger. The power to save is heightened when life is threatened.

In the novel *Destination Biafra*, Debbie, the army officer, marveled at the resources of women; their seeming passivity when husbands are around contrasts with their wisdom and resourcefulness when left alone. This is illustrated by the incident of a woman refugee whose husband was taken away by the army and shot. When Debbie first saw the family, they were sitting under a tree, and she notices that the woman had her

> head resting passively on a pole, the way she lifted her eyes as if they were so weighty ... the way she spoke in a whisper.... And now look at the same woman, a few days after the death of her husband. (Emecheta 1981: 207)

The same widow had the energy and the presence of mind to slap a young mother who, through hysteria, kept on crying and saying, "I can't look after my children by myself, I want to die" (Emecheta 1981: 207). To encourage the young woman to stop indulging in self-pity, she said to her:

> Your husband has given you children ... don't you think you have to make sure you live so that you can look after them? But because men also gave us their name, you forget your father's name and in the process of letting your husband provide for you, you have become dumb and passive. Go back to being yourself ... farm ... sell your body.... Your children have to live. (Emecheta 1981: 207)

These were the words and actions of a woman seemingly passive when faced with the task of encouraging and comforting a young mother whose husband had just been shot and who was bewailing her condition.

It seems that women caring for women and children is normal, women caring for men is a duty, but women do not expect men to take care of them beyond the material provisions laid down by culture. A woman in labor, whose husband and sons are reluctant to leave her alone, dismissed them as follows: "Why should you stay away from work just because I am having a baby? Are there no women in our clan any more? Have I become a coward who cannot give birth to a child?" (Emecheta 1977: 17) The narrator then suggests that "perhaps she did not want to alarm her family unduly" (Emecheta, 1977: 17), while, for my part, I wonder how many wounds, minor and serious, had been inflicted on her by these men in her life. Women do not expect much from men so they shield themselves from getting hurt by neglect.

Living for Others

The power expected of women is the power to live for others: to die that others might live. Buchi usually associates this power with wives and mothers, but daughters are not exempted. June, the protagonist in *Gwendolen*, wondering whether or not to tell the truth about her condition to the authorities, who were about to consign her to a home for the mentally disabled, decided not to do so. Her reason was that

> If she said that she was being locked up in a ward for the mentally sick so that her father would not be put away in a jailhouse, this woman might not understand.... She wanted to hate the two of them (mum and dad). But if she did, then she'd have nobody to love. She had to love people around her. She had been brought up that way. To dispense love. She had been brought up to nurture not to destroy. (Emecheta 1989:152)

Similarly, at the end of her days, Nnu Ego, the epitome of *The Joys of Motherhood*, when she was asked not to saddle herself with children in her retirement, she confessed that she did not know any other life.

Women do not demand much from men and are therefore not vulnerable to their callousness. In *The Joys of Motherhood*, one woman says to another, in an attempt to cheer her up, "All men are selfish, that is why they are men" (Emecheta 1979:139). This spirituality, one that is informed by the saying "She that is down needs fear no fall, she that is low, no price." Such sentiments shield women from disappointment by giving them low expectations, especially from men. Women do not expect them to look after children. In Igboland, rural husbands bring yams and mend roofs, urban ones give housekeeping money to which wives always have to add, mostly by selling things if they are not salary earners. Ekejuiba writes

> I grew up in an environment in which the working mother was the norm. Women routinely shared costs and responsibilities of household welfare. Children, women and men worked side by side to produce food for the family and to sell the surplus. (Ekejuiba 1995:47)

A young wife, who finds life in Lagos with her washer-man husband hard, is told:

> You want a husband who has time to ask you if you wish to eat rice, or drink pap with honey? Forget it, men here are too busy being white men's servants to be men. We women mind the home, not our husbands. Their manhood has been taken away from them. The shame is that they do not know it. (Emecheta 1979:51)

Buchi seems to suggest that under colonialism and urbanization even the occasional expression of affection that African men used to demonstrate has declined. In *Head above Water: An Autobiography*, Buchi Emecheta expresses how she has come to accept her lot: a single woman living for her children who may not care for her during her old age. "To give and not to count the cost" seems to be the fountain of spirituality for her and many African women. Buchi originally dedicated *The Joys of Motherhood* to her children, but upon reading it, the daughter who defied her threatened to burn the book. So she dedicated to it "All Mothers", which was most appropriate!

For women in Buchi's hometown Ibuza, living for others never ends. When they die they are buried with the necessities for keeping house in the world beyond, if the spouse has preceded them. Buchi says her heroine Nnu Ego's "love and duty for her children ... were like her chain of slavery" (Emecheta, 1979:186). What do women do about this situation except to run to prayer? So Buchi prays: "God, when will you create a woman who will be fulfilled in herself, a full human being, not anybody's appendage?" (Emecheta, 1979:186) Children feed on the lives of their mother, mothers have to give them all. "And if I am lucky enough to die in peace, I even have to give them my soul" Nnu Ego laments. "They will worship my dead spirit to provide for them. If things go wrong my dead spirit will be blamed.... When will I be free?" (Emecheta, 1979:187)

Power from Tradition

Buchi Emecheta also seems to suggest that the power of Nigerian women is such that it is not allowing them to be sucked into certain aspects of westernization. Where traditional provisions for inheritance safeguard women's economic independence, she would have them preserved. But whereas, in *Kehinde*, it is Western law that does that, she maintains that the essential thing is that a woman is worthy of material prosperity. In *The Slave Girl* one woman challenges another who wanted to make demands that were not customary saying: "But you are woman, how is it that you want to inherit the girl? It is not your right!" (Emecheta1977:185) And the storyteller comments: "In Ibusa, women are usually more conservative than men" (Emecheta, 1977:185).

If the bride price is related to getting land through one's sons, and having a say in your husband's patrilineage, then you will not have children before a proper marriage has been concluded (Emecheta 1981). For her, personally, the bride price is not a *sine qua non*, so she writes in *Head above Water: An Autobiography*: "my daughters ... God help me, nobody is going to pay any 'bleeding price' for them. Their marriage will not depend on the highest bidder nor would they marry because they are looking for a home. She did that" (Emecheta, 1986:127). Similar words are put into the mouth of Debbie, the heroine of *Destination Biafra*:

> Debbie would not be advertised like a fatted cow. She will not go into a marriage of unequals. She wanted to do more than child breeding and child rearing and being a good passive wife to a man whose ego she must boost all her days, while making sure to submerge every impulse that made her a full human. Before long she would have no image at all, she would be as colourless as her mother.... She told herself, she must make a move to fashion a life for herself.... She was going to help the Nigerian army – not as a cook or a nurse, but as a true officer. (Emecheta 1981:44)

Buchi overstates her case with the choice of the military but she does make her point. Debbie did not see herself in a life in which she would marry a rich man and "start breeding and continue breeding till menopause" (Emecheta 1981: 117). So marriage is affirmed but on terms that affirms the personhood of a woman. Choice will be a non-negotiable factor.

Traditional provision for taking care of widows and orphans are, according to Buchi, empowering for women. She would advise that men abide by them as the King of Shavi who, in his sarcasm, tells his councilor to abide by the traditions lest women pray to the goddess to send disaster. The King was speaking in relation to the tradition of compensating the first wife when a husband wants to bring in other wives (Emecheta 1983). It is also significant to note that women will not act directly. They will bring down the wrath of the spirit world when treated unjustly. "My wife wants a cow before I can take a new wife, so please give her a cow. Otherwise she'd go and invoke her sister, the goddess of Ogene" (Emecheta, 1983: 43). The Queen Mother of Shavi had argued that if the women abide by the traditions of Shavi, so should the men.[1] This reciprocity was a traditional source of power for all, and women could expect the whole community to side with them with regard to such a well-known practice.

Buchi Emecheta points to the ruinous effect of westernization on African men, but seems to put the onus on women to cope with the results. In the *Joys of Motherhood* (1979) a wife is counseled to accept the new form of marriage imposed on her by city life. Buchi blames the fact that "husbands and wives grow apart, live in different worlds" to strive to make money "for survival and finery" through the modernization of the economies of Africa. She very wisely leaves this challenge open. Do Africans have the option to distance themselves from the global economic system when "the birds of fire" arrives in Shavi without invitation bringing strange people and strange ways and wares? What power do women have to transform this? Both they and their men are faced with situations that their fore-bearers did not know, have to cope as best they can. The situation showing women's power is in their involvement in shaping new norms in society. Buchi's women, whether located in Ibusa or elsewhere, do just that using different strategies.

The Power of Sexuality

Buchi seems to point to a secret power that accompanies women. The narrator of *Destination Biafra* says of a man whom "his wife knew him well. She was silent and passive whenever he was around, but in her shrewd retiring way she had discovered methods of getting around him" (Emecheta 1981: 72). There are several such insinuations in these novels that women's power lie in their sexuality. In the same novel Debbie is given the assignment to go to Biafra to convince the army commander (with whom she had studied in Cambridge and who had a soft spot for her) to drop his weapons and make peace. She was told not to meddle in things bigger than her. She was reminded that she was being sent on this delicate mission because she was a woman: "You might use your feminine charms to break that reserve of his" (Emecheta, 1981: 118).

In *Double Yoke*, Buchi Emecheta demonstrates this explicitly through using what was then a common allegation in university campuses. Women at that time could turn a discussion on its head by calling attention to the sexual

harassment of women by men. By writing *Double Yoke*,
Buchi was chastised by many readers.[2] She, however, did
not invent this situation, neither was she the first to cast
such insinuations. In Nigeria of the oil boom "bottom power"
(gaining advantages by giving sexual favors) was on all lips
and a successful woman in any field was suspected to have
used this power.

On the other hand, in her writings, women are at their
most vulnerable for the same reason, their sexuality. They
are reminded of this often. Politicians, whom Debbie had
arrested, say to her, "Whatever you do, however much you
are armed and in command now, you are still a woman"
(Emecheta 1981: 75). In the end she was raped and later
ridiculed for having been raped by a fellow officer, the same
one who accompanied her to undertake the assignment and
who had just attempted to rape her. For this officer, his
only regret was that: "My mother would die if she hears I
had anything to do with a thing like that" (Emecheta, 1981:
168).

Whereas Buchi wrote a whole book on bottom power,
she seems unable to bring herself to associate rape with
her own people, Igbo men. The only occurrence of this was
the marital rape inflicted upon Nnu Ego during her first
night with a husband who was a total stranger. It was
suggested that this conjugal rape was done intentionally to
prevent her escaping from a man who did not appeal to
her, and that it was for her own good since her fertility was
in question. The other two were attempted rapes, one to
ensure marriage - a customary marriage by kidnapping -
and the other by a spiteful Hausa man who was a soldier.

Rape, according to Emecheta's work, is perpetrated by
aliens, a white visitor and two Jamaicans - Africans
brutalized by slavery, who had become alienated from
African values. This seems to me to be only part of the
picture. Such a presentation demonstrates African women's
deep-seated patriarchal upbringing, which leads them to
shield their men from outside criticism. They know that
shame kills faster than disease and they want their men to
live (Emecheta 1977). June's baby was her father's, but as
a Jamaican woman she was more African and it is in Africa

where her ancestors are from that "babies are a woman's greatest achievement" (Emecheta 1989: 154).

The story of the rape and murder of two nuns could not be swallowed by one of the women refugees. She simply refused to believe that this was a reality.

> Dorothy insisted in a vain effort to wash away the sins of the men of her race who wore borrowed army uniforms, promoting an equally borrowed culture. A culture that did not respect the old.... Accepting the death of her child, but not able to understand the abuse of the helpless old." (Emecheta, 1981: 213)

Certainly she could not accept the rape of an old woman by an African man, even one in army uniform.

Buchi felt obliged to explain why African men would rape women of all ages in all circumstances during war. She writes, that in the distant past, African women were treated almost as men's equal, but with the arrival of colonialism their traditional claim to equality had been taken away. Now with the coming of independence young women like these (women army officers) were determined to play their part in the new nation: this, in turn, was making the army boys more brutal to women caught in any helpless situation. This is because of war, and in a war situation men lose their self-control. So what is the transforming power that will be adequate to confront this evil? Should rape be excused because it is war? Or does Buchi mean that women entering that tradition would say is man's domain is tantamount to war, and that rape is men's weapon against women who insist on women's full participation in shaping culture? If this is so, then a woman's femininity is an aspect of her sexuality that renders her vulnerable so that men, who have little beyond being male, exploit to threaten, subjugate and marginalize her from the use of whatever transforming power she may possess.

The Power in Observing Limits

Women's power is in knowing when to turn from men to children and finally to self. To know the difference between what can be changed and what cannot is an essential part of wisdom. In *Destination Biafra* a woman talking to other women about their politician husbands, points to their shortsightedness and their arrogance. "How old grown men make such blunders, and yet elevate themselves with such arrogance that one could not reach them to tell them the truth?" (Emecheta, 1981: 240) This particular wife had a mind of her own. She did not want to perish with her husband. She intended to live to see her children's children. She was not going to "die for another person's bad dreams" (Emecheta, 1981: 240). In the end these politicians' wives who seemed not to have a mind of their own devise a scheme to save themselves and their children from the devastation that accompanied the failure of Biafra.

The fact that a husband is "another person" empowers a woman in the end. In recent times, especially under the influence of Christianity and its insistence that "a man and a woman are joined in holy matrimony until death do them part" women have become more strongly identified with the "household" as their husband's spouse. Christianity, colonial policy, modern bureaucratic systems and development praxis, promoting the notion of male household head-ship and life-long virilocality, have contributed immensely to women's loss of material security from her kin (Ekejuiba 1995). There was a time when a woman died in reality in some communities, and in most symbolically, when her husband died. There was a time when a woman was expected to feel like a half person when without a husband. But Buchi, whose heroine Kehinde fretted because it seemed that without Albert (her husband), she was "only a half person" ended up with a Kehinde who came to realize that claiming her rights did not make her less of a mother, and nor less of a woman. If anything, it made her more human.

In *Gwendolen* the feelings of a woman who finally managed to take a holiday by herself were described as a new life, away from her husband, living by herself with no mother to look after (she had just died), no children to feed (they had been left with their father) and no man to cook for was, at first, disconcerting. She felt frightened. She was like a person without roots. "She knew that good women were not supposed to live for themselves. They were expected to remain alive for others ... to live for themselves was not to be" (Emecheta 1989: 3). Nnu Ego knew no such limits. Nnu Ego, on the other hand, was like so many not so well informed Christians who thought that the kingdom of God was just around the corner, and that Jesus Christ was coming the next morning. Reality was too painful to accept. So she kept on boasting of her absentee sons until she died quietly by the wayside. But she did get her big funeral, the ultimate joy of motherhood (Emecheta 1979).

There has to be a limit to the self-giving propensities of African women. In *Joys of Motherhood* Nnaife makes it sound as if sexual intercourse was the supreme expectation of women. "What are you complaining about?" asked he to his aggrieved wives. "Don't I sleep with you?" (Emecheta, 1979, p. 134) Is this solution to all marital challenges? For women, however, it seemed that the sole purpose was to have children, preferably sons, and if they were not forthcoming then it became a bothersome act. Emecheta reviews this in *Head above Water: An Autobiography*:

> It is very possible not to regard sex as the main reason for our existence. Women are capable of living for so many reasons and there is a lot more for African women to busy themselves with. (Emecheta 1986: 70)

Many of her characters lived for marriage and for children and would abide by the dictates of culture to achieve this end. But even here Buchi says there is a limit to compliance with tradition. Marriage is portrayed as the *raison d'être* of African women. From her autobiography we read that "a married women is a full dog, an unmarried one is a hungry dog" (Emecheta 1986:75). Women are expected to find fullness and contentment in marriage. So Buchi finds occasion to present her readers with a critique of the legal prostitution involved in the system of "Home Daughter" (Oduyuye1996)[3], illustrated through the life of Ona, Nnu Ego's mother. Here priority is given to children to contribute to the homestead of one's father. However, it is also believed that children do not do well outside the protection of the paternal spirit. Ona, whose father was keeping her as a home daughter, "had to leave her people. Not because she was allowed her love for Agbadi (a recognized lover) to rule her action but because she wanted the safety of her child" (Emecheta 1979: 28). It is fortuitous that her desires and those of some aspects of her culture agreed. It stands to reason that at the point of death she should, in turn, say to Agadi "However much you love your daughter, Nnu Ego, allow her to have a life of her own, a husband, if she wants one. Allow her to be a woman" (Emecheta 1979: 28). This is obviously Buchi's voice, an argument against legal prostitution, and one for women's choice in marriage.

The Power of the Hearth and the Hoe

Much research links African women to food security. As food producers, they are the hardest hit by the vagaries of the African climate, especially where food farming depends solely on the natural fertility of the soil and rain from above. They are the most vulnerable during famine, for all look to her hearth to fill their stomachs and a stomach does not understand famine. Hoeing is a backbreaking task, yet women, pregnant or carrying babies on their backs, still hoe. There are many stories warning them against leaving babies under trees or in the care of others while they hoe. Women have to hoe and they have to carry their babies so they hoe carrying their babies (Obbo 1995). The power of African women to give life and to defy death is an often-explored theme. Where AIDS take its toll, women get together to save orphans of stricken parents, for AIDS has become a matter of concern for all parents.

There is power in stoicism and abstemious life, but in most African countries, it often spells pain and death for women. Women's health is often impaired by this tradition of living for others. Health, hearth, and hoe have to be together if women are to continue with their capacity to give and preserve life. The costs of women's nursing of family members, their scavenging to feed the family, and to reproduce the human race even under conditions where AIDS has such an impact are scarcely taken into account.

The willpower to transcend these circumstances is neither publicly recognized nor appreciated and women are not empowered to enhance the quality of the life they reproduce and struggle to preserve.

With this extensive exposure of African women to risk one cannot help but ask where the locus of power is in these precarious conditions? Women are vulnerable to sexually transmitted diseases. Under these conditions, to be empowered is to have the knowledge of how to avoid them and where to seek cure. Above all, it is to have the right and readiness to say no to an infected man, no matter what bride price he has paid. Bride price was paid to produce more life, not to terminate the life of the woman. The only power left is the power to resist, maybe even unto death, for that may be the transforming power required. Resistance to male excesses often takes the form of not fighting back, but finding other ways of punishing men (Ekejuiba 1995). The Akan will ridicule a man who fights or beats a woman by telling him to go find his match in a man. Women protect their property by fending off men, for "cursed is the man who sits on the seat of a woman" or one that a woman has sat on. There were stools for men and stools for women. The power of evenhandedness and reciprocity to transform is the power of the powerless.

Conclusion

The power of a woman is in her head-ship and management of her hearth-hold. Buchi Emecheta has herself become such a woman not by choice but by force of circumstances. For many women even the contribution of the husband, the putative head of a household may not be forthcoming. As heads of hearth-holds women may achieve financial independence and prestige, and exercise power in the public sphere. Women in these positions have as much possibility as men for philanthropic acts, the seeking of political office and for pursuing other sources of prestige. They do not have to submit to abusive life-denying marriages. But most, in fact, invest their all in the people around them and in that lies their power. Even economically vulnerable women will spend her all on her hearth-hold. In her personal influence lies her power.

Sisterhood as an empowering aspect of the diverse traditions of Africa is to be found throughout her writings. But she is not starry-eyed about it. She knows that caring can become interfering. She uses an example of sisters who are consoled by seeing others in worse situations than themselves. She portrays sisters who want to make others conform to their way of resolving difficulties. Some help others to cope in an expected traditional way, and using other aspects of traditional practice to help out. By and large they resent the empowering aspects of tradition that give women the possibility of seeking support from other women. During the last hour of pregnancy and the first weeks of motherhood, help comes mainly from other women. In our most vulnerable situations we hope for the solidarity and healing presence of other women. Sisterhood is empowering, but there is also vulnerability that only spiritual powers can deal with.

Women's power also lies in the power of sisterhood. Buchi introduces white people into *Destination Biafra*, and they appear mostly in her work *The Rape of Shavi* to demonstrate the global nature of sexism. By so doing, she could be stating her hopes for humanity in global terms. Thus in *Head above Water: An Autobiography*, Buchi speaks of how the black woman of South and the white woman of the North will come together and try to build a better world and raise up better sons.

There is a vulnerability that does not empower but simply adds to the oppression of women. We need the power of God to transform this and work for its elimination. We may be able to articulate the true meaning of power by following the model of Jesus Christ. We may even be able to demonstrate how this transformed power works, but to transform the mentality of those who lord it over others, we depend on the power of the Holy Spirit.

In our Circle for Concerned African Women Theologians, we wish to pray for the transforming power of God so that women and men together may be children of the household of God. We pray and work for the transforming power of God to infuse our relationships with the rest of creation with care and respect. May the transforming power of God so permeate us that we might become instruments of transformation. Together with the women of Buchi Emecheta's novels we hope and pray that: "God will not let any evil spirits come to our house" (Emecheta, 1979:30).

Endnotes

1. Buchi Emecheta does not use the designation Queen Mother in the same way as the Akan of Ghana. Among the Akan the Queen Mother is a ruler in her own right often an aunt or some other women in this matrilineal age, certainly not his mother nor his wife. In Shavi the Queen Mother is the first wife of the king.

2. Conversations and tapes of interviews with Buchi Emecheta, Belgium, 1996.

3. It is interesting that Emecheta does not deal with "female husbands". The closest she comes to exposing women's power over women is in Emecheta, B. (1977). *The Slave Girl.* London: Allison and Busby. For a discussion of this, see Amadiume, I. (1987). *Male Daughters, Female Husbands: Gender and Sex in an African society.* London: Zed Books. Cf. p. 48 of Ekejuiba, F. I. (1995) "Down to Fundamentals: Women-Centred Hearth-hold in Rural West Africa" in D. Bryceson (Ed.), "*Women Wielding the Hoe: Lessons from Rural Africa for Feminists Theory and Development Practice*" Oxford: Berg. "Many women of my mother's generation survived childless marriages by manipulating the flexible gender division of labour.... She later became a 'female husband' by 'marrying' her own wives who increased the 'hearth hold' by producing four more children for her." See p. 250 of Vuorela, U. (1995) "Truth is Fantasy" in D. Bryceson (Ed.), *Women Wielding the Hoe: Lessons from Rural Africa for Feminists Theory and Development Practice.* Oxford: Berg.

References

Chukwuma, H. (1989). In H. C. Otokunefor, & O. C. Nwodo (Eds.), *Nigerian Female Writers: A Critical Perspective*. Lagos: Malthouse Press, 2-17

Ekejuiba, F. I. (1995). "Down to Fundamentals: Women-centred Hearth-hold in Rural West Africa" in D. Bryceson (Ed.), *Women Wielding the Hoe: Lessons from Rural Africa for Feminists Theory and Development practice* . Oxford: Berg, 47-62.

Emecheta, B. (1977). *The Slave Girl*. London: Allison and Busby.

Emecheta, B. (1979). *The Joys of Motherhood*. London: Allison and Busby.

Emecheta, B. (1981). *Destination Biafra*. London: Allison and Busby.

Emecheta, B. (1983a). *Double Yoke*. New York: George Braziller.

Emecheta, B. (1983b). *The Rape of Shavi*. Ogwugwu Afor.

Emecheta, B. (1986). *Head Above Water: An autobiography*. Ogwugwu Afor.

Emecheta, B. (1989). *Gwendolen*. William Collin.

Obbo, C. (1995). "What Women Can Do: AIDS Crisis Management in Uganda" in D. Bryceson (Ed.), *Women Wielding the Hoe: Lessons from Rural Africa for Feminists Theory and Development Practice*. Oxford: Berg, 165-178

Oduyoye, M. A. (1996). *Daughters of Anowa: African Women and Patriarchy*. New York: Orbis Books.

Talitha Cum! to the New Millennium: A Conclusion

Talitha Cum! to the New Millennium: A Conclusion

Nyambura J. Njoroge

The Wake Up Call

When almost seventy African women theologians gathered in Accra, Ghana, in October 1989, and collectively resolved to construct theologies and ethics from their faith experiences and social, cultural location, their wake up call was the story of the twelve year old girl (Ms Jairus) presumed dead in Mark 5:21-43. These women agreed to be alert, to "Get up", "Arise" and contribute to the ongoing construction of African theologies and ethics which have been and are dominated by men. Mercy Amba Oduyoye, in her keynote address, emphasized the need for a "two-winged" theology, through which both women and men could communicate with God. Since then African women theologians have been making every effort to ensure that this wake up call has not gone unheeded. As a result, at the end of twentieth century and the start of the second millennium, we can talk about theologies of African women. In this concluding section we are extending this wake up call to all those who care for Africa and its much-needed ministry for healing and well being. We need theologies and ethics that will give us the space to breathe, reflect, get well, grow and serve our continent.

Unheeded Quest: Humble Beginnings

Having listened to the voices in the preceding chapters, let us briefly reflect on the journeys African women have walked to arrive at the point where they are writing theologies and ethics that reflect some of the issues with which women are struggling. We should also identify some of the related critical issues that demand our attention in the new millennium. In 1999 I was asked to give a lecture on ecumenism and theological education in Africa. In the course of reading and preparing for this lecture I came across the name of Mina Soga of South Africa, the first woman delegate to the International Missionary Council (IMC)[1] held in Madras, India, in 1938. Efiong Utuk, a Nigerian ecumenical historian, has this to say about Soga:

> A little shy and reserved, Mina Soga spoke on why African women must be given equal opportunity in education and evangelical leadership. Realizing that Christian missionary was dominated by men insofar as most missionaries and delegates to this conference were men, Miss Soga wished that many women missionaries would be trained and sent to Africa. Additionally, she asked the Conference to pray and plan for the day when African women will take a prominent part in ecumenical conferences. (Utuk 1991:205)

These words remind us that African women's quest and desire to be equipped for and included in the ministries of the church and ecumenical movement is not only a thing of the 1990s, when the Circle of Concerned African Women Theologians (hereafter the Circle) began to gather and mentor women to study theology, research, write and publish. Unfortunately, the missionaries and the African church did not see or feel the urgency to heed Mina Soga's well-articulated request and prayer. No doubt African women have played a significant role in the shaping of the African church and the ecumenical movement but most of those involved have done so without much needed pastoral and theological training. Few African women theologians have held prominent leadership positions in their individual churches or in the ecumenical organizations at the national, regional and international levels. Obviously this is one area that demands critical research, analysis and documentation as we enter the new century and millennium. In particular we have to analyze how women's faith and commitment have impacted on the shaping of African Christianity, churches, ethics and theologies. But one is left wondering what the African church and its ecumenical bodies would be like today if the missionaries and African church leaders had taken Soga's words seriously.

In reality, if African women had not asserted themselves and claimed their rightful place in the leadership of the church and position at the ecumenical table, it would be unthinkable to talk about African Christian women theologians today. We would do well to remember that in 1963, prior to the gathering of the first general assembly of All African Conference of Churches (AACC) in Kampala, the first consultation of African Christian women was held. At this meeting the issue of the ordination of women for the ministry was discussed, among other things. In Africa, allowing the ordination of women for ministry also implies opening doors for women to undertake pastoral and theological training. This is because in most missionary-founded churches the practice has been and is to accept students to theological institutions only if they are candidates for ordination. Given this reality, many women and men who wish to acquire pastoral and theological training, but not necessarily for ordination, are denied entry to theological institutions. Fortunately, at the dawn of a new millennium, this trend is slowly changing, as some churches are training women in seminaries and Bible schools while still debating whether to accept the ordination of women to the priesthood. In addition, since the 1980s, more commercially oriented theological institutions (universities and seminaries) have been established and women are allowed to enroll in them. These institutions belong to the missionary-founded churches as well as to the Evangelical, Pentecostal and Charismatic churches. After the Kampala Conference, some women leaders of church women's organizations, as well as others who had acquired status in secular professions, spearheaded the campaign and struggle for the ordination of women and their inclusion in the leadership of the churches, whether ordained or as lay people. This was undertaken largely with the support of some of the emerging group of African male ecumenists.[2] In this regard, we must add that the ecumenical movement has played a significant role in supporting the struggle of African women to achieve visibility and full participation, including the gaining of scholarships for theological education. However, research on the contribution of the ecumenical movement in the empowerment of African women theologians is necessary and overdue. The same applies to research on African women's contributions in the ecumenical movement.

A large number of African women theologians have pursued their theological studies in the religious departments and theological faculties of state universities. A few of these women end up teaching and lecturing in the same religious departments and theological faculties of state universities or in high schools. To a large extent, however, many churches seem to ignore women and men who are educated in theology in these state universities when they consider people for leadership in their churches, particularly for teaching in and leading theological institutions operated by churches. Some of the churches do not even recognize them as theologians, even though they might be committed and active church members. On the other hand, we find a significant number of ordained male theologians teaching in the religious departments and theological faculties of state universities, but there are few ordained women theologians in this category. In the 1990s, only a handful of women theologians were teaching in seminaries and Bible schools. This is a matter that demands critical attention on the part of the churches. The number of African women with a Bachelor of Divinity degree, the basic degree that prepares candidates for ordination or specific ministries in the church, is still relatively small despite the increasing number of ordained women.[3]

Given this state of affairs, there is urgent need for theologians working in the state- and the church-controlled sectors and church leaders to engage in serious conversations on how to work together and how to contextualize pastoral and theological studies in the churches. Contextualizing these studies means taking women more seriously and admitting them to the status of theological students, educators and administrators, including the posts of principal and academic dean. The existing theological associations could provide such a forum for discussing such matters.[4] Needless to say, to date theological associations have been male-dominated in leadership and in participation, but the trend is slowly changing. One great advantage of utilizing theological associations is that they have a wide ecumenical representation, and are also inter-religious since religious departments teach Christianity, Islam, African Traditional Religious and, to a lesser extent, Hinduism. Such a forum could provide the space where theologians and church leaders could engage in mutual learning, criticism and understanding of other denominations, faiths and religions. At the same time it is hoped that this kind of interaction will provide the opportunity for theologians and church leaders to discover emerging writings, such as theologies by African women, and to integrate them in the curricula as necessary. Without such efforts, the voices heard in this volume will remain unheeded, as was Mina Soga's plea and prayer for women to be equipped for church ministries and ecumenical engagement. It is not enough to publish books that may not even reach the libraries of our theological institutions and churches. The majority of the women and men leading and working as pastors in the fast growing African churches have not encountered these emerging theologies. It is, therefore, a matter of urgency to create space where African theological educators and church leaders can seriously consider what is happening in the theological world and pastoral ministry.[5] This must be done for the sake of delivering well-informed and articulated theological and spiritual guidance and nurture, which is relevant, empowering and healing.

The Kairos Moment for African Women-Articulated Theologies

Nevertheless, we would do well to remember another occasion, which is little known or talked about when we reflect on the beginnings of African women theologies and ethics. In 1978, the same year I enrolled in a seminary to prepare for the ordained ministry, I had the opportunity of attending the Consultation of Women Theology Students, organized and sponsored by the Sub-Unit of Women in Church and Society, of the World Council of Churches. Brigalia Bam of South Africa was the staff person responsible for the Sub-Unit and fifty-three women attended the consultation at Cartigny, Switzerland, in July 1978. Eight women were from Africa: two theological teachers, one pastor and five students from Egypt, Ghana, Nigeria, the Democratic Republic of Congo (former Zaire), Kenya and South Africa. In a regional report from the African group it was stated:

> Pleased to discover one another, they determined that, once back in Africa they would look for the other women in Africa studying theology and bring as many as possible together in a consultation of African Women in Theology. The African consultation would be a way to share the experience of Cartigny, to find out just what women theologians are doing in Africa, to question the meaning of ministry and women's part in it, to look critically at theological education in Africa, to encourage women to become more active in the emerging theologies and to discover how the church can be more responsive to the issues and needs of women. Their hope is that such a meeting would encourage more women to take an interest in theology, and would be a contribution to the World Council of Churches' study: "The Community of Women and Men in the Church".
>
> These eight women also intend to keep in touch with the other women who attended the conference at Cartigny, and with the World Council of Churches. (Scott & Wood 1979: 45)

Mercy Amba Oduyoye, the most seasoned and senior participant in the African group, carried this dream and vision with her and for ten years did the best she could to bring about the fruits of our determination and commitment. I would say this was the *kairos* moment for African women and the real beginning of the construction of theologies and ethics from their faith experiences and perspectives. In the process, the launching of the Circle took place in October 1989 in Accra, Ghana, which was the genesis of our current talk about theologies and ethics of African women.

At this juncture, we should also mention that the Ecumenical Association of Third World Theologians (EATWOT), launched in 1976, has played its role in providing fora where African women theologians have discovered one another. EATWOT did, indeed, begin as a male-dominated association as Virginia Fabella (1993) has so well demonstrated in *Beyond Bonding: A Third World Women's Theological Journey*. But those few women who were involved from its early years spoke out against their marginalization and the exclusion of their experiences and faith perspectives. To remedy this they created the women's commission in January 1983. Fabella has highlighted the activities and issues addressed by African women in the commission between 1984 and 1986. No doubt these occasions provided room for African women to develop strategies which later helped in the creation of the Circle.

As noted earlier, these women were motivated by the story of Ms Jairus as they invoked their will to arise, to wake up, to make a difference by writing theologies that are women constructed and articulated. Above all, they demand inclusive communities for women and men in our religious institutions. We need however, to recall that the story of Ms Jairus is intertwined with the story of the unnamed woman who had suffered from hemorrhages for twelve years. This, too, has inspired African women to assert themselves, claim their right to healing and well-being, and to let faith in God drive them to do the unthinkable. The will to arise from exclusion, marginalization, oppression, exploitation, betrayal and to make a difference has its motivation in these two women and their encounter with Jesus who uttered life-giving words: "Daughter, your faith has made you well; go in peace, and be healed of your disease" (Mark 5:34); and "Little girl, get up!" (Mark 5:41). Today, when HIV/AIDS and other diseases are claiming many lives in Africa, these words of Jesus need to be shared more than ever before.

On the other hand, the birthing process of the Circle coincided with the launching of the Ecumenical Decade of Churches in Solidarity with Women, 1988-98 (hereafter the Ecumenical Decade) by the World Council of Churches (WCC) in Geneva, Switzerland. It is not proposed here to assess how the Ecumenical Decade has influenced African women. It did provide more opportunities for women to gather, to undertake Bible studies and theological reflection and to learn what other women the world over are doing with regard to such matters as empowering women for ecumenical leadership and theological education. In addition, more women have received theological scholarships to undertake masters and doctoral studies through the Ecumenical Theological Education program of the WCC, a commitment that continued even after the Ecumenical Decade. Churches, theological institutions and ecumenical bodies have been challenged to take women seriously as equal partners with men in the life and mission of the church and in the ecumenical movement. Of great significance is the fact that African women like, women elsewhere, were empowered to speak out against violence against women in the family, church and society. In 1996, the Kenyan Chapter of the Circle published a collection of articles under the title *Violence Against Women: Reflections by Kenyan Women Theologians,* (Wamue & Getui 1996).

The Way Forward

Given our prevailing circumstances in Africa, however, writing and publishing theologies and ethics by women is not enough. The greatest challenge facing us and the churches and theological institutions in Africa is to ensuring that these voices are heeded. They have to be subjected to critiques and articulated in the life and mission of the churches, in the theological institutions, in the ecumenical movement and in society as a whole. African women theologians need to converse with males and to listen to critical voices if they are to grow and get well. As Musimbi Kanyoro, the coordinator of the Circle (1996-2003), asserted in a high-spirited sermon at the Decade Festival marking the conclusion of the Ecumenical Decade in Harare, Zimbabwe, in November 1998, we need to move from solidarity to accountability (Kanyoro & Njoroge 1998).[6] Denise Ackerman has observed that accountability requires awareness, "a waking up". Becoming aware and accountable means doing away with ignorance and the withholding of life-giving information. Theologies and ethics are needed which ensure that every woman, man, youth and child is given every opportunity to experience life in its fullness. Such trends demand hard work, determination, boldness, courage and faith in God. They also mean listening to the scriptures anew and engaging in socio-cultural critiques that leave no stone unturned in our collective search for healing, well being and fullness of life.

We must also ensure that these theologies and ethics reach the classrooms of our theological institutions and that more women are engaged in teaching theology and other related fields. Fundamental to all this is the urgent need to transform our curricula and courses in theological institutions to enable us to address the critical issues facing our continent. At the heart of extreme poverty experienced by so many of our people, is the imperative need to teach theology and economics. Do the scriptures have a message for us in the new millennium as globalization continues to condemn our people to misery, violence and death? Ross Kinsler and Gloria Kinsler (1999) have provoked us Christians to take biblical Sabbath and Jubilee seriously in their new book *The Biblical Jubilee and the Struggle for Life*.[7] Violence on the continent is another issue that demands a strong "wake up" call. What do the scriptures and African religions and cultures have to say about peace making and values that will enable us to overcome violence?[8] Equally urgent is the need to focus attention on the devastating consequences of the HIV/AIDS pandemic. Such challenges require that we revisit the way we train and prepare women and men for pastoral ministry.[9] Can we construct liturgies that will enable our people to begin a journey of healing and well being in the midst of poverty, violence and disease?

In his book, *Development and The Church of Uganda: Mission, Myths and Metaphors*, Kodwo E. Ankrah (1998) has eloquently demonstrated the need for theological institutions to include developmental ethical studies in their curricula. The same proposal could be made for environmental and ecological theology. In similar vein, people with disabilities have drawn the attention of theological institutions of the need to take seriously the challenges they, and their families, face throughout their lives. This requires the construction of appropriate theologies and ethics, especially those in the field of pastoral theology.

These life-destroying issues and challenging realities demand that we call to account our leaders. Leadership crises and conflicts, which hamper many churches and other church-related bodies in Africa, should not continue unchallenged. It is tempting to critically analyze political leadership on the continent, and to point out how it has failed and betrayed the people. At the same time we complain about the power struggles and poor leadership in our churches. Theologies and ethics that ignore the fact that leadership is a crucial aspect of our faith are incomplete. Lack of good leadership in our religious institutions will adversely affect how these emerging theologies and ethics are received. This must be of concern to all.

The issues identified above should help to shape theologies by African women and men in the new century and millennium, but they do not make up an exhaustive list. Certainly the issues highlighted adversely affect many people on the continent: they are also issues that concerned Jesus then and now. Accountability requires that we wake up to the occasion, listen to the cries of God's people and together create alternative ways of living our lives guided and empowered by the Holy Spirit. This promise is as much ours now, as it was to the followers of Jesus in the first century and millennium.

Fortunately, African women have taken the wake up call seriously and are creating spaces and institutions to empower women. They are also ensuring that theology students and church workers are exposed to gender studies and women-articulated theologies. For instance, in Ghana, the Ghanaian Chapter of the Circle held a conference in October 1999 to celebrate the 10th Anniversary of the Circle. They also began the process of raising funds to build Talitha Cumi Centre to house the Institute of African Women in Religion and Culture, which is currently housed in the Trinity Theological Seminary, Legon.[10]

In South Africa, Isabel Apawo Phiri (April 2000) is responsible for the Program on Women in the Church at the Society of the Centre for Constructive Theology. In September 1999, Pauline Muchina of Kenya and Jana Meyer (January 2000) from the USA helped to facilitate the first ecumenical seminar on African women's theologies in Maputo, Mozambique. This gave birth to the Portuguese-speaking (Lusophone) Circle Chapter. These women decided to hold similar seminars every year, if funds allowed, to bring together participants from Mozambique, Angola, Cape Verde and Guinea Bisseau. Prior to the Maputo seminar, Muchina and Meyer (January 2000) had facilitated another seminar at the Kalahari Desert School of Theology, which is based at the Moffat Mission, Kuruman, South Africa.

In Kenya, Esther Mombo, the Academic Dean and lecturer at St. Paul's United Theological College, Limuru, and Emily Onyango, the Dean of Students and a lecturer at the same college facilitated the first ecumenical two-week conference for ordained women in July 2000. The College is also being assisted by the Kenyan Chapter to equip its library with books on women's theologies and other related subjects. This was initiated by Musimbi Kanyoro and Nyambura Njoroge. In faith and through action and commitment such as these, Africa will surely get up, arise and get well to feed its children and to bring life in its fullness. *Shalom!*

Endnotes

1.   IMC was formed in 1921 and in 1961 it became part of the World Council of Churches.

2.   For further discussion on the struggle for ordination of women in the Presbyterian Church of East Africa, Kenya, see my book, *Kiama Kia Ngo: An African Christian Feminist Ethic of Resistance*

and Transformation. Accra, Ghana: Legon Theological Studies Series.

3. To address this shortfall in 1998 the World Council of Churches launched a fundraising campaign to establish the Sarah Chakko Theological Endowment Fund to provide scholarships to women of the South to undertake the first degree in theology.

4. Since the early 1960s with the assistance of the World Council of Churches, Theological Education Program, theological institutions in the South (Third World) were encouraged to create theological associations to provide a forum where theological educators, students and churches could critically look at the curriculum and how it could be made relevant to the needs of the people. In Africa there are more than ten sub-regional associations as well as the umbrella regional one, the Conference of African Theological Institutions (CATI). Most of these associations meet annually or biannually. On 14-18 August 2000, African theologians held the first Theological Conference in Nairobi, Kenya, organized and sponsored by CATI, AACC, Circle, EATWOT-Africa (Ecumenical Association of Third World Theologians) and the OAIC (Organization of African Instituted Churches). The Conference was attended by religious scholars from state universities, theological seminaries and ecumenical officials/ staff of AACC, World YWCA, WCC, OAIC, UBS (United Bible Societies). Unfortunately among those missing were church leaders, even those who are theologians in their own right.

5. Such space can be created by the theological associations, national council of churches and regional ecumenical organizations like AACC, OAIC and UBS.

6. African women theologians were among those who prepared Bible Studies that were used at the Decade Festival as well as their editors.

7. Ross Kinsler and Gloria Kinsler have provoked us Christians to take biblical Sabbath and Jubilee seriously in their book *The Biblical Jubilee and the Struggle for Life.*

8. To accompany churches and societies in the struggle to overcome violence the world over, the World Council of Churches launched the Decade to overcome Violence (2001-2010) in February 2001.

9. A Conference on HIV/AIDS curriculum development for theological institutions in Southern and Eastern Africa was held in Nairobi, Kenya, June 2000, which was co-sponsored

by WCC, UNAIDS (United Nations AIDS) and MAP (Medical Assistance Programme) International.

10. See Report of African Women Theologians and Jubilee 2000 Celebration (5-10 October 1999). (2000). *Ministerial Formation*, 88, 57. See also The Ghana Project of Women's Ministries Program Area (2000) *Dream, Woman Dream...Dream Africa's Dream: An Invitation to a Partnership with African Women*. Published by Women's Ministries Program Area in National Ministries Division, Presbyterian Church (USA) A Ministry of the General Assembly Council.

References

Ankrah, K. E. (1998). *Development and the Church of Uganda: Mission, Myths and Metaphors*. Nairobi: Acton Publishers.

Fabella, V. (1993). *Beyond Bonding: A Third World Women's Theological Journey*. Manila, Philippines: A joint publication of the Ecumenical Association of Third-World Theologians and the Institute of Women's Studies.

Kanyoro, M. R. A., &. Njoroge, N. J. (Eds.). (1998). *A Decade of Solidarity with the Bible*. Geneva: World Council of Churches.

Kinsler, R., & Kinsler, G. (1999). *The Biblical Jubilee and the Struggle for Life*. New York: Orbis Books.

Muchina, P., & Meyer, J. (January 2000). "African Women: The Spirit is Upon You!" in *Ministerial Formation 88*. Geneva: World Council of Churches Publications, 35-46.

Phiri, I. A. (April 2000). "Empowerment of Women Through the Centre for Constructive Theology" in *Ministerial Formation, 89*. Geneva: World Council of Churches Publications, 46-53.

Scott, J., & Wood, B. Y. (Eds.). (1979). *We Listened Long, Before We Spoke* (Report of the Consultation of Women Theological Students, Cartigny, Switzerland, July 1978). Geneva: World Council of Churches Publications.

Utuk, E. (1991). *From New York to Ibadan: The Impact of African Questions on the Making of Ecumenical Mission Mandates, 1900-1958*. New York: Peter Lang.

Wamue, G., & Getui, M. (Eds.). (1996). *Violence Against Women: Reflections by Kenyan Women Theologians*. Nairobi: Acton Publishers.

Selected Bibliography

Ackermann, D., Draper, J. A., & Mashinini, E. (et al.). (1991). *Women Hold up Half the Sky: Women in the Church in Southern Africa*. Pietermaritzburg: Cluster Publications.

Amadiume, I. (1997). *Reinventing Africa: Matriarchy, Religion and Culture*. London: Zed Books.

Bailey, R. C., & Pippin, T. (1996). "Race, Class and the Politics of Biblical Translation" in *Semeia 76*, Atlanta, Georgia: Scholars Press, 1-6.

Banana, C. (1993). "The Case for a New Bible" in *Rewriting the Bible: The Real Issues*, eds. L. Cox, & I. Mukonyora, 17-29. Gweru: Mambo Press.

Bird, P. A. (1982). *The Bible as the Church's Book*. Philadelphia: Westminster Press.

Boulaga, F. E. (1984). *Christianity Without Fetishes: An African Critique and Recapture of Christianity. (Translated from French by Robert R. Barr)*. Maryknoll, New York: Orbis Books.

Brueggemann, W. (1991). *Interpretation and Obedience: From Faithful Reading to Faithful Living*. Minneapolis: Fortress Press.

Bruns, G. L. (1992). *Hermeneutics: Ancient and Modern*. New Haven: Yale University Press.

Bujo, B. (1992). *African Theology in its Social Context*. New York: Orbis Books.

Croato, S. J. (1995). *Biblical Hermeneutics: Toward a Theory of Reading as the Production of Meaning* (R. R. Barr. Trans.). New York: Orbis Books.

Day, P. L. (Ed.). (1993). *Gender and Difference in Ancient Israel*. Minneapolis: Fortress Press.

Dube, M. W. (1996). "Woman, What Have I to Do With you? A Post-Colonial Feminist Theological Reflection on the Role of Christianity in Development, Peace and Reconstruction" in Isabel Phiri, K. Ross, & J. Cox (Eds.), *The Role of Christianity in Development, Peace and Reconstruction*. Nairobi: AACC, 244-258.

Dube, M. W. (1997). "Praying the Lord's Prayer in the Global Economic Era." *The Ecumenical Review*, 49(4). Geneva: World Council of Churches Publications, 439-450.

Dube, M. W. (1998). "Reading for Decolonization: John 4:1-42" *Semeia*, 75. Atlanta, Georgia: Scholars Press, 37-59.

Dube, M. W. (1999). "Searching for the Lost Needle: Double Colonisation and Postcolonial African Feminisms" in *Studies in World Christianity*. Edinburgh: Edinburgh University Press, Vol. 5, Part 2, 213-222.

Dube, M. W. (2000). *Postcolonial Feminist Interpretation of the Bible*. St Louis: Chalice Press.

Egbuji, I. I. (1976). "The Hermeneutics of the African Traditional Culture". Unpublished doctoral dissertation, Boston College, USA.

Fabella, V., & Oduyoye, M. (1988). *With Passion and Compassion: Third World Women Doing Theology*. Maryknoll, New York: Orbis Books.

Fall, Y. (Ed.). (1999). *Africa: Gender, Globalisation and Resistance*. New York: Aaword.

Getui, M. N., & Obeng, E. (Eds.). (1999). *Theology of Reconstruction: Exploratory Essays*. Nairobi: Acton Publishers.

Gibellini, R. (ed.). (1994). *Paths of African Theology*. London: SCM Press.

Imasogie, O. (1983). *Guidelines for Christian Theology in Africa*. Accra: African Christian Press.

Kanyoro, M. (1997). "A Life Of Endless Struggle or Stubborn Hope: An African Feminine Perspective on the Jubilee" in *The Ecumenical Review*, 49(4). Geneva: World Council of Churches Publications, 399-410.

Kanyoro, M. R. A. (Ed.). (1997). *In Search of a Round Table: Gender, Theology and Church Leadership*. Geneva: World Council of Churches.

Kanyoro, M. R. A., & Robins, W. (1992). *The Power we Celebrate: Women's Stories of Faith and Power*. Geneva: World Council of Churches.

Kinoti, G. (1994). *Hope for Africa and What Christians Can Do*. Nairobi: AISRED.

Kinoti, H. W., & Waliggo, J. M. (Eds.). (1997). *The Bible in African Christianity: Essays in Biblical Theology*. Nairobi: Acton.

Kirwen, M, C. (1979). *African Widows.* Maryknoll, New York: Orbis Books.

Kitzberger, I. R. (Ed.). (2000). *Transformative Encounters: Jesus and Women Reviewed.* Leiden: Brill.

Larom, M. S. (Ed.). (1994). *Claiming the Promise: African Churches Speak.* New York: Friendship Press.

Lind, C. (1995). *Something is Wrong Somewhere: Globalization, Community and the Moral Economy of the Farm Crisis,* Halifax: Fernwood.

Mananzan, J. M., Oduyoye, M. A., Tamez, E., Clarkson, J. S., Grey, M. C., & Russell, L. M. (Eds.). (1996). *Women Resisting Violence: Spirituality for Life.* Maryknoll, New York: Orbis Books.

Maluleke, T. S. (1997). "Half a century of Christian Theologies of Africa: Elements of the Emerging Agenda for the 1st Century" in *Journal of Theology for Southern Africa, 99,* 4-23.

Maluleke, T. S. (1997). "Smoke-screens Called Black and African Theologians: The Challenge of African Women Theology" in *Journal of Constructive Theology, 3(2),* 39-63.

Martey, E. (1993). *African Theology: Inculturation and Liberation.* Maryknoll, New York: Orbis Books.

Mbugua, J. (Ed.). (1994). *Our Time Has Come: African Christian Women Address the Issues of Today.* Grand Rapids: Baker Book House.

Mbula, J. (1975). "Continuing Elements in African Traditional Religion in Modern Africa: The Case of Maweto Marriages in Ukambani." Paper in manuscript form, Department of Philosophy and Religious Studies, University of Nairobi.

Mugambi, J. N. K., & Magesa, L. (Eds.) (1990). *The Church in African Christianity.* AACC Challenges Series. Nairobi: Initiatives.

Njoroge, Nyambura J. (1997). "Woman, Why are You Weeping?" *The Ecumenical Review,* 49(4), Geneva: World Council of Churches, 427-438.

Njoroge, Nyambura J. (2000). *Kiama Kia Ngo: An African Christian Feminist Ethic of Resistance and Transformation.* Accra, Ghana: Legon Theological Studies Series Project in collaboration with Asempa Publishers.

Ogunyemi, C. O. (1996). *Africa Wo/man Palava: The Nigerian Novel by Women.* Chicago: The University of Chicago Press.

Parker, G., & Pfukani, P. (1975). *History of Southern Africa,*. Padstow: Unwin Hyman.

Parsons, N. (1982). *A New History of Southern Africa,* London: Macmillian.

Plaskow, J. (1991). *Standing Again at Sinai: Judaism from a Feminist Perspective.* San Francisco: Harper.

Pobee, J. S. (1994). *Culture, Women and Theology.* Delhi: ISPEK.

Pobee, J. S., & von Wartenberg-Potter, B. (1986). *New Eyes for Reading: Biblical and Theological Reflections by Women from the Third World.* Geneva: World Council of Churches.

Ranger, T. O. (Ed.). (1968). *Aspects of Central African History,* New Hampshire: Heinemann.

Russell, L. M. (Ed.). (1985). *Feminist Interpretation of the Bible.* Philadelphia: Westminster Press.

Russell, L. M. (1987). *Household of Freedom.* Philadelphia: Westminster Press.

Russell, L. M. (1987). *The Church in the Round.* Philadelphia: Westminster Press.

Schüssler Fiorenza, E. (1992). *But She Said.* Boston: Beacon Press.

Schüssler Fiorenza, E. (1999). *Rhetoric and Ethic: The Politics of Biblical Studies.* Minneapolis: Fortress Press.

Segovia, F. (1991). *Farewell to the Word: The Johannine Call to Abide,* Minneapolis: Fortress Press.

Segovia, F., & Tolbert, M. A. (Eds.). (1995). *Reading From This Place: Social Location and Biblical Interpretation in Global Perspective.* Minneapolis: Fortress Press.

Schneiders, S. M. (1991). *The Revelatory Text: Interpreting the New Testament as Sacred Scripture,* New York: Harper.

Smith, A. (1999). "Cultural Studies" in J. Hayes (Ed.), *Dictionary of Biblical Interpretation A-J* . Nashville: Abingdon Press, 236-238.

Spivak, G. C. (1990). *The Post-Colonial Critic: Interviews, Strategies, Dialogues.* New York: Routledge.

Staley, J. L. (1988). *The Print's First Kiss: A Rhetorical Investigation of the Implied Reader in the Fourth Gospel.,* Atlanta: Scholars Press.

Talbert, C. H. (1984). *Reading Luke: A Literary and Theological Commentary on the Third Gospel.* New York: Crossroad.

Tannehill, R. (1990). *The Narrative Unity of Luke-Acts: A Literary Interpretation.* Philadelphia: Fortress Press.

Tamez, E. (1979). *Bible of the Oppressed.* New York: Orbis Books.

Tamez, E. (1987). *Against Machismo.* Oak Park: Meyer/Stone.

Tamez, E. (1989). *Through Her Eyes: Women's Theology from Latin America.* New York: Orbis Books.

Weems, R. (1988). *Just a Sister Away: A Womanist Vision of Women's Relationships in the Bible.* San Diego: Laura Media.

Weems, R. (1995). *Battered Love, Marriage, Sex and Violence in the Hebrew Prophets.* Minneapolis: Fortress Press.

West, G. (1995). *Biblical Hermeneutics of Liberation: Modes of Reading the Bible in the South African Context.* Pietermaritzburg: Cluster, Rev. ed.

West, G., &. Dube, M. W. (1996). "Reading with: An Exploration of the Interface Between Critical and Ordinary Readings of the Bible" in *Semeia 73.* Atlanta, Georgia: Scholars Press.

World Council of Churches. (1997). *Living Letters: A Report of the Visits to the Churches During the Ecumenical Decade of Churches in Solidarity with Women.* Geneva: World Council of Churches Publications.